Mitchell Leisen:
HOLLYWOOD DIRECTOR

Mitchell Leisen:
HOLLYWOOD
DIRECTOR

David Chierichetti

PHOTOVENTURES
PRESS

Published by Photoventures Press
3700 Eagle Rock Blvd.
Los Angeles, CA 90065

Printed in the United States of America

Typesetting Production by Michael Bifulco
Cover Design by Graphico

ISBN: 0-929330-04-8

Acknowledgments are due to all of the "cast of characters," also to Dr. Howard Suber of UCLA, the staff of The American Film Institute at Greystone, in particular Helen Seitz, to Philip Chamberlin, Rosalia Woodman, Howard Mandelbaum, Mark A. Vieira, Packy Smith, Matt Marchand, Robert Cushman, Sheila Roman, Laurel Taylor, and most of all, to Mitchell Leisen.

For my best friends:
Isabel Gillespie Hall
and Antonio Chierichetti

CONTENTS

FOREWORD
TO THE 1973 EDITION

I am very pleased to learn of the book David Chierichetti has written about Mitchell Leisen. Mitch was one of the greatest directors this town has ever known and a serious study of his whole career has been long overdue.

I've yet to meet anybody who had as many talents as Mitch. You name it and he could do it: painting, sculpture, costume design, interior decoration, navigation and nightclub staging. Mitch could have been the top man in any of these fields, but he chose instead to concentrate on motion picture directing, a wise move since it was the one career which could fully utilize all of Mitch's talents. But it was more than just his versatility that made Mitch great. To every film he brought his unique perception and sensitivity, and many of the films he made—*Death Takes A Holiday, Hands Across The Table, Easy Living, Midnight, Arise My Love, Hold Back The Dawn, To Each His Own, Golden Earrings*—are coming to be regarded as classics. His record is one of the most distinguished in the industry, and as performers, we were always very proud when he cast us in one of his pictures.

Above all else, Mitch was my friend. Friend is not a word I often use, but it certainly applies to Mitch. Through good times and bad, he was steadfast. For all his importance, he was never too busy to help. All of us whose lives were touched by his are the richer for it.

Mitch was a highly complex person, and although many people worked with him and were acquainted with him, few could claim to know him well. Three years ago, David Chierichetti began what must be one of the most exhaustive researches ever done on any director. For endless hours he interviewed Mitch, and then he sought out all of us who had ever worked with him. David is a very dedicated scholar and his persistence has paid off. The result of his labor is the major rediscovery of one of Hollywood's rare geniuses. We will be hearing more about David—and Mitch—in the future.

Dorothy Lamour

Hollywood, California
December 13, 1972.

Cast of Characters

Appearing in this Book *(in order of appearance):*

ALLAN DWAN: Veteran director who worked with Leisen on *Robin Hood.*

NATALIE VISART: Leisen's mistress who succeeded him as costume designer on Cecil B. DeMille's productions.

FREDRIC MARCH: Star of three of Leisen's earliest films: *Tonight Is Ours, The Eagle And The Hawk* and *The Death Takes A Holiday.*

EVELYN VENABLE: Lovely leading lady of *Cradle Song* and *Death Takes A Holiday* .

CHARLES LANG: Master cinematographer who worked with Leisen on *Cradle Song, Death Takes A Holiday, Midnight, No Time For Love, Practically Yours* and *The Mating Season.*

ERNST FEGTÉ: Art director on *Death Takes A Holiday, Swing High, Swing Low, Easy Living, Artists And Models Abroad,* and *Frenchman's Creek.*

ELEANOR BRODER: Leisen's secretary from 1934 to the end of his life. Although Broder was a lesbian and always addressed and referred to her boss as "Mr. Leisen," she was actually a much more constant companion to him than his wife or the great loves of his life.

RAY MILLAND: Appeared in Leisen's *Four Hours To Kill, Big Broadcast Of 1937, Easy Living, Arise My Love, Lady In The Dark, Kitty* and *Golden Earrings,* and subsequently hired Leisen to direct episodes of his television series, *Markham.*

FRED MacMURRAY: Star of *Hands Across The Table, Thirteen Hours By Air, Swing High, Swing Low, Remember The Night, The Lady Is Willing, No Time For Love, Practically Yours* and *Suddenly It's Spring.*

DOROTHY LAMOUR: Appeared in Leisen's *Swing High, Swing Low, Big Broadcast Of 1938* and *Masquerade In Mexico;* he staged her nightclub acts in the '50s.

CLAUDETTE COLBERT: Who was gowned by Leisen in *The Sign Of The Cross* and went on to star for him in *Tonight Is Ours, Midnight, Arise My Love, No Time For Love* and *Practically Yours.*

OLIVIA de HAVILLAND: Nominated for the Academy Award for her performance in Leisen's *Hold Back The Dawn;* later won the Oscar in Leisen's *To Each His Own.*

ARTHUR HORNBLOW JR.: Producer of many of Leisen's films, including *Easy Living, Artists And Models Abroad, Midnight, Arise My Love, I Wanted Wings* and *Hold Back The Dawn.*

CHICO DAY (aka Francisco Alonso): Second Assistant Director on *The Big Broadcast Of 1938;* Assistant Director on *Remember The Night, Hold Back The Dawn, The Lady Is Willing, Lady In The Dark* and *Darling, How Could You,* among others.

CONSTANCE MOORE: Leading lady in *I Wanted Wings* and *Take A Letter Darling;* Leisen staged her nightclub acts in the '50s and '60s.

MACDONALD CAREY: Was directed by Leisen in *Take A Letter Darling, Suddenly It's Spring, Dream Girl, Bride Of Vengeance* and *Song Of Surrender.*

EDITH HEAD: Served her apprenticeship with Leisen, Howard Greer and Travis Banton in Paramount's wardrobe department; later while

Head Designer at Paramount collaborated with Leisen for the costumes and fashions in most of his '40s films.

PHYLLIS LOUGHTON SEATON: The wife of director George Seaton, she was the head of Paramount's school of contract players in the '30s, later was dialogue coach on *I Wanted Wings, Lady In The Dark,* all of Paulette Goddard's films with Leisen, *Frenchman's Creek, To Each His Own, Song Of Surrender* and *Captain Carey, U.S.A.*

JOAN FONTAINE: Star of *Frenchman's Creek* and *Darling, How Could You!*

RAY LIVINGSTON: Songwriter, who with collaborators and/or Victor Young contributed songs to such films as *To Each His Own, Golden Earrings, Captain Carey U.S.A.* and *Red Garters.*

JOHN LUND: Made his debut in *To Each His Own,* then did *Bride Of Vengeance, No Man Of Her Own, The Mating Season,* and *Darling, How Could You?* with Leisen.

RICHARD MAIBAUM: Producer of *Song Of Surrender, Bride Of Vengeance, Captain Carey U.S.A.* and *No Man Of Her Own.*

YVONNE WOOD: Designed the Mens' costumes for *Red Garters.*

PAT CROWLEY: Replaced Anna Maria Albergetti in *Red Garters* at the same time Leisen was fired.

ANNE BAXTER: Star of *Bedevilled.*

MALVIN WALD: Wrote the script for the *Shirley Temple Storybook* episode "Mother Goose".

RODDY McDOWALL: Appeared in the *Twilight Zone* episode, "People Are the Same All Over".

DOUGLAS BENTON: Associate producer of many *G.E. Theater* episodes, gave Leisen his last job directing three *Girl From U.N.C.L.E.* shows.

PREFACE
TO THE 1995 EDITION

Twenty-one years ago, *HOLLYWOOD DIRECTOR: The Career of Mitchell Leisen* was published as part of the Curtis Film Series. Since the text was also my Masters' Thesis at UCLA, its appearance in print represented the end of a long chapter of my life.

It began when I was ten years old and my mother, on her way to the beauty parlor, dropped me off at Paddock's Bookstore in Glendale, California, as she had done many times before. This time, however, my eye landed on a large volume entitled *"A Pictorial History of the Talkies,"* by Daniel Blum. From that moment on, I was obsessed with old movies. I subscribed to *Films in Review* magazine and began haunting the used bookstores in Los Angeles looking for old fan magazines.

Along the way I learned that there was another teenager who was similarly obsessed living in Teaneck, New Jersey named Leonard Maltin and he published a magazine called *Film Fan Monthy*. We began corresponding; I wrote articles for *Film Fan Monthly* and we visited each other during school vacations. When I went to New York, Leonard would take me to the Theodore Huff Society, the Museum of Modern Art and Movie Star News. When he came to Los Angeles, I drove him around to conduct interviews for his magazine and the books he was already writing. When, in the summer of 1969, Leonard told me that he had an appointment to interview Mitchell Leisen, I made up my own list of questions. I had just seen *To Each His Own* and marveled at its period authenticity. I had also been very frustrated when *Lady In The Dark* ended and nobody had ever really sung "My Ship."

The interview, which appeared in *Action Magazine,*(the periodical of the Director's Guild of America), and the January 1970, *Film Fan Monthly,* went beautifully and as we were finishing Leonard asked Mr. Leisen if he had prints of any of his films. Leisen produced a list and Leonard asked if we could see *Murder At The Vanities* and *Swing High, Swing Low.* The next night we were back, along with my friend Mae Woods and what I saw on the screen, especially the final moments of *Swing High, Swing Low* absolutely knocked me out. Leisen was very gratified to see that three college students enjoyed his films so much.

The late '60s had already seen an explosion of interest in American Films as art and popular culture and "oral history" was becoming a big buzz word in film study. Mae Woods had already taken a class at UCLA in Oral History Methods and was in the process of transcribing Peter Bogdanovich's taped interviews with John Ford, Allan Dwan and Orson Welles. Within a few days, I decided I would conduct an oral history with Leisen. Even though I was not even a student in the Film Department at UCLA, I burst into Dr. Howard Suber's office at UCLA and persuaded him to give me class credit for this endeavor. Next was funding from the Louis B. Mayer American Oral History Project which was administered by the American Film Institute. Moving into that magic realm, where I worked alongside the celebrated film historians Kevin Brownlowe and David Shepard and attended the screenings and seminars set up for the AFI Fellows was all I'd ever dreamed of and more.

Leisen thoroughly enjoyed it too. Once or twice a week we would drive up to the Doheny Mansion (then the AFI's West Coast Headquarters) in my beat-up 1951 yellow Plymouth Coupe (Leisen dubbed it the "Yellow Peril") and screen one or two of his films. A day or so later, we would sit down together to tape our interview, a job he took very seriously. After it was typed up, he would review and correct it. He was in very poor health already, emphysema was causing him to gasp for breath and and he was suffering from an intense pain in his left leg. Not long after we had screened all the films the AFI could obtain for us, he was hospitalized and the leg was amputated. He was so weak I was not allowed to visit him, so the project was considered finished.

I had not thought about publishing the interviews as a book. However, I made a trip to London and Mae Woods asked me to deliver Bogdanovich's manuscript on Allan Dwan to his editor at November

Books who thought the Leisen interviews would make a good book too, but before the contracts were signed, November Books had gone out of business.

Returning to Los Angeles, I re-enrolled at UCLA and started writing my thesis. I had a wonderful interview with Olivia de Havilland done in Paris and I began interviewing as many of Leisen's co-workers as could be found. His longtime secretary, Eleanor Broder was of great help, both with her own memories and by putting me in touch with many others. Dorothy Lamour gave me a wonderful interview, wrote the preface to the book and also persuaded Ray Milland and Fred MacMurray (who was very unwilling) to see me. Eventually Leisen, by now living at the Motion Picture Country Home, was strong enough to be interviewed about all the pictures we failed to cover in our previous talks.

I was working at the AFI Library when one day out of the blue I got a call from Leonard Maltin. The Curtis Publishing Company had decided to do a series of film books, and had named him editor. Did I want the Leisen book to be included in it? I was delighted. The book appeared early in 1973, was well received and I felt succeeded in bringing about a greater appreciation for Leisen's talent.

Unfortunately, the Curtis Film Series disappeared as suddenly as it had appeared. Overnight, *HOLLYWOOD DIRECTOR* became a rare collector's item. Over the years, I learned more about Leisen (some people were franker about him after he died). I asked Leonard for permission to reprint which he generously allowed. At first no publisher wanted to print it in its entirety (let alone expanded), but then I talked with John Dorman of Photoventures Press and here we are.

In preparing this edition, we added to the original interview copy while deleting none. The sections pertaining to Leisen's personal life have been expanded; now that his mistress Natalie Visart and her husband, Dwight Taylor have died, her decades long relationship with Leisen can be discussed more freely. I also have a better perspective about Leisen's lover, Billy Daniels.

Regrettably I did not speak much with Leisen himself about his emotional life. He probably would have discussed it frankly with me, but schooled as I was about motion pictures, I did not have enough life experience at that time to deal with what he would have told me. Bisexuality was and is not very well understood. Thus I have pieced together as well as possible a picture of his complex relationships with his wife, Stella Yeager, Natalie, Billy and the others from incidental information gathered along the way. Natalie had talked a great deal to her daughter Laurel Taylor about this relationship. Laurel and some of Leisen's male lovers have been very helpful in gaining a better insight into what really happened.

As before, my hope in writing this book is that it will draw attention to Leisen's remarkable career and contribution to American Films.

David Chierichetti

Hollywood, California
March, 1994

Mitchell Leisen:
HOLLYWOOD DIRECTOR

James Mitchell Leisen about the time he arrived in Hollywood.

WHO WAS
MITCHELL LEISEN?

When Mitchell Leisen died October 28, 1972, his was a name that few people knew. Film buffs have seen his *Lady In The Dark, Easy Living, Midnight* and *Hands Across The Table,* and perhaps a few of them wonder how the same man who directed these flamboyant entertainments could also have made the somberly beautiful *Death Takes A Holiday.* The very sophisticated know that he was the costume designer on several of Cecil B. DeMille's epics and might ponder that it is unusual for a costume designer to become a film director. He is more or less forgotten today, and it is a pity, because his career was unique and of great importance in the annals of American film history.

In a town where success is most often measured by the dollar sign, Leisen held the untouchable position of fifteen years of solid box office hits without a single failure. Stars clamored to be in his pictures which as a whole comprise one of the most varied *oeuvres* of any American director.

Leisen's extraordinary success was due to several factors: his complete understanding of all the major and minor elements which make up a film, his infallible good taste, and his own driving personality which made him always restless for new worlds to conquer. In his first years as a director, Leisen was fortunate, for the most part, in being assigned stories which interested him and competent, if not great, actors. He knew exactly what he wanted in terms of costume design, art direction,

1

sound recording and all the other elements of the cinematic craft, and he surrounded himself with a staff which could realize his concepts to the most minute detail, leaving him free to concentrate on his scripts and the performances of his actors. Many of his early projects seemed to the front office to have no great potential, but in Leisen's hands they blossomed beyond their expectations and he was rewarded with bigger budgets, a high paying contract and much greater freedom of operation.

He shared with Michael Curtiz and a handful of other directors the instinct of knowing just how to make all camera movement underline the points of the story. His films were not flashy with technique, but down to the slightest nuances, everything in the frame and on the sound track was carefully calculated for a certain effect. In terms of content, Leisens's films as a whole are far too varied to make any facile classification possible. Indeed, his individual works are often too complex to fall easily into the usual categories. Is *Murder Of The Vanites* a comedy, a murder mystery or a musical? Are *Swing High, Swing Low* and *Arise My Love* comedies or melodramas?

There are some elements, however, which bind his works together. Some contemporary critics see him as a cynic, and certainly it is true that *Hands Across The Table*, *Midnight* and *Practically Yours* have a certain cynical and pessimistic feeling. Yet Leisen's overwhelming romanticism overrides this, and optimism more than balances the pessimism. In Leisen's films, the most antagonistic of couples find true love and seem to live happily ever after (*Swing High, Swing Low, Midnight*); a long-suffering unwed mother is miraculously reunited with her child (*To Each His Own*); and a most fastidious Englishman finds in a filthy gypsy woman the love of his life (*Golden Earrings*). Leisen's films also shared a pictorial quality which is lushly romantic, from the dazzling highlights of *Tonight Is Ours* and *Midnight*, through the splendid colors of *Lady In The Dark* and *Frenchman's Creek* to the luminous low-key lighting of *The Eagle And The Hawk*, *Golden Earrings* and *Song Of Surrender*.

Like George Cukor, Leisen is sometimes classified as a "woman's" director. It is true that Leisen often made his actresses lovelier than they appeared in the films of other directors, and he could stretch the thin talents of some of them into quite credible performances, but it is also true that he worked equally well with men. Leisen's careful training helped groom both Fred MacMurray and Ray Milland for stardom. Surely Charles Boyer's performance in *Hold Back The Dawn* is as fine as Olivia de Havilland's, and Claude Rains' work in *Song Of Surrender* is masterful. Like a great many books, plays and other movies of the '30s and '40s, Mitchell Leisen's films were remarkably middlebrow, a quality contemporary popular culture seems to have lost. The great masses could follow Leisen's plots and dialogue, and yet there were certain nuances of the performances, certain extraordinary compositions of the image that intrigued the more sophisticated urban audiences and won praise from critics. The ingredients of films like *Swing High, Swing Low* and *Remember The Night* were essentially the same as for countless other films of the era, yet scene after scene revealed unexpected beauty in ordinary things, and new depths of emotion from familiar players.

Above all, Leisen's pictures entertained. He was a man very much concerned with the quality of life and the human condition, and such ponderings found their way into his films, but only subliminally. On the surface there was a story that interested the audience and characters it could care about. And Leisen's films moved. As filled as they often were with details of historical research and finely detailed acting, the plots moved so fast that nobody had much time to notice; yet these details were perceived subliminally and greatly enriched the films.

In his era, Leisen was pre-eminent on the Hollywood scene. The whole town turned out twice a year for the openings of his lavish revues at the Coconut Grove and invitations to Leisen's parties were so much sought after that Sonja Henie had to enlist Darryl Zanuck's help in order to get invited. His New Year's 1946 shindig cost him $52,000 and was so enormous that Leisen had to lease a building on La Cienega Boulevard and convert it to a ballroom. The building thereafter housed the multifaceted Leisen Enterprises where Leisen turned out stunning gowns as favors to his stars, staged nightclub acts and conducted an interior decorating business which was the subject of a monthly column in *Photoplay* magazine. He was also co-owner of Mitchell and Haigue, one of Beverly Hills' most stylish tailor shops. Ray Milland told me, "He had so much talent in all artistic directions, I think one thing kept dissipating the other. He was always enthused about a new project to the point where he never stopped trembling."

James Mitchell Leisen was born October 6, 1898 in Menominee, Michigan where his father was a partner in the Leisen and Hennes Brewing Company. His parents were soon divorced and he went to live with his mother and her second husband in St. Louis. At the age of five, he was operated on for a club foot. The operation left him slightly lame for many years and the foot continued to bother him throughout his adult life.

James Mitchell Leisen at age six in Menimonee, Wisconsin.

An introverted child, he spent his time making models of lavish theaters and arranging flowers. He was sent to military school and although his foot ruled out induction into the First World War, he was hired by the Army to drill new recruits.

After living for awhile with his Kansas City socialite aunt, Myrtle Irene Mitchell, James returned to St. Louis to study architecture and commercial art before entering the Church School of Fine and Applied Arts in Chicago. He began receiving commissions there, designing the ballroom of the Edgewater Beach Hotel and decorating the Powers Theatre. A set he designed for the Playshop Players at the Philistine

Theater was later enlarged and adapted for Carolyn Cole's vaudeville act, "No Sabe." He also worked for the Junior League Follies in Kansas City.

Coming to Southern California around 1919, Leisen happened into a job designing costumes for Cecil B. DeMille. He devoted much of his leisure time to amateur theatricals, designing stage sets and acting occasionally for the Hollywood Community Theatre. Soon he was designing sets for William DeMille's films and acquiring a broad knowledge of the motion picture craft. He was called upon in various capacities for many Paramount films in the early '20s. Even then the competition in Hollywood was keen, but right from the start, Mitchell Leisen was a success.

As rewarding as his professional life was, Leisen's personal life was troubled and he seemed to find little contentment outside of his work. He had the reputation of being quite a ladies' man, probably because of his long affair with Marguerite DeLaMotte which began when Leisen visited the set of Douglas Fairbanks' *The Three Musketeers* in 1920. DeLaMotte was the leading lady and he reportedly had boldly told her that he wanted to visit her at home that night. She warned him that she had a chaperone, so he offered to get a ladder to come in through her bedroom window! This was the beginning of an affair that was to last for several years and soon a gossip columnist reported that they were "secretly engaged," (a euphemism for having an affair.) However, the *Los Angeles Times*, on July 29, 1921 reported, "After all, Marguerite DeLaMotte isn't to marry Mitchell Leisen as so often reported. She sent word to that effect yesterday. So there's another nice romance spoiled." The "romance" was hardly spoiled as it continued for several more years. She later married actor John Bowers, but Leisen said in 1969 that he remained in touch with her throughout her life. Even more mysterious was Leisen's sudden marriage to Stella Yeager in 1927, which was held at Cecil B. DeMille's ranch with the wedding party dressed in Russian flavored costumes. Yeager was a mezzo-soprano who used the name of Sondra Gahle professionally. Although Ray Milland characterized her as a "horror" and said her singing was "lousy," Leisen seldom said an unkind word about her. He once related quite proudly that when she sang in *Rigoletto* with the San Francisco Opera Company on its annual trip southward to Los Angeles' Shrine Auditorium, a critic noticed that Stella had stayed on pitch when Lily Pons didn't.

Leisen rented and refurbished a lavish house for Stella in Paris where she studied singing and they would visit each other from time to time.

Mitchell Leisen and Stella Yeager on their wedding day.

When World War II began, she returned to California and although they didn't live together again, she visited his sets and he sent her lavish presents.

One explanation for Leisen's sudden interest in Stella was that she had "the face." Throughout his life, he seems to have been fascinated with women who had a certain look, blonds with strong jaws and strong, sometimes even hooked noses. Carole Lombard had that look, as did Constance Moore. The telling clue to this is in a sketch he drew for one of Mary Pickford's costumes for *Dorothy Vernon Of Haddon Hall* and another for a never filmed production of *Faust,* both some years before he met Stella. Although Pickford didn't have a hooked nose, he drew her with one. Leisen's own nose was long and pointed and he had it shortened. He encouraged Stella to have the hook removed from her nose, and he later related that the operation was mostly successful except that she looked as if she was smelling something bad when she smiled. Later he advised Natalie Visart to have her nose fixed but changed his mind when he realized she'd have to modify her pointed chin as well.

With his love of music, Leisen clearly enjoyed being married to an opera singer. He went so far as to try to interest Paramount in letting him direct a film of Bizet's *Carmen* to star his wife. He paid for an elaborate test himself although nothing ever came of it.

Author's note: Perhaps another reason Leisen married Stella was that Stella was very tolerant of the men in his life. So many people have asked me what he told me about Hollywood's gay scene in the '20s that I regret now that I never asked him about it specifically but there is some evidence that he was involved right from the start. Going through his memorabilia, I found a picture from a handsome man, dated 1919 bearing the cryptic inscription, "You're all right Mitch, even if they are silk." Photos from Ramon Navarro and Ivor Novello also bore affectionate inscriptions. Leisen told me he once traveled from Los Angeles to New York in a stateroom on a train with his costume designing protege Gilbert Adrian. Adrian woke him up in the middle of the night by tickling his nose with a feather and Leisen's raised eyebrows conveyed to me the idea that he and Adrian subsequently had sex.

The funniest story about Leisen's not always satisfied desires concerned Joel McCrea. Leisen found McCrea tremendously beautiful when he was called upon to costume him for his small part in *Dynamite,* but he took great pains during the fittings to avoid touching McCrea and possibly revealing what he was thinking. Maybe McCrea sensed what was on Mitchell's mind anyway for some weeks later, Leisen and his wife ran into McCrea and Gloria Swanson while both couples were waiting for their limousines after a performance of the Los Angeles Philharmonic. Much to Swanson's consternation, McCrea yelled across the street, "Haven't you heard, Mitch? I can be had now!"

Fond as he was of Stella, the love that persisted throughout his life was Natalie Visart. The fact that they couldn't marry was painful to both of them. He usually referred to her as "Mrs. Taylor" in deference to her husband, who he respected.

Born (in 1909) and raised in Chicago, Natalie suffered from respiratory problems, so her father, a doctor, sent her out to the Hollywood School For Girls in 1920. There she met another new student, Katherine DeMille, who had recently been adopted by the DeMille family.

This photograph of Leisen was inscribed to Natalie Visart: "To Nat, How's about it? Mitch '33."

The DeMilles became very fond of Natalie and soon she was spending weekends and school vacations at their home. Leisen was also a frequent dinner guest at the DeMille house, but Natalie's memory was that she didn't meet him until the filming of *The Volga Boatman* in 1926. By 1929 they were sleeping together. Mitchell gave Natalie a beautiful piece of jewelry which she longed to wear to a DeMille dinner party but didn't dare for fear that the family would catch on to what was happening.

Aside from physical attraction, Natalie and Mitchell had much in common as both were well educated and loved art and music. The society boys that Natalie dutifully dated on her visits home to Chicago didn't begin to compare. As Mitchell started to direct his own films and began phasing himself out of DeMille's unit, he groomed Natalie to take his place as a costume designer, a fact that other costume designers working for DeMille, such as Ralph Jester, did not appreciate at all. Finally in 1938, she was assigned to design *The Buccaneer* on her own. As her professional life improved, Natalie's personal life remained

Leisen and Visart dance at C.B. DeMille's birthday party, December 5, 1937.

difficult. Being a devout Catholic, she could not marry a divorced man. Moreover she suspected that Eddie Anderson, a pilot who had taught Mitchell how to fly and was now sharing his home, was more than just a roommate. Evelyn Venable would say many years later, "I entertained them both [Leisen and Anderson] in my home and hadn't the vaguest idea of what their relationship really was."

Natalie enjoyed the fascinating company that her relationship with Mitchell brought to her. Often they spent the weekend at Zeppo Marx's ranch in the San Fernando Valley with Clark Gable and Carole Lombard, and Robert Taylor and Barbara Stanwyck, two other not-yet-married couples trying to keep a low profile. Fred MacMurray's first wife Lillian was chronically ill and Natalie spent a lot of time with her during the periods when she was confined to her bed, literally running Lillian's household. And then there was Leisen's frequent producer, Arthur Hornblow Jr. whose wife Myrna Loy remained close to Natalie for all of her life.

> **Author's note:** Myrna once invited me to a Broadway play followed by dinner at Sardi's and no matter how much I tried to change the subject, all Myrna wanted to talk about was what Natalie and Dwight Taylor were doing. In response to my suggestion that Natalie's relationship with Mitchell might have been more or less platonic, Myrna replied, with one of those pauses for which she was famous, "Oh no, they had .... a *relationship.*"

The era of the '30s and '40s provided Mitchell with the opportunity to work in a medium perfectly suited to the expression of his many artistic talents but the social mores of that time, even in liberal Hollywood, did not allow him, in the end, to fulfill his diverse personal needs as fully. It was typical of Leisen to think that somehow he could manage to have it all, balancing relationships with Natalie, his wife and Eddie Anderson at the same time. Raised in a conservative Catholic family, Natalie was also very sophisticated and she made allowances for Mitchell's homosexual drives as long as his main interest was Eddie Anderson. She could tolerate that relationship because nobody knew about it — their mutual interest in flying gave them a reason to be together often and Mitchell got Paramount to hire Anderson as his Assistant Director. Natalie began living openly with Mitchell and according to Eleanor Broder, he started taking hormone shots in the hope that they would cure his homosexual impulses. (They didn't.)

War clouds in Europe in 1937 brought the possibility that Stella

Natalie Visart, Dorothy Lamour, Martha Raye, Leisen and Shirley Ross at Leisen's birthday party on the set of *The Big Broadcast of 1938*. Paramount's caption said, "as a rib to Director Mitchell Leisen, Shirley Ross and Dorothy Lamour staged a fake fight that started in the morning and ended at the hair pulling stage in the late afternoon when Leisen jumped in between them to separate them. It was all because of Leisen's birthday but it left the director weak." About a month later, Leisen suffered a heart attack and nervous breakdown which would change the course of his life.

would return to Los Angeles and reassert her position as Mitchell's wife. Eventually she did come back, settled in San Francisco and reentered Mitchell's life to some extent. One newspaper clipping from 1940 says that Leisen and two dancers from his nightclub revue, Evangeline Kirby and Billy Daniels, were all set to visit Stella in San Francisco, but the plans were canceled when he was ordered to Texas to take over *I Wanted Wings*. Leisen had first hired Daniels for the nightclub act in the mid-'30s and his affection for him increased as his relationship with Anderson was winding down. These tensions all came to a head when Leisen was shooting *The Big Broadcast Of 1938*, late in that year. Eddie Anderson fell in love with Shirley Ross, one of the film's stars, and began going off to her dressing room at the end of each day's work, rather than staying for the usual production meeting. It infuriated Leisen that Anderson was neglecting his duties, but it also broke his heart as he realized he was losing him. The night *Big Broadcast* finished shooting, Leisen suffered a serious heart attack.*

---

*Even though Natalie and Eleanor Broder always blamed the impossible behavior of W.C. Fields for the heart attack, the departure of Eddie Anderson was probably a bigger factor.

Leisen's recovery was long and difficult. As he slowly resumed his work, some noticed that Leisen's personality was changing. Where he had once been very agreeable and easy to get along with, he was now increasingly arrogant and bossy. Of his behavior in the '40s, Roddy MacDowell now says, "I didn't meet him myself until much later, but I was aware that some people really hated him. He knew that his pictures made a lot of money and big stars wanted to work with him so that put him in a position of considerable power which some people felt he abused."

Part of Leisen's change in personality was to make his relationship with Billy Daniels known to everybody whether they were interested or not. It was sometimes hard for Daniels to keep the image Mitchell desired for him. For one thing, Mitchell had two toupees especially made for Billy: one curly and one straight. Daniels found them highly uncomfortable when he was rehearsing, so he would take them off and then have friends warn him if Mitchell was on his way over to the dance studio! He was a talented dancer and choreographer and although Leisen got him work at Paramount (eventually he choreographed all the musical shorts), most observers thought he did it well. He later worked with Betty Grable and at various other studios.

Natalie Visart decided that there was no room for her in this situation and accepted a short term job with Lily Dache in Paris. The threat of war and the fact that DeMille needed her for *Northwest Mounted Police* led to her return to Paramount in 1939. Mitchell wanted her back in his life. She tried to ignore him but could not; the Paramount lot was too small and Eleanor Broder, Leisen's secretary, was one of her best friends. They did not live together again but saw each other throughout the War years. When Barbara Stanwyck asked Mitchell to design her wardrobe for the independently produced *Meet John Doe (1941),* he persuaded her to use Natalie. DeMille got Paramount to offer her a full time contract, but she turned it down, saying, "When you don't need me, Edith [Head] would have me picking up pins off the workroom floor!" Instead, she signed a contract with producer Hunt Stromberg and continued with DeMille.

Sometime during this period, Natalie found she was pregnant with Leisen's child. (Her daughter now thinks it was in 1943.) This created a great crisis in both their lives. Now both wanted the child very much, yet they couldn't get married. Suddenly, she miscarried.

Coincidentally, Paramount sent Leisen the script for *To Each His Own,* a story of an unwed mother trying to get her child back. Nobody could

Leisen and Billy Daniels, late '40s.

Leisen and his secretary Eleanor Broder.

understand why he hated it so much. His agent, Charles Feldman, (who apparently did not know what had happened) persuaded him to reconsider. By the time she saw the film, Natalie had married Dwight Taylor and was pregnant with her son Peter Taylor. She said that it made her "very uncomfortable" but she sent word to Mitchell that she thought he had "done it very well."

The marriage of Natalie Visart and Dwight Taylor came about rather suddenly. Myrna Loy had returned to Hollywood after two years in New York and Dwight Taylor was one of the writers on her new picture, *The Thin Man Goes Home* (1944). His wife was hospitalized for alcoholism in the Menninger Clinic and Myrna knew Natalie was extremely depressed, so she invited them both to a party she was giving. At first Natalie refused to come, so Myrna called Katherine DeMille and said, "You get her here or else!" As the two women walked in Myrna's door, Natalie noticed Dwight and said, "You see that man over there? I'm going to marry him." And she soon did. The Taylors lived in New York most of the time, but Natalie kept in touch with Mitchell. Although most of his screenplays *(Gay Divorcee, Top Hat)* were about idle sophisticates, Dwight Taylor was a kindly man, who did not resent Mitchell.

Once Natalie was married, Leisen seemed to throw all caution to the wind. One young man, who worked in Paramount's mailroom, later told that he was amused to read about Leisen's devotion to art. "When I knew him, all he wanted to talk about was sex. Every time Eleanor Broder called the mailroom and asked for something to be picked up, I'd get the other fellows to let me be the one to go to Mitch's office. I noticed that Eleanor always managed to have the door between her outer office and Mitch's office closed when I arrived so I wouldn't get to talk to him. One time, however, it happened to be opened a little, and although she tried to get rid of me fast, Mitch heard me out there and rather angrily told her to let me come in. We got to talking and he

Natalie Visart, Mitchell Leisen and the author at USC on May 15, 1972.

invited me and my (male) lover to spend the weekend on his yacht. He was a very highly sexed person."

It is hard to gauge now whether Leisen's blatant homosexual behavior of the late '40s was part of his problems with Paramount. Songwriter Jay Livingston thinks it wasn't. He recalls overhearing a conversation between screenwriter Bob Hartman and Y. Frank Freeman, one of the top executives of the studio. Freeman, who came from the South and was often consulted to make sure Paramount pictures didn't offend Southern sensibilities, commented, " I just don't understand Mitch Leisen." Hartman replied, "He's a homosexual." Freeman: "What does that mean?" Hartman: "He has unnatural sexual practices." Freeman: "Does that mean he's unfaithful to his wife?" Even if Leisen's homosexuality did contribute to some of his unpopularity with certain executives, it was also an undeniable aid in building Leisen's well-known rapport with certain bisexual leading ladies.

Being bisexual was part of Leisen's general unhappiness and life would have been easier for him if his desires had been wholly one way or the other. Once, when talking about Marlene Dietrich, he suddenly abandoned his usually breezy raconteur style of talking and said solemnly, "You have to understand Marlene is double-gaited. You just have to accept that about her." The "You just have to accept that" part was really referring to himself. During this time, the side that most people saw was wild and promiscuous, but there was another side that wanted to settle down and have children.

Leisen's liaison with Billy Daniels continued into the early '50s. Hoping to further Daniels' career, Leisen suggested that he be allowed to direct a musical short, in addition to doing the choreography. The picture was primarily directed by Leisen himself who reasoned (incorrectly) that once Daniels' name was on a film as director, he would get other offers to direct. However, the industry seemed to know who had really directed it and no offers came in. Daniels went back to choreography.

Shortly afterwards, Daniels developed a medical problem which caused him to gain a lot of weight. After a period of working in Europe, Daniels returned to Los Angeles . Mitchell told him their relationship was over but that he could sleep on a cot in his studio on La Cienega Boulevard. When Daniels died soon thereafter, Leisen told people he had committed suicide with prescription drugs. Other accounts attributed the death to a heart attack.

During this time, Leisen was getting the reputation of being "always on the make" even with men who were undoubtedly heterosexual. This behavior was partly responsible for his being fired from the film *Bedevilled* in 1954; and the reputation he had (also of being extravagant) made it hard for him to get jobs, even with Charles Feldman's considerable influence behind him.

Both Dwight and Natalie tried very hard to make their marriage work. Laurel Taylor says, "I don't think she really "got" my father intellectually in the same way that she did Mitchell, but she loved him very much. She faced a lot of serious problems with my father, especially financial ones. Although she and Mitchell also had many problems, she didn't have the day to day troubles of paying the bills and raising the kids that she had with my dad." It was during a very difficult period in 1971 that Natalie came back to Los Angeles for an extended vacation. She once again became Mitchell's constant companion. It was only when Leisen died that Dwight Taylor moved out from New York City.

Billy Daniels (circa 1947)

THE BEGINNING
WITH DEMILLE

MITCHELL LEISEN: I never could decide what I wanted to be. All of the fellows I knew in college were planning to go into their fathers' businesses, but I didn't have any father and I couldn't make up my mind. I had a cousin named Kathleen Kirkham who was a stage actress and had done some films too. I saw her once when she was back in Chicago and she said there was a real scarcity of leading men in Hollywood due to the first World War. I had done some acting with a little theater company in Chicago, so I thought, "Why not give it a try." I was working for the architectural firm of Marshall and Fox in Chicago, but they were having a slow period, so they gave me some time off and I went out to Hollywood.

Ruth St. Denis and Ted Shawn were old friends of the family, so I stayed with them at their studio on Alvarado Street. I remember sticking some peacock feathers in the back of my pants one night and doing an imitation of Ruth's favorite dance, much to the annoyance of all present. Somehow I managed to get a small part as an actor in a picture starring Olive Thomas. Don't ask me what the title was. I didn't get anywhere as an actor.

One night Ted asked me if I'd like to go with them to a dinner at the Smalley's. Philip Smalley was the husband of Lois Weber, the only woman director in Hollywood at the time. I sat next to a very charming woman at dinner, and I went on and on, telling her all about myself. I didn't realize it then, but she was Jeannie MacPherson, Cecil B. DeMille's scenarist. A couple of nights later, I was down at the pier at Venice, at the Old Ship Cafe and I happened to see this same woman I had met at the Smalley's. I went over to ask how Mrs. Smalley was (Mrs. Smalley had had a broken arm that had been badly set and needed to be rebroken and reset). My new acquaintance said she'd like to have me meet Mr. Cecil B. DeMille.

I was so thrilled because I had been raised on *The Woman God Forgot* and all the DeMille spectacles. After the introductions, DeMille said, "Miss MacPherson tells me about the wonderful work you do. I'd like to have you come and work for me. Get in touch with Miss MacPherson at the studio and she'll tell you what I want."

I thought it would be a good chance to see the inside of his studio, so I went. DeMille was doing *Male And Female,* and he wanted some costumes designed. I had never designed any costumes in my life, but I thought, "What the hell." I went through Ted Shawn's library of art books and the public library, and I made three sketches. I took them to DeMille and he asked me what I wanted for them. Taking a wild flyer, I said, "$300 apiece." He said, "Well, just wait in the outer office." He came back and said, "I'll give you a hundred dollars apiece for these and a year's contract for a hundred dollars a week." I told him I had a job in Chicago and I'd have to see if could accept his offer.

Marshall and Fox were waiting for the Drake Hotel contracts to come through. I wired Benny Marshall about my job offer and he wired back, "No sign of Drake Hotel contracts, go ahead and take it." I signed a piece of paper, and two weeks later I got a wire from Benny saying, "Just signed the Drake Hotel contracts, come back at once."

I went to DeMille and said, "I'm terribly sorry, but I have to go back to Chicago" He said, "You have a contract with me." I replied, "But Mr. DeMille, I have a job in Chicago, this is just movies." He said, "Well, it may be just movies to you, but it's still a legitimate contract and you are under contract to me." So I've been here ever since.

A year later, I asked Miss MacPherson, "Whatever in the world did you tell DeMille about me? If I didn't know I could design costumes, how did you know? She answered, "You had such interesting hands I knew you could do something."

I started with *Male And Female.* It was from a play called *The Admirable Crichton,* but DeMille had to change the title because he got several letters from exhibitors saying they didn't want any more navy pictures and who was this Admiral Crichton anyway? I worked on the flashback

Thomas Meighan and Gloria Swanson in Leisen's costumes for *Male and Female* (1918).

sequence entitled, "When I was a King of Babylon and you were a Christian slave." DeMille approved of my sketch and then told me I had to do fifty or more and supervise the making of them! I had never made a dress before in my life and I didn't know the first thing to do. Clare West was the head of wardrobe at the Lasky studio and she wasn't about to have me making anything in her workroom. She stuck me in a little room about 4' by 6' with six seamstresses, and I sweated the whole thing out myself.

I finally hit upon the idea of making the train in batik. I painted the pattern on the fabric with plain, ordinary beeswax, then I dyed it, being very careful not to crack the wax, or the pattern would have had a crackled effect. Where there was wax, the cloth didn't take any dye. Then I pressed the material, melting the wax and leaving a pattern. We embroidered with pearls for the peacock's eyes.

We did Tommy Meighan's costume for the king and one for Bebe Daniels who was the king's mistress. Bebe was a fairly tall girl, but Gloria Swanson is a very small person, very short. I wanted to give her high heels to give her more stature. I couldn't just put French heels on her, which were in style at the time, because it would have been a terrible anachronism. I finally hit upon the idea of making wooden clogs for her that were in the shape of Babylonian bulls standing on their forelegs with wings that came up on the sides of Gloria's feet and held them on.

I did clothes for some other pictures, but I forget what they were. I did some of the clothes for the Cinderella Ball in *Fool's Paradise* and Natasha Rambova did the others. One of hers was a black dress for the Fairy Godmother that had little electric lights all over the skirt. After about a year, I went to DeMille and said, "Look, I'm not a dressmaker. I've studied architecture, how about letting me do something in the art department?" He said, "What can you do? Anybody can design a beautiful palace, but can you make a livery stable that smells?" I said, "I don't know, but I want to try." DeMille said, "I'll tell you what I'm going to do. I'll put you with my brother William for a year and you can dress his sets."

Explaining the basic difference between his pictures and William's, Cecil always said, "It's arithmetical. William always brings his pictures in under budget and on schedule. The only trouble is that we can't sell them." William was a very plodding, conservative guy, the complete opposite of Cecil who was the flamboyant member of the family. They couldn't think alike at all. William was very studious, very conscientious. He was having a quiet love affair with his scriptwriter, Olga Printzlau. I was the set dresser on *Conrad In Quest Of His Youth* and a Barrie play; I don't remember the name of it.

I think it was Midsummer Madness. *There is a scene in* Conrad In Quest Of His Youth *where Thomas Meighan is in a British railroad station and at the very edge of the frame there is a little sign that says Bovril. Without that sign, that station could have been anywhere. Was that your doing?*

MITCHELL LEISEN: Probably. That was my training with Cecil. He always used to say: "The camera has no ears. If you want to say it, get it on the screen." That is advice I've used throughout my career, in talking pictures as well as silent. No matter what, get it on the screen. The visual image carries more impact than the dialogue.

I was working with William one day when Cecil sent for me in a rush and I went down to his stage. He had a special stage on the end of the lot and nothing was ever on that stage but DeMille's sets. DeMille pointed to his set and said, "What is it?" I said, "It looks like tenement rooms to me." DeMille yelled, "That set dresser's a goddamned stupid bastard. It's supposed to be a very fashionable girls' school. Fix it!"

I said, "Wait a minute, Mr. DeMille. You know this can't be done in five minutes. We have to repaint and repaper the whole thing. We have to get new drapes for it." He said, "All right, how long will it take?" I said, "Well, with any luck, I can have it ready for you tomorrow morning." With that, he dismissed the company and I flew.

I worked on it all night with the painters and the drapery department, and by 8:00 a.m. the next morning, the truck with the new furniture still hadn't arrived from town. I was going crazy; all hell would break lose if he got there and it wasn't done. Five minutes before DeMille came back on the stage, the furniture arrived. He took one look at it and said, "Now that looks like something," and I was back in his unit as set dresser.

Was DeMille as much of a sadist as he's sometimes described?

MITCHELL LEISEN: No, everybody adored him that ever worked with him. He might raise holy hell on the set, but often that was to put fear into the actor by criticizing me or the prop man. The minute we walked off the stage, he couldn't have been more charming. He'd even apologize for blowing his stack: "There was nothing personal in that." I'd say, "I know, don't worry, I've been with you long enough to know that."

Did he direct the actors much? Do you think he was a good director?

MITCHELL LEISEN: For the type of thing he did, he was very good. DeMille had no nuances. Everything was in neon lights six feet tall: *Lust, Revenge, Sex.* You had to learn to think the way he thought, in capital letters. Roy Burns was his business manager, and whenever he and I went through a new script to figure the costs, he'd say, "Here it is again, two squirrels in a tree, makin' love to each other." Script after script had the same crap in it. It wasn't until Jeannie MacPherson left and he got another writer that he saw the light and stopped doing the same old shit over and over again.

He directed the actors well. He had very positive ideas of what he wanted, and he wasn't satisfied until he got it. He used to say that no woman could be an actress until she had had her heart broken. Wallace Reid was the stud of the studio, and whenever DeMille had a new sweet young thing under contract, he sent Wally over to "make her a woman" as they said in those days.

Paul Iribe was DeMille's French art director. I used to have knock-down fights with him and he'd fire me. DeMille didn't fire me so much. At the end of the day, Iribe would suddenly drop everything on my shoulders and go home. I remember one time I worked all night long trying to get a set for a big carnival sort of thing. At 6:00 a.m. in the morning, I decided that I would go home and take a bath, and then come back and finish what had to be done. I fell asleep on the bathroom floor and I didn't wake up until 10:00 a.m. I tore back to the studio and Iribe was in flames because he had to go in there and finish this thing up. That was one of the times I got fired; maybe it was the last, I can't remember. Eventually I heard Douglas Fairbanks needed somebody to do costumes, so I took that job instead of trying to get back in Iribe's good graces.

What are your feelings about DeMille now?

MITCHELL LEISEN: I owe him everything I ever learned about making pictures. The most important thing of all is the power of concentration, never deviating from your objective. Once he started on a project, he concentrated on that and thought of nothing else. Through him, I learned how to be the same way.

ROBIN HOOD - 1922

MITCHELL LEISEN: Fairbanks was really interested in this. He was fascinated by the period and was very knowledgeable about everything in it. Once he got wound up in a project he couldn't stop. But he played all the time too. When some athletes came by, he would stop everything and race or play tennis. If Fairbanks wanted to play that day, you didn't shoot, that's all. He had a Turkish bath and a pool with a 500 pound cake of ice in it. We had to go in every night after work and take a steam bath and then dive into the ice cold water! Then we lolled around the dressing room while Abdul the masseur gave everybody a massage. Unfortunately, the massage table had hot wires on it and it would give you a shock every once in awhile.

I lived at Pickfair for weeks on end. Charlie Chaplin, Harry Davenport and I drove up there with Doug almost every night for dinner. Mary would go to bed right after dinner and we'd run a picture. Douglas would fall sound asleep during the picture and just as it ended, he would wake up and say, "Best picture I've ever seen in my life." Then everybody would go upstairs to bed and climb into the Rolls Royce the next morning and go to the studio. I started wishing I could spend a night at home for a change, so I said, "Douglas, I've got to go back home and get some clean clothes." He said, "I've got plenty of clothes here, what the hell do you need?" I had more underwear and shirts of Doug's.

I have always been a fiend for authenticity and *Robin Hood* was as correct as I could make it. Each knight had a tabard he wore on his chain mail which had his crest on it. His shield had the same crest, his helmet carried it and so did the banner on his spear. These were all sets, and they had to go together all the time. I did hundreds of them. The chain mail was knitted out of hemp, ironed flat and silver leafed.

One of the tough things was to get Douglas' long-haired wig to fall naturally. The first wig was so stiff, no matter what he did with his hair, the wig stayed the same. I got a German wig maker, who was the father of the Westmore boys, and we made the wig out of the finest toupee hair. He worked and worked with it, a magnificent job of wig making, but the result was if Doug shook his head, the hair just flew all over the place, so we had to watch out for that.

ALLAN DWAN: Mitch was always a gentleman. He was a grade above most people on the Paramount lot in terms of education and manners, but he wasn't a snob. He was very friendly and everybody liked him. Later on, when he was directing his own pictures, I think there were times when he didn't come down from his pedestal enough for the common tastes, but Mitch's exacting standards were great for the DeMille pictures, and *Robin Hood* too.

I had known Mitch at Paramount because we often had two or three companies working on the same stage and everybody knew everybody else. Mitch was officially with the DeMille unit, but anybody at Paramount who needed him could use him. I vaguely remember that he helped me stage a typhoon for some Paramount picture. DeMille thought very highly of Mitch and depended on him a great deal, right from the beginning.

There was quite a slump in the business when we did *Robin Hood,* and I think the only reason we got Mitch away from DeMille was that DeMille wasn't shooting at the time. Wilfred Buckland came to us from the DeMille unit too, and he was officially the art director, but Mitch helped him a lot dressing the sets, especially anything that involved

Director Allan Dwan (with hand on chin), cameraman Arthur Rossen (hand in belt loops) and Mitchell Leisen on the set of Douglas Fairbanks' *Robin Hood* (1922).

draping fabric. When we shot the tournament sequence, some fellow came in and built the platform for the King to sit on, but it was Mitch who draped all the material around the sides and made the canopy above.

It was Mitch also that made the enormous drape that Doug Fairbanks slid down to get away from the villain in the balcony. The drape was 70 feet long; it hung from the top of the set and had to be carefully arranged to conceal the slide in back of it which was really how Doug got down. There was nowhere you could go to buy any cloth that large. Mitch made it out of burlap and painted it himself to look like tapestry. Doug was in Europe when we built the set and his first reaction was, "Get rid of it, it's too big to compete with," but then I slid down the drape and Fairbanks was all for it. Mitch also made tapestries for the walls by painting burlap and they looked more genuine on film than the actual tapestries we borrowed from museums.

As a coutourier, Mitch was superb. If he had wanted to, he could have gone on to become another Dior. Getting all those costumes was a real chore. He rented whatever he could, but nobody in town would have that many things in stock, so he had to make the rest. He supervised a factory of seamstresses.

Many of the scenes had thousands of extras. Every morning, a mob would come to the gate and my assistants and I would pick out the people we knew and Mitch chose from the others the ones that looked best to him. We usually started the day shooting the close shots of the principals while Mitch got them dressed, and then we did the longer shots. He had many assistants to help him, but they all filed past Mitch for inspection. When they weren't okay for some reason, Mitch told his assistants how to fix them up. We told him when we'd need the extras, and he always got them on the set by that time.

I relied on Mitch to compose the group scenes and arrange the extras in a way that did justice to his designs. He had to go out on the stage one day and show the men how to use their spears and shields. He always paid particular attention to the skirts of the women and how they were draped. Once he fussed with the veils of the women for such a long time, making them fall just so that I finally said, "I don't care if these broads are wearing bed sheets, we've got to start shooting."

In one scene Fairbanks was being chased by a crowd of women. The girls got tangled up in the skirts, so they just hoisted them up in order to run. No medieval woman would have dreamed of doing that, but I didn't have time to fool with them, so I called Mitch over and said, "Teach them to move," and he did.

When we shot the wedding scene from the balcony, we only had about three hundred extras in that day. Fairbanks said, "You didn't get enough people, that's a very big set." I said, "We have enough, just wait and see." Mitch and I went to work. We spread them all out about an arm's width apart, but from the angle we were shooting, they looked tightly packed in. I went up to the balcony and looked at it through the viewfinder. Wherever I saw a patch of empty floor, I told Mitch and he put a woman in there with a big skirt that filled it up.

ROSITA - 1923

MITCHELL LEISEN: Then I went over to Mary Pickford's unit to do the costumes for *Rosita*. I didn't think it was the right thing for Mary to do, in terms of the period or anything else. It was Lubitsch's first

Mary Pickford in one of Leisen's costumes for *Rosita* (1923).

picture here which made it very difficult for everybody because he could hardly make himself understood.

Despite all the problems with the story, I really loved designing the gowns for *Rosita*. My love of detail came out in designing those Empire dresses, particularly Irene Rich's, which had long velvet hangings. Some of the trains were nine feet long. The women would wrap them around themselves and throw the end over their partner's shoulder when they danced. To make them hit the floor just right and lay out there without pulling back into ugly lines was quite a problem.

THE COURTSHIP OF MILES STANDISH - 1923

MITCHELL LEISEN: I don't think I ever even saw the picture. All I did was the costumes and I left when I got back into DeMille's good graces.

The picture was terrible. It was a dull story to start with, and it was very badly designed. Charlie Ray built the Mayflower in the middle of the block, and then he couldn't photograph it because all of Hollywood was all around it. It was completely the wrong part for Charles to undertake, and he bankrupted himself doing it.

Charlie was a very funny person. He was probably the most famous hick character on the screen, but he couldn't stand the idea of being a hick, so in his private life, he went completely berserk in extravagance. He had a huge house out in Beverly Hills, at the corner of Sunset and Benedict Canyon. We would go out there for lunch one day, and the whole garden had, perhaps, tulips. Then we'd go the next weekend, and they'd be camillias. The flowers were just in pots stuck in the ground and covered over. They'd take them all out and put something else in. The upholstery in the drawing room cost $125 a yard.

His wardrobe was all cutaway and striped trousers on Sunday. There was a footman and a chauffeur on the Packard limousine. His wife Clara never paid less than $300 for a pair of shoes, and there were a hundred pairs in her closet. At one of their dinner parties, Rosa Ponselle stood singing on the stairway in the hall while everybody sat in the living room. I think Clara paid her $5,000 to do it.

Charlie did such crazy things. We complained that there was no place to eat around the studio. I said, "Why don't we have a luncheon club? We could get a cook, use that empty building over there and all put in so much money a week to pay for it." We wound up with a hammered beam gothic room, with an antique banquet table, a $6,000 set of pewter and dishes, a butler, a footman and a cook. Nobody ever put in a dime; Charlie paid for the whole thing.

Once I said, "It would be kind of fun to do some plays Sunday afternoons out here in the garden." I went over the next Sunday, and he had built an open air theater with clipped hedges for wings. He hired a coach from UCLA and we started with Euripides. That lasted a fast five weeks! Instead of doing something fun, we had to go through a whole course of Greek tragedy and everybody got bored to death.

The fabulous thing was their last party. Clara had blue lacquer tables made for it and there were strolling musicians. That was the day they declared bankruptcy. I was sitting next to her that night and I said, "Clara, for God's sake what's this all about?" She said, "You might as well go down with all flags flying." That was their philosophy.

After their crash, Clara opened a dress shop on Sunset Boulevard. Charlie would not go back to the hick character for anything, so he tried to become a nightclub singer. He couldn't carry a tune for hell nor high water. Years later, when I was directing a picture of mine, I looked outside to the end of the set, which was a hotel, and the doorman was Charlie Ray, doing extra work. I went over and talked to him. That was the last I ever saw of him and I never knew what happened to him after that.

THE THIEF OF BAGDAD - 1924

MITCHELL LEISEN: I stayed on with Fairbanks for his next picture, *The Thief Of Bagdad,* but Wilford Buckland left, so we had to look for a new art director. I don't know where I first met William Cameron Menzies, but he was doing advertising illustration. I asked him to do some sketches for *The Thief* and he brought some fabulous drawings in. Fairbanks flipped over them and gave Bill Menzies his first job as an art director. I designed the costumes in keeping with Bill's sets and sort of supervised Bill. All of his drawings went over my desk for approval, and I looked on at the construction of the sets. The art director, the set dresser, the costume designer—we all worked together as closely as possible.

The shot where Douglas and Julanne Johnstone rode through the air was not a trick shot at all. The carpet was on top of a big steel plate

Douglas Fairbanks and Julanne Johnston in Leisen's costumes for *The Thief of Bagdad* (1924).

suspended 30 feet off the ground by four piano wires. There were 3,000 people below and Doug and Julanne were really riding the thing; we didn't use doubles. To make the carpet fly, the boom just swung across the set and the camera was right behind on the same boom, getting it all. Four piano wires, that was all! We really held our breaths during that one.

We had 3,000 extras a day for *The Thief,* and I had to design different costumes for all of them. Western Costume made them and they charged us the full cost of making the costume as a rental and they got them all back when it was over. The costumes were much more complicated than *Robin Hood* had been. We had a hundred Chinese soldiers' uniforms, all identical and very intricate. There were a hundred copies of something else. The principal problem with the extras on this was to keep the men from wearing long trousers rolled up under their costumes which would suddenly unroll in the middle of a take and spoil everything.

DOROTHY VERNON OF HADDON HALL - 1924

MITCHELL LEISEN: We really spent the money on that one. Mary Pickford found out that Blanche Sweet had just made a renaissance era film that had a gown which supposedly cost $25,000, so Mary wanted one that cost more. I gave her one that cost $32,000. It was embroidered with real pearls.

I knew Claire Eames and when I found out she was going to play Queen Elizabeth, I called her up long distance in New York City and said, "How do you see her, Claire?" She said, "Like the whole Spanish Armada in full sail." I said, "Great." I made every garment completely authentic, even the underwear. The reason Elizabeth always sat that way is because the front of her costume was a solid board with a long point that came down between her legs. She couldn't sit any other way. With all those uncomfortable clothes, Claire had to move as Elizabeth moved, she couldn't walk any other way. It took us fully a half hour every day to dress Claire because each garment was put on exactly as it was done in Elizabeth's day. The farthingales had to be put on, the sleeves tied in and the ruffs gotten on.

Mary's costumes were so heavy they were almost more than she could bear, but she insisted on them. I used to carry her onto the set in the morning to conserve her strength. The sheer weight of her costumes was so great that she lost a lot of weight by the end of the day. She pulled on the bodice and complained that it was too loose and told me to take it in. I argued, but I had to do it, and the next morning, after she had eaten breakfast and had more water in her system, it was too tight and we had to let it out.

I always felt sorry for Mary. I don't see how anybody could bear the terrible pressure she was under. She and her mother and the hairdresser used to wash her hair everyday and use up a whole bottle of shampoo. One wall of her dressing room was covered with shampoo bottles except some of them were filled with whiskey which was the same color as the shampoo. When Fairbanks wasn't looking, she and her mother would drink. I think he knew, but he couldn't figure out where she was hiding it. I don't think her marriage to Fairbanks was happy then, even though they loved each other very much. He was tremendously jealous of any man that even talked to her. One day after we finished shooting, he saw me carrying her back to her dressing room, and made some remark inferring that she and I were interested in each other roman-

Mary Pickford in two of Leisen's gowns for *Dorothy Vernon Of Hadden Hall* (1924).

Leisen's sketch for *Dorothy Vernon Of Hadden Hall*. The back of the sketch says, "ok Miss Pickford - 2/2/23." The face in this rendering looks very much like Stella Yeager who Leisen had not yet met.

tically. It was preposterous and I was furious. I said, "How dare you insult her that way!" Somehow we finished the picture, but I never worked with either one of them again. When they were doing *The Taming Of The Shrew,* Mary called me up because she was very upset about the way her costumes looked. I went over there and gave some advice, but I didn't want to get involved.

THE ROAD TO YESTERDAY - 1925

MITCHELL LEISEN: I went back with DeMille when he started his own studio. We had a train wreck in *The Road To Yesterday* that was terribly difficult to set up. I had all the bits and pieces wired so that when I pushed a button, it would all fall apart. Jetta Goudal was supposed to jump across the wreck and every time we tried to shoot it, she'd chicken out and not do it and we'd have to spend the rest of the day piecing it back together again. This went on— for I don't know how long— until she finally did it.

THE VOLGA BOATMAN - 1926

MITCHELL LEISEN: DeMille was hesitant to make me a full fledged art director right off the bat, but he agreed to let me be art director on all the program pictures the studio made, while continuing as set dresser on the DeMille spectaculars. Another man was assigned as art director on *Volga Boatman,* but after we started shooting, some problem developed between him and DeMille, and I was allowed to take over.

DeMille was very anxious to see the palace set where the banquet takes place, but I pleaded with him not to go down there until it was dark. He thought I was stalling because I hadn't gotten it ready in time, but he waited. We went down together that day after we'd finished shooting on another set, and I knocked on the door. A liveried footman opened it and we went in. I had used a highly polished black marble floor, perhaps the first time that was ever done, and there were torches everywhere which reflected in the floor. Best of all, the banquet tables were loaded with the most fantastic food I could find. C.B. said, "I can see why you wanted me to wait." He called the whole company down and had a feast.

The scene where the mob storms the palace and the roof caves in was very dangerous to stage. I rehearsed the extras all morning, but just to be on the safe side, I decided to put on a Cossack uniform and get right into the scene so I could direct them in case anything unexpected happened. You could talk as much as you wanted during a take of a silent film, and I felt that being right in the scene would give me the best possible vantage point. So C. B. yelled, "Roll it"; the roof caved in; and all the extras ran around just as they'd been told and nobody got hurt, except me. One of the balsa wood columns fell right on my head and knocked me out cold!

Volga Boatman was Adrian's first picture as a costume designer. Doing the art direction on several pictures at the same time, I didn't have time to do the costumes as well, and I didn't particularly want to either, so DeMille gave me permission to find another designer. When I was in New York, somebody introduced me to Adrian, who was just out of high school. I liked his sketches and so did DeMille, and he was hired.

I could tell from the beginning that he had enormous talent. He didn't know enough about sewing, so I still had to supervise the fitting and the sewing at first, but all of the creative traumas were right in Adrian's lap right from the start.

THE KING OF KINGS - 1927

MITCHELL LEISEN: At the beginning, I was the set dresser and the art director was Paul Iribe. He and DeMille came to a parting of the ways very violently one night, and DeMille told me to take over. I said, "Uh huh, wait a minute. I'll let you know tomorrow morning after I find out where we stand." The Crucifixion was coming up and Iribe had made no plans for that at all. He was just going to go out on a mountain at night and shoot it. He had made no provision for the storm. I sat down on the floor of the office to see what he left me and there was nothing. So I said, "I will take over this picture, Mr. DeMille, but if you ever mention Paul Iribe's name again, I'll walk right out." From that day on, I had the reins.

There were no special effects using dupe film and tricks in those days; the only way you could show something was to actually do it and photograph it. There was something called the Williams Process in which they took a positive print, painted out certain parts of it, and made a dupe negative, but that always left a wavy black outline and I said, "We can't have Christ on the cross with a wavy black outline."

The worst problem was how we were going to keep Christ on the cross. I practically went up the wall for two weeks trying to figure out how to do this. We tried a bicycle seat, and he couldn't stand the pressure, and besides when he died, he couldn't sag and really collapse. I was about to throw in the sponge. Then, I was having dinner one night and my wife's earring came off. It was one of those screw earrings. I said, "Oh my God, of course!" I made casts of H.B. Warner's hands, and I molded the blood running down in steel. It had a leather pad at the back of the hand and a nail screwed into the steel and pressed into his palm. When he died, he just collapsed, taking the full weight onto his hands.

There were spectators all over the place, but I never allowed anybody to see Christ get up on the cross or get off of it. I dropped a curtain in front of it, and when they were in place, we'd raise the curtain. Harry Warner was never allowed to smoke on the stage, nor was anybody else in the cast. They also had to sign agreements that they would behave themselves for the next year and not get divorced or cut up in a nightclub.

We had an opening day ceremony in which Rabbi Magnum, Father Lord, representing the Catholic church, a Greek Orthodox priest and a Buddhist priest all came in and said a prayer. Whenever DeMille started to get apoplectic about something, I would say very quietly, "There's a bishop right behind you." That was my one revenge for all the hell I got from him most of the time.

THE GODLESS GIRL - 1929

MITCHELL LEISEN: We had a big fire scene in that one and I had to burn the whole thing down but protect all the people in the scene. I fireproofed everything, the set, the furniture, the actors' clothes. I even flame proofed their hair and make-up. I worked out every movement and every flame until I was satisfied there was no danger.

We started the take and the whole thing worked out beautifully. Nobody was burned at all except the leading man, who touched a spotlight and burned the whole palm of his hand.

DYNAMITE - 1929

MITCHELL LEISEN: That was DeMille's first talkie, and working with that crude sound equipment was murder. There was no way you could dub in any sounds later; all the sound effects had to be recorded during the take.

The cave-in in the coal mine was tremendously difficult to rig up.

Charles Bickford examines Leisen's version of a DeMille bedroom and bath in *Dynamite* (Photo taken 2/26/29).

Kay Johnson and Conrad Nagel in train tunnel for *Dynamite* before it caves in. (Photo taken 4/14/29).

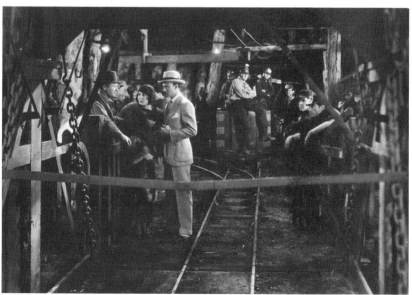

Nothing could touch the mikes or they'd go out and we wouldn't have any sound. I set it all up so that the mikes were concealed and papier-mâché rocks would fall, and sound effects men banging things next to the mikes to make more noise. I made vents and put big pieces of cardboard covered with coal dust behind them and on a cue, the prop man was supposed to turn a fan onto the dust and blow it in so it would look like the dust was rising from the impact of the boulders on the ground.

I gave the cue and the rocks crashed, but when I cued the prop man, he turned his fan in the wrong direction and he blew the dust right into DeMille's face instead of onto the set.

Did you have to take it over to get the right effect?

MITCHELL LEISEN: Are you kidding? We made do with the take we had. Carole Lombard was originally announced for the role Kay Johnson played. DeMille made a test of Carole and decided she wouldn't do, much to my disappointment, since Carole and I were already close friends and this was her big chance. But she made it anyway, without DeMille. Kay was a very talented lady from Broadway, and a lot of fun to work with, but she didn't quite set the screen on fire.

MADAME SATAN - 1930

MITCHELL LEISEN: That one was hell. Metro didn't have enough sound stages for all the pictures they were shooting, so each stage had three companies who worked eight hour shifts. The first company worked from eight in the morning to four in the afternoon, then they left and another company came in until midnight, and then the last bunch worked from midnight until eight in the morning. This meant that we had to dismantle the entire set every night before we left, and then reassemble it as quickly as possible the next day so we could start working without losing much time. To make matters worse, the party on the graf zeppelin was all in two-color Technicolor which required an enormous amount of light and was so limited in its range it was harder to design than it would have been in black and white. The strain was so great I had a nervous breakdown and had to quit entirely for awhile. But it was a long picture, and they were still shooting when the doctors let me come back and work an hour a day.

Cecil B. DeMille rehearses Kay Johnson, Roland Young and Reginald Denny in scenes from *Madame Satan*. Assistant director Mitchell Leisen, at left.

NATALIE VISART: Katherine DeMille and I were both very fond of Mitchell from the time we first got to know him on *Volga Boatman,* and we were terribly concerned about Mitch when he had the nervous breakdown. When we mentioned it to C.B. at dinner one night, he just shrugged and said, "I'm not worried, he's tougher than anything and he'll be back right away." Mitchell did come back, and much too soon, we thought. If he hadn't pushed himself so hard when he was young, I'm sure he would have enjoyed better health when he grew older.

THE SQUAW MAN - 1931

MITCHELL LEISEN: Art directors often have a lot to say about how a scene will be lit and set up in terms of the movements of the actors and camera. I had been setting the cameras for DeMille for a long time because he wanted to get as much as he could out of my sets. DeMille's natural inclination was to always shoot the master take straight on, so that when we started breaking it down for close-ups and over the shoulder shots, you'd have to reverse the angle and there'd be no set behind them. No matter how big my sets were, he'd get stuck, and I'd be summoned from wherever I was to bail him out.

Now that we were at M-G-M and I was no longer supervising the DeMille lot's program pictures, I stayed on the set with him all day long, and more and more I was expected to stage all of the action, which left DeMille free to concentrate on the actual performing.

THE SIGN OF THE CROSS - 1932

MITCHELL LEISEN: C.B. DeMille left M-G-M after *The Squaw Man* and took a long trip to Europe. He laid off the whole staff, including Anne Bauchens, who had been his cutter since he started. It had been up to me to choose the extras and some of the bit parts, so I knew the boys in the casting department at Metro. I asked them if they could use me as an extra, just to keep a little money coming in. I did that for a year, off and on; I was even an extra in one of Garbo's pictures. I also played a scene with Heather Angel in something, but I forget what it was.

Then DeMille came back and made a new deal with Paramount. The studio agreed to release the thing [*The Sign Of The Cross*] but C.B. had to put up the money himself. Boy, then the pennies were pinched! He had paid me $800 a week at M-G-M, but now it was the Depression and I got a fast $100 a week. I hadn't done many costumes after I brought Adrian out for *The Volga Boatman,* but Adrian stayed at M-G-M when we went back to Paramount. DeMille got somebody else, but they disagreed about something, so he asked me if I would do the costumes too. I said, "Yes, for an additional financial consideration." He gave me $25 more a week.

DeMille had seen some spectacular German picture in Europe and he just couldn't understand how they got so much production for so little money. I said, "We can do it too, if you just shoot what I give you and don't try to do anything more."

I used every trick I could think of. The arena was a miniature. We built several flights of stairs with ramps at each level so the people walked in and that was all. As the crowd entered the arena, we panned straight up because there was nothing on either side. We had a tiny segment of the arena, and when you see close-ups of the spectators, we used a prism lens which turned it over and doubled the size of the crowd.

Claudette Colbert in Leisen's costume for *The Sign Of The Cross* (1932).

Fredric March and Elissa Landi from an elaborate sequence staged by Leisen for *The Sign Of The Cross*.

For the opening scene, where Rome is burning while Nero fiddles, we built a balcony and right next to it was all of Rome in miniature. The perspective and lighting were such that Laughton appeared to be on a hill overlooking Rome at a great distance. We set parts of the miniature on fire and eventually burned it all up. Of course they didn't have fiddles in those days, so we gave Nero a harp.

That scene where Claudette Colbert takes a bath in ass's milk was something else again. DeMille wanted the milk to just barely cover her nipples, so the day before, I had Claudette stand in the pool and I measured her to get the level just right. We had compressed air blowing up from the bottom to make it foamy, and Claudette said, "Ooh, it tickles!" It was real powdered milk.

The compressed air and the heat from the lights made the milk start to spoil very quickly. Claudette said, "This bath is turning into cheese!" We finished up and got her out of it. She got cleaned up and we went to dinner. Without the air, the surface of the clabber became very smooth. While we were eating, one of the New York executives was taking a tour around the set. He thought the white stuff was a marble floor, so he stepped right on it and slowly began to sink! He was the most awful mess you ever saw.

Making the costumes for Claudette was a real pleasure. She has just about the most beautiful figure I've ever seen. I slit her skirts right up to the hip to show her marvelous legs. She didn't have a stitch on underneath.

We couldn't get the lions to do anything when we shot the carnage in the arena. The trainers guaranteed that the lions had been starved for days. I got a lamb carcass, dressed it in a costume and chained it to the ground so they wouldn't pull it up and expose what it really was. They let the lions loose and they just walked around as if they were saying, "What have you been doing since our last picture together?" That was all. After awhile, they sort of lined themselves up along the carcass and began lapping up the blood. The trainers got in there with chairs and whips, but nothing would stir them up. We hardly got any usable footage at all and DeMille was tearing his hair out.

All through the picture, DeMille had kept telling Roy Burns, his business manager, "Let me know when we run out of money. I won't spend spend one penny more." We were out in the arena, with pygmies being slaughtered, when Roy came out and said, "We've just used up the budget. You haven't got a dime." DeMille yelled, "Cut" and we stopped right then and there. We didn't even finish that day.

The extensive renditions of set designs that DeMille usually expected were not possible on the quickly made *Sign of the Cross.* Leisen made this sketch for the bath on onion skin paper.

Claudette Colbert in the "bath that turned to cheese."

LEISEN WITHOUT DEMILLE

MITCHELL LEISEN: DeMille hadn't minded my working on *Tonight Is Ours* or *The Eagle And The Hawk* because he wasn't in production, but he expected me to come back when he needed me. Manny Cohen, who was the head of the studio, wouldn't allow it. He said, "He's a good director and he's getting better all the time." DeMille was furious. He thought it was my fault, and he didn't speak to me for a long time. Then he saw *Cradle Song* and he thought it was the greatest thing he'd ever seen in his life. It was just the kind of thing he couldn't do, a little picture, told with nuances. Then he was very proud of me and we were great friends from then on.

But he had grown to depend upon you a great deal. How did he get along without you?

MITCHELL LEISEN: He had a hard time at first. He could never figure out how I got so much production value out of a set. He didn't understand lenses. He wanted to see everybody's eyelashes, so he never used any lens smaller than a 2". A 2" lens doesn't give you much depth of focus, but with a 25mm or a 35mm you get tremendous depth of focus.

He went to Honolulu for *Four Frightened People* so he could shoot a real bamboo forest. It was murder because it was all in lava and they had to lay tons of sawdust to even walk through. He shot it all with a 2" lens, so you saw the people but the whole background was nothing. He had gone all the way to Honolulu and none of all this expense showed on the screen.

I knew they were in trouble over there because I got a telegram from Roy Burns and he signed it, "One of the four frightened people." After DeMille had cut the picture, he had to go to New York for some reason and couldn't attend the preview. He asked me to go and telegraph him the results. I went and the audience reaction was terrible. I didn't know how I could ever tell the truth politely, but fortunately I bumped into Manny Cohen in the lobby and he said, "Forget it. I'll send him the bad news."

NATALIE VISART: I don't think C. B. ever got over the loss of Mitchell. He had to hire about ten people to cover all the things Mitchell did by himself, and he was never satisfied. To have to follow in Mitch's footsteps was an impossible task.

When the studio made it clear that DeMille was not going to have

Robert Montgomery, Ray Milland and dress extra Mitchell Leisen in M-G-M's *But The Flesh Is Weak* (1931). His one line of dialog: "Did you like the play, Joan?"

Mitchell for *Cleopatra*, Mitchell agreed to help DeMille find somebody to do the costumes. They looked everywhere; they even delayed production, but they still couldn't find anybody. Mitchell had been working with me, and he persuaded C.B. to take me on as sort of an apprentice. Travis Banton did some of Colbert's gowns, Ralph Jester did some other things, but there was still nobody in charge of the overall wardrobe and DeMille was getting desperate. He wasn't satisfied with the art direction either. I knew that he was so desperate that he would go to any length to get Mitch back. Mitchell was just as determined; he would not do spectacles in any capacity. I found him in wardrobe one day and told him what was going on. He and I had had a quarrel and we weren't speaking. He thanked me for the warning, and he managed to get out of it somehow.

The Crusades was another collaboration among myself, Travis Banton, Ralph Jester and others, but starting with *The Plainsman*, I was head costume designer. Mitchell told me I would waste my time by making a lot of sketches because DeMille didn't know what he wanted and could never decide. I adopted Mitch's practice of taking one sketch in, saying, "This is the way it's going to be, C.B.," and generally that was the one he used.

I must say that Mitchell taught me everything I know. He made me do careful research. He said if I couldn't imagine how the material would drape, I had to drape it before I made a sketch. While he was training me, he could always tell exactly how far I had progressed. If I complained I couldn't do something, he would say, "You know how, " and I had to do it by myself, but he could tell when I was really stumped and then he would help me out.

Of course C.B. thought Mitchell was really doing all the work and letting me take credit, but Mitchell straightened him out about that. Mitchell did do a couple of sketches for *Cleopatra*, just to keep his hand in, and they were used. He had some ideas for *The Crusades* too. One day he said, "I've got a great idea for the Wanton." I said, "There's no wanton in this script." He said, "Well, there should be. Every picture needs a wanton." He sketched out a girl in a burlap dress, with one breast uncovered and wearing clog shoes. Mitchell always wanted to put the women in clogs. I had my sketch artist paint it, and I wrote "Suggested by Mitch Leisen" on the bottom. Ralph Jester, who was supervising costume designer, was jealous of Mitch and he erased that. DeMille didn't approve it and it was never used, but I've always remembered, "Every picture needs a wanton."

TONIGHT IS OURS - 1933

The speed with which *The Sign Of The Cross* was shot had made it necessary for DeMille to delegate more of directorial responsibilities to Leisen than he had ever done before, and as DeMille was willing to give credit where it was due, the front office became well aware that Leisen had been completely responsible for the staging of several prolonged scenes. These included the long lyrical moment when Fredric March and Elissa Landi first meet at the well, and the sequence where the camera pans across the set, picking up Claudette Colbert playing with her pet leopard, and then Fredric March coming in the door. Since DeMille was no longer in a position to demand that his staff be kept idle on salary until the next DeMille picture, Leisen knew he would be sent back to the art department, and to avoid this, he began looking for another director he could assist with camera work and staging as he had assisted DeMille. Stuart Walker, a highly successful producer-director of stock companies, had not adjusted well to the motion picture medium, and when Leisen proposed to assist him on his next picture, ultimately titled *Tonight Is Ours,* the front office concurred.

As shooting began, Leisen blocked the actors and the camera movement, carefully avoiding any infringement on Walker's responsibility, which was the performance of the dialogue. The actors, however, had little confidence in Walker and since Fredric March and Claudette Colbert both knew Leisen well from *The Sign Of The Cross,* they began to seek out his opinion and ignore Walker. Leisen seized the opportunity, and after the first few days, Leisen was wholly the director while Walker sat alone on the set offering occasional suggestions about pronunciation and phrasing.*

The finished picture was one of the most brilliant debuts any American director has ever made and remains Leisen's most exquisite work. Based on Noel Coward's play *The Queen Was In The Parlour,* it is a Ruritanian romance seemingly in the Lubitsch manner, but with the important difference that Leisen takes his characters seriously throughout and Lubitsch always played his tongue-in-cheek.

---

* This account comes from Leisen and Natalie Visart and may not be fair to Stuart Walker. When I asked cinematographer Karl Struss to recall what had happened he would only say it was an uncomfortable situation and he didn't want to talk about it.

Claudette Colbert in her costume for the opening scene of *Tonight Is Ours*, designed by Travis Banton.

Paul Cavanaugh and Claudette Colbert in *Tonight Is Ours*.

Claudette Colbert portrays the Duchess of a small country who goes to Paris for a spree. She meets a charming American (Fredric March) at a masked ball, they fall in love and are about to marry when she is forced to return to her native land and assume the duties of queen. A year of trouble passes, while the queen prepares to marry a neighboring nobleman she does not love for political expediency. The revolutionaries, however, demand that she marry a commoner, and when March reappears, she consents to marry him and all ends happily.

The plot was already too sugary for 1932, but Leisen managed to make it work by having his actors play it as if they believed every word of it and with his all-pervading sense of elegance and romance. The initial scene at the masked ball is dazzling with brilliants and serpentines. Leisen could have staged the next sequence, in which Colbert relates how she married royalty, in any available room, but instead he placed his actors in a rowboat, drifting in and out of weeping willow trees on a glistening lake. As Colbert describes her wedding, we see a brief flash of an elaborate wedding, lifted out of *The Love Parade*, followed by a very close and even briefer shot of Colbert surrounded by a similar crowd and wearing a dress like the one Jeanette MacDonald had worn in *Love Parade*. Later in the film comes a good example of Leisen's brilliant technique in the movement of the camera. The queen is dining with her fiance and a small retinue at a long banquet table. Starting at the left end of the table, Leisen slowly pans down, catching a phrase from each conversation as he goes by. When he reaches the end of the table, the camera backs up until the whole table is in view, and then backs out of a door, which closes behind it. In this way, Leisen managed to get a lavish feeling while hiding the fact that his set only had one wall and a door.

MITCHELL LEISEN: We shot that in eighteen days for $86,000, and that was quite a feather in my cap. Stuart Walker had no idea what a camera was for, or about, or anything else. They had put a guy with him to direct the camera on his first picture, and I think they were 28 days over schedule! So when Walker came up to do *Tonight Is Ours,* I said, "Why don't you let me do that job?" and the head of the studio said, "O.K., go ahead." Claudette and Freddy were plugging for me, accepting my directions and paying no attention to Mr. Walker at all. I just quietly pushed him into the sound booth and said, "You listen to the dialogue and if you don't like the way it's going, we'll talk it over."

Lubitsch had done *The Smiling Lieutenant* and all the Chevalier things and Paramount was loaded with these beautiful French interiors, so I used his sets all the way through it. I changed the lighting, moved the furniture around and did everything I could to make them look different, of course. The set for the party scene was only about 8' by 10', and we didn't get very many extras, but it seems much bigger because the serpentines filled in a lot of it.

Claudette and Freddy were wonderful together. They both had extensive stage training, and you had to keep them from projecting too much at times, especially in the close-ups. The closer the camera gets, the less you project until you get a really big close-up and then all you have to do is think. Thoughts alter the muscular structure of the face and you are able to read the thoughts going through their minds without dialogue. One of my shots of Freddy was so close I cut off his forehead and chin. He said, "You can't get that close to me," and I said, "Yes I can. Remember your face is going to be thirty times normal size, so whisper your dialogue, don't project at all." He did it.

I learned about photography as we went along. I'd tell the camera-man, Karl Struss, "Let's go in, I want to get closer" and he'd say, "Let's

just change the lens." Instead of a 30mm, he'd put a 2" on, and I could
see the difference.

THE EAGLE AND THE HAWK - 1933

Although Leisen's second film was also credited to Stuart Walker,
Walker seems to have had even less to do on *The Eagle And The Hawk*
than he had had on *Tonight Is Ours,* and when *The Eagle And The Hawk*
was reissued in 1939, Paramount rewrote the advertising to say
"Directed by Stuart Walker and Mitchell Leisen." Unfortunately, at the
same time, the film was recut to comply with the Hays Office's dictums,
and the most militant anti-war scenes were removed, so that the film, as
it exists today, takes an ambivalent stand on war and is a far cry from
the statement Leisen originally made. Nonetheless, Fredric March's
performance as a war hero who commits suicide when he can no longer
bear to be idolized for killing is magnificent, and Carole Lombard's
performance as "The Beautiful Lady" who listens sympathetically to
March's tale of terror is a highlight of her early career.

MITCHELL LEISEN: After *Tonight Is Ours,* I was sent back to the Art
Department and assigned to some ghastly Sylvia Sidney picture that
took place in the deep South. Don't ask me what the name of it was.
One day, the script for *The Eagle And The Hawk* came through for us to
start work on the sets. I read it and I was dying to direct it. It was the
only time in my career when I ever felt I just *had* to direct anything.
  Bayard Veiller was the producer, so I busted into his office and told
him I wanted to make it. He said, "Billy Wellman's on his way over here
and I don't even want him to see you here, so get out!" I was very
discouraged and I said, "Well, I think I'll splurge and have lunch at the
Ambassador Hotel." While I was down there, I got a call to come back
to the studio. It seemed that Mr. Wellman didn't like the script at all
and wanted to change the whole thing. Veiller said, "If you want to do
it, go ahead," but the studio was a little leery that I might not know
enough about dialogue, so they put Stuart Walker on it to assist me
with that end of it. I stuck Stuart in the sound booth again, and he
didn't say a word through the whole thing.
  It was such a strong anti-war story. It [the 1939 reissue] played for
seven months after we declared war, and I was sure they were going to
arrest me, but I didn't realize then how much they'd cut out. It became

Jack Oakie, Fredric March and Sir Guy Standing in *The Eagle And The Hawk.*

a completely different picture. In the love scene between Carole and Freddy March, originally he said, "You're awfully kind" and she said, "I want to be kind, your place or mine." Then I cut to the next morning, when he wakes up and finds she's gone, but she left her gardenia in the hollow in the pillow where her head had been. All that was cut out.

And the end! The whole reason I wanted to do this script so much was for the end. When March commits suicide, Cary Grant gives him a Viking funeral by putting him in his plane and making it look like he'd been shot down in action. March becomes a hero in spite of himself. In the end, you see a plaque in March's hometown; that's where the film ends now, but originally, we pulled back from the plaque, until we see Cary Grant, walking by with a bottle in a paper bag. He has become a bum, and he will regret all his life the mockery he made of March's death.

Carole was a little younger here than in the other pictures I did with her, and I think the shots of her leaning against the mantle, watching the agony March is going through were particularly beautiful. Carole was already an established leading lady, and it was unheard of for somebody of her stature to accept such a small part, but I asked her to do it and she agreed.

Cary Grant wasn't like he is today, I'll say that. If you remember the scene where the bomb hits the roof and all the timbers fall in, well, I'd rehearsed that very carefully so everybody had a safe place to go. Except Mr. Grant, who was off tap dancing in a corner and wasn't paying much attention. The special effects department touched the wire off accidentally, but everybody dived into their positions except Mr. Grant. He just stood there looking up and got it right in the face so badly they had to send him to the hospital.

I got all my stock footage from Bill Wellman's *Wings*. I ran seventy reels of dog fights to pick out the shots we finally used, and then we shot our stuff to match.

Paul Mantz had quite a collection of antique planes including two original DeHavillands which were called the Flying Coffins because

Fredric March and Carole Lombard in *The Eagle And The Hawk*. Her final line, "Your place or mine" as well as the following shot of her gardenia on his empty pillow was removed when the picture was reissued in 1939. (*Photo courtesy Photofest*)

they had an unfortunate habit of bursting into flames at the slightest excuse. Eddie Anderson, who doubled for Freddy March, had been my flying instructor when I learned to fly. He and I went out to the airport to get the planes. Eddie started to take the first one off the ground and it just warped out of shape, so we decided to truck them out instead. We had to recondition them before we could shoot anything. One of them was pretty good and we used it for everything. When you saw two of them on the ground we used the bum one too.

The scene where Sir Guy Standing and Freddy walk along in the dark was actually shot at sundown so that we got that night effect. Once in awhile they would hit a light, but most of the time they were in complete shadow. We opened the camera lens up as wide as we could and somehow we got enough exposure.

From the beginning, it was clearly understood on all sides that I was the director of *The Eagle And The Hawk*, and it was Stuart Walker who was assisting me. When we finished, however, Stuart pointed out a clause in his contract that stated he would always get full directorial credit no matter what, and since I didn't have any contract at all, there was nothing I could do about it. The studio was just as furious as I was. Now I happened to know that Stuart had set his heart on directing both *Cradle Song* and *Death Takes A Holiday*. I didn't know anything about *Cradle Song*, but when the studio asked me what I wanted to do next, I said *Cradle Song* just to get back at Stuart. After I'd been shooting that a couple weeks, they asked me what I wanted next, and I said *Death Takes A Holiday*. Those turned out to be two of my favorite pictures, so at least Mr. Walker had good taste, even though he couldn't direct a picture.

FREDRIC MARCH: Mitch is 100% right in saying that he directed *Tonight Is Ours* and *The Eagle And The Hawk*. Mitch was great in assisting C.B. on *The Sign Of The Cross* and although I don't remember *Tonight Is Ours* too vividly, I know he certainly did the major job of directing *The Eagle And The Hawk*.

I remember telling them so at the front office, and soon after that they asked me if I'd care to do a film with Mitch as the sole director. I readily agreed; it proved to be *Death Takes A Holiday*. I'll always be grateful to Mitch for that picture.

Mitch has been kind enough to thank me several times for the boost I gave him with the front office, and that kind of thank you doesn't happen too often in Hollywood.

CRADLE SONG - 1933

Leisen's first incontestable directorial credit, *Cradle Song* is a sublimely beautiful work. It marked the debut of Dorothea Wieck, the German star whose performance in *Maedchen In Uniform* had made her known in the United States and convinced Paramount that she might be another Dietrich. Her physical resemblance to Dietrich was wisely ignored, however, in the selection of *Cradle Song* as her first vehicle. Wieck was ideally suited to the part of the angelic Sister Joanna, which Eva LaGallienne had created on Broadway.

Leisen lyrically contrasts Joanna's boisterous family life with the serenity of the convent to which she goes. The singing choirs of nuns, the beautiful garden and complete lack of contact with the outside world bring Joanna peace, but cannot gratify her maternal instinct. But a foundling is left at the convent, and she persuades the sisters to let her raise her there. The little girl grows up and Leisen compared the evergrowing child with the timelessness of the convent.

Evelyn Venable made her film debut as the grown-up child. She does not appear until the middle of the film, and Leisen cleverly creates suspense by playing her first scene with her back to the camera, allowing us to hear her voice without letting us see her. Her identifying close-up is delayed further by having the nuns hear her sing in the garden as they sit inside, and then following them as they slowly walk outdoors and find her perched high in a tree, looking over the convent wall.

As she drifts into the world outside and falls in love, Leisen makes the girl more and more lovely, by dressing her in frilly organdy and photographing her through an embroidered wedding veil which slowly lifts to reveal her face. Evelyn Venable's glowing voice and projection of innocence coupled with intelligence was a rare and beautiful thing in the era of Mae West and *Gold Diggers Of 1933*.

EVELYN VENABLE: I arrived in Hollywood in August of 1933, and it had already been decided that I would be the girl in *Cradle Song*. I was sent to Nina Moise for breathing and diction lessons which I didn't need, so I went right into the part. Miss Moise was listed as Associate Director on *Cradle Song* and I know she worked a great deal with Dorothea Wieck to control her accent, but the rest of the actors had very little contact with her. We were completely directed by Mitch.

Mitch was the most sensitive person I ever knew. He knew in-

Leisen took Dorothea Wieck, Evelyn Venable and Sir Guy Standing on a flight in his plane during the filming of *Cradle Song*.

stinctively just what you could contribute, and he worked with you until he got it. There wasn't anybody Mitch couldn't reach. He was a great director from the actor's point of view.

CHARLES LANG: *Cradle Song* was the first one of Mitch's pictures that I photographed. From the cinematographer's point of view, Mitch was

Leisen lunched with Dorothea Wieck and Evelyn Venable during the shooting of *Cradle Song.*

a great director to work with, though he always had very definite ideas about what he wanted. He'd tell me what lens to use, and I'd do it unless I had some good reason not, and then I'd have to tell him. Or he'd suggest a couple of things and ask which was better and why. He picked up knowledge very quickly. About the only thing he didn't control was the lighting. He left that to me and always gave me plenty of time to get what I wanted. There was never any, "When will you be ready?" with him.

Dorothea Wieck had a face like Dietrich, small boned but with very sharp features. You lit Dietrich with one very high key light, far away and very little or no fill light, which was what gave that fantastic modeling to her cheekbones and eye sockets. We could have done the same thing with Wieck, but we wanted a softer effect so we used more fill. She was really stunning.

DEATH TAKES A HOLIDAY - 1934

Leisen's sense of visual imagery was used to even greater advantage in his fourth film, *Death Takes A Holiday,* than in *Cradle Song,* and, tackling

Did Mitchell Leisen film a walk-on part for *Death Takes A Holiday* as he had in *Cradle Song?* That would explain his costume. Evelyn Venable wrote this caption for her scrapbook: "Mitchell Leisen 'auditioning' with Evelyn Venable."

subject matter that was even more profound, Leisen created a film that was superb in all departments and an enormous commercial success.

The raw materials Leisen had to work with on *Death Takes A Holiday* were all first rate. Maxwell Anderson participated in the adaptation of his own successful Broadway play (derived in turn from a Spanish work by Alberto Cassello) and the cast headed by Fredric March, Evelyn Venable and Sir Guy Standing, was very well chosen. Although he had a moderate budget of $317,000 and a fast schedule of 27 days, Leisen was greatly aided in the execution of his visual concepts by the masterful cinematography of Charles Lang and the art direction of the very talented Ernst Fegté. The pictorial quality retained the lyrical aura of *Cradle Song,* infused here with a strong feeling of fantasy, it had a too-beautiful-to-be-real effect.

The film opens with a familiar device of the early '30s, which was already fading from use by 1934. After the credits, we see a close-up of Sir Guy Standing holding an armful of chrysanthemums. White lettering at the bottom of the frame identifies, "Sir Guy Standing as Duke Lambert." Leisen pans over to Helen Westley as Standing passes her the heaps of mums. She is introduced in the same manner, as is the rest of the cast. Then the camera moves to a church where Evelyn Venable as Grazia, kneels in prayer. Gazing dreamily at her fiance, Corrado (Kent Taylor) she says, "I hoped I would be finished before you missed me," indicating that Grazia doesn't seem to control her own destiny. She is the only one of the party who is not frightened by an inexplicable black shadow which pursues the cars as they drive back to their palazzo. For their entrance into the palazzo, Leisen had Charles Lang pull farther and farther back in one of the most elaborate crane shots ever devised. Lang picked the group up at the door, and always preceding it at the same distance, followed it down an enormous corridor lined with the tombs of dead ancestors for several minutes, finally turning a corridor as the group enters the magnificent salon.

Grazia strolls out into the garden, where an indescribable sensation passes over and she faints. She is carried into the house and revived, but she cannot explain what happened. ". . . an icy wind seemed to touch me, only it wasn't a wind," she says.

The guests retire, and as he is putting out the lights, the Duke is suddenly confronted with a black apparition. He fires his pistol at it, but to no effect. The apparition speaks and reveals that it is Death, come to Earth to seek the reasons that cause men to fear Death so, and

Evelyn Venable and Kent Taylor in the opening scene in the church, "I hoped I would be finished before you missed me."

to find what joys of living are so profound as to cause a desire to prolong life. Death decides to take human form, assuming the identity of Prince Sirki, a houseguest the Duke had awaited.

No person, animal or plant dies during the next three days, during which Death enjoys all earthly pleasures. He is pursued by two beautiful women (Gail Patrick and Katherine Alexander) and wins constantly at the races and in the casino. He fails, however, to find any quality of human life as profound as death.

In the evening of his third and final day, the Duke gives a big party. Both ladies are at their most seductive, but they run in terror when they perceive something of Prince Sirki's true nature. Grazia is not afraid of her love for Sirki. They disappear together into the garden where their love is consummated.

They return and console Grazia's terrified mother and friends. As the clock strikes twelve, Death relinquishes human form and is once again the black apparition. He says, "Now you see me as I really am." Grazia replies, "I have always seen you that way. I love you." "Now I know that love is stronger that death," is Death's final word, as Grazia walks up the stairs to him. They disappear and a breeze scatters newly fallen leaves across the stairs. Death's holiday is over.

Beyond its great beauty, *Death Takes A Holiday* is a profound philosophical statement. Surprisingly, perhaps, the concept of death is completely existential. Although Grazia is apparently very religious, no mention is made of heaven as the hereafter. Death is viewed simply as a cessation of life. While there are some vague references to an eternal life, they are not necessarily indicative of Christian beliefs.

Fredric March is perfectly cast in the title role. His masterful presence and commanding voice give just the right feeling of all-knowing wisdom to Death's speeches, and March's histrionic technique of overplaying some scenes is just right for the larger-than-life aura of the inhuman Prince Sirki. The role of Grazia, who neither understands nor attempts to suppress her subconscious wish to die, is as pivotal and basically unplayable as Death, but Evelyn Venable matched March's virtuosity. Lines that are spooky and incredible on paper become reality when Miss Venable speaks them. Grazia knows intuitively but cannot verbalize all the answers of eternity which her friends fear to discover. She is indifferent to pleasure and seems to absorb few of the realities of life. Her only reality is that which she shares with Sirki, a reality that can be only speculation to the others.

Sir Guy Standing, Kent Taylor, Kathleen Howard and all the others contribute fine acting in the other roles. All of the beauty of the cinematography and art direction notwithstanding, it is the actors' performances of Maxwell Anderson's extraordinary script which make *Death Takes A Holiday* a great film. Working for the first time without any co-director or dialogue coach, Leisen proved unquestionably that his skill in directing actors was just as strong as his visual orientation. *Death Takes A Holiday* was Leisen's first big commercial success, and thereafter his position at Paramount was secure.

MITCHELL LEISEN: Evelyn Venable had a very charming quality to her voice; it was a very rich voice. Grazia is a hard role to play, and indeed to write. Maxwell Anderson and I had quite an argument over this. He said Grazia had no motivation. I said that Grazia had every motivation; having just done eight years of psychiatry, I was full of "motivation." Her motivation is simply that she does not want to live. She wants peace and quiet, which is symbolized to her by death. I said to Max, "Just take the attitude that this girl has gone out into the garden at

Fredric March and Sir Guy Standing in *Death Takes A Holiday.*

night, gotten pneumonia, and doesn't have the will to live." In the introduction, I showed the whole cast at a wine festival, loud and raucous and everybody having a ball. Then we find Grazia in the church, with the choir singing. I wanted to plant, from the very beginning, the character of this girl who only wanted peace and quiet.

I cast Kent Taylor as her fiance because he resembled Freddy March so much. They looked almost exactly the same, and I wanted to get the effect over that March represented Death, and Taylor was Life. She loved them both, but she loved Death more.

There was quite a cast in there. The mother was Kathleen Howard, from the Metropolitan Opera Company. There's a very amusing story about her. I was entertaining the Maharajah and Maharanee of Indor one night; my wife was in Paris at the time, so I asked Kathleen to be the hostess. They arrived and I said, "Your highnesses, may I present. . ." and I went completely blank. I looked at Kathleen and I said, "What's your name?" She could have killed me!

The effect of Death being transparent was very difficult to do because we wanted to do it right in the camera instead of having the lab put it in, and we had to keep him within two or three feet of Sir Guy

Standing, who had to remain solid. We duplicated certain pieces of the set in black velvet. Then we put a mirror in front of Freddy that was only 30% silvered so that you could shoot through it. In order to make him transparent, we simply lit up certain portions of the black set which reflected in the mirror superimposed over Freddy, giving the appearance that he was transparent. Shooting through the mirror had a tendency to make a slightly soft focus, but soft focus was considered very artistic at the time.

The costume was many layers of chiffon from charcoal grey to black. His face was made up like a skull and there were tiny lights under the hood to light up the face. The shadows hovering over the cars were printed in by the Special Effects Department. The only place we could find real Italian Cypress trees was out in Newhall, and they were only on one side of the road, so we had to always use the same angle.

The other women were very interesting. Gail Patrick was a healthy young American girl, who can't see Death at all. It never enters her head. Katherine Alexander is the neurotic woman who comes face to face with Death and is terrified. She climbs the wall screaming and yelling when he says, "Look deep into my eyes and tell me what you see." His face changes into a skull and she goes berserk. That was done with red make-up. Under red light, the make-up didn't show and he looked normal. Then by dissolving the red light out and bringing the green light in, the make-up slowly began to show until his face became a skull. Loving symbolism as I do, I played that scene in the long corridor, which has sarcophagi and statues of dead emperors. It is a background suggesting death.

The scene when they arrive back from the festival at the beginning of the picture and walk down the long hallway was one very long take. Charlie Lang is a fantastic cameraman, but he is probably the slowest cameraman in the world. I don't know how he's been getting along recently when we don't have the schedules we used to have, but he keeps working all the time. It took him seven hours to light that. There were ten or twelve people in that scene, all moving forward, with the camera trucking ahead of them. All the lights had to be set for each position, each mark on the floor that they would hit at different times. Originally that same take swung right into the living room without a break; now it cuts to a different angle which I don't remember.

I thought the scene where Grazia has fainted and they're all clustered around her was very nicely composed.

MITCHELL LEISEN: I just had to rehearse and rehearse to get them into a position where they're not blocking each other. They had to hit their mark and lean in just so far enough so as not to block the lights or get their face into a position that threw a shadow on somebody else's face. I was practically on a close-up of Grazia, yet you never have the feeling that there was a deliberate hole left there to see her. If I may brag a bit, it was kind of a tour de force to get so many people into such a close shot.

Several times they've asked me to do a stage play and I've refused because the direction of a play and the direction of a film are two completely different things. In a play, you're working out of a cone to a proscenium arch that's at least thirty feet across. On the screen, it's just the reverse. You're working down to the point of the cone, to a proscenium arch the size of your lens, approximately two inches. As you get closer to your camera, the action becomes more mental and less physical. With a close-up, the actor only thinks. Subtle changes take place in the musculature of the face from the thoughts. If an actor had an expressive face, as Garbo did, it was quite wonderful. You could run a close-up of her for twenty minutes, and see all the changes taking place in her face and eyes. Carole Lombard had the same quality, and to some extent, so do most actors. The principal problem then is to get them to think what their character would be thinking.

CHARLES LANG: Mitch had a tremendous feel for the cameras; I guess it was because of his experience as an art director. He always placed the cameras himself. I'd give him the finder and he'd tell me what angles he wanted. He liked a slightly high angle on the women, which I like too. It plays up the eyes and obscures the chin and neck a bit.

Mitch knew how to get the most out of the sets. He always staged the action so that the actors were against an interesting background. He told me how he wanted the camera to move, and it was up to me to find a way of doing it.

MITCHELL LEISEN: The front office gave me full control. Whatever I wanted, went. I remember Joe von Sternberg found out I was planning to have a collection of sarcophagi in the hall of the palazzo, and he went screaming bloody murder to the front office. He said I was stealing his thunder, that he was going to do the same thing in *Scarlett Empress*. I never paid any attention to what he was doing and this was wholly coincidental. All I know is that I shot it that way and apparently he didn't.

But weren't you both working with Hans Dreier who might have suggested the same thing to both of you?

MITCHELL LEISEN: Hans Dreier had nothing to do with *Death Takes A Holiday*. He was the head of the Art department and his name was in the credits of every Paramount picture, regardless. I worked directly with the unit art director Ernst Fegté who is one of the most brilliant art directors of all times. Perhaps Hans supervised Ernst a little, but I know I had no contact with him at all.

I'd move heaven and earth to get Ernst Fegté on one of my pictures. I'd even postpone production until he was available. With other art directors, it was often difficult to get them to do anything themselves. They knew I had been an art director, and they expected me to tell them exactly what I wanted. I had to tell them, "Look, this is your job, not mine. Make up some plans and then I'll go over it with you." It was even worse with wardrobe. I ended up doing some of the clothes on practically all of my pictures.

I would go up to the art department and see Ernst and his blueprints. Sometimes I sketched some detail on the back of an envelope or I said, "Make this room larger, we'll have a lot of people in this scene," but otherwise, I left it to him. He supervised all the construction. I looked in occasionally, but it was his job. He was on the set most of the time we were shooting the picture so if something didn't work right or photograph right, he was there to correct it. Roland Anderson is another very talented art director, and so is Bill Ihnen, who is Edith Head's husband and was with us on *Cradle Song*. They could do it themselves without much assistance from me.

ERNST FEGTÉ: To me, Mitch's career was like a star that got brighter and brighter until it exploded and the remnants fell to earth. I very rarely ever had to make a sketch for him. He's just about the only director I've ever known who could read blueprints. I'd have my draftsman make the plans up with all the elevations, and he could read them and visualize the whole thing. We thought so much alike, we must have had similar educational backgrounds. We were both fascinated by history and art and had to have everything absolutely authentic. He knew I would do everything pretty much the way he wanted, and while he was interested in my ideas, he never got very involved with the sets during pre-production. He was much more concerned about getting the script ready and he spent all his time working on that.

The climax of the film, Prince Sirki leads Grazia to her death.

I first knew him when he was with us in the Art department at Paramount. I admired his work on *Sign Of The Cross* very much and from then on, I always paid attention to whatever he did. The whole department had to watch the dailies from every picture being shot on the lot, and I could tell that he had set up some of the scenes of *Sign Of The Cross*. When we saw the dailies of *Tonight Is Ours* and *The Eagle And The Hawk,* I knew it had to be Mitch who was directing them, and not Stuart Walker, because it was all done with Mitch's flair for setting up action and moving the camera. I was very excited when I learned I was going to do *Death Takes A Holiday* with Mitch.

The greatest art director Hollywood has ever had was Hans Dreier. He taught us that every picture must have something visual on the screen that the public will always remember, and we only have a few seconds of a long shot to do it. Sometimes we do it with architecture, sometimes with set dressing, sometimes just with colors. But you have to be a showman — Mitch is a showman and I am a showman. As head of the department, Hans had to make the assignments, and although he and Mitch never got along, he knew that the chemistry between Mitch and me was just right. Every so often in the heyday times, a group of compatible people got together on a picture and they were so sensitive and aware of each other's talents that it was wonderful. *Five Graves To Cairo* was like that for me, and so was *Death Takes A Holiday*. Mitch, myself and Charlie Lang were an unbeatable combination.

Mitch is my pet kind of director. Some directors, like Fritz Lang, know exactly how they are going to shoot when they walk on the set. There are others like George Marshall, Victor Schertzinger and David Butler who shoot it any old way and don't pay much attention to the set. Then there are guys like Mitch who just have an infallible instinct. When Mitch came on the set in the morning, he had no preconceived notion as to how he'd do that day's work. He'd have the whole crew leave the set, except for myself, the cameraman and the actors. He blocked the actors and while they walked through the scene, he watched them through the viewfinder from all different angles. Then it would slowly evolve. "If she comes in from the left, then we'll have the mantle behind her in the two shot. Good." He decided what he wanted behind the close-ups and then staged the master scene so it all matched. His pictures cut together perfectly.

Where did I get the ideas for the set? Some were pure imagination and some pure fact from research. The stone mantle was an exact copy of something I found in a book, but the hallway was pure imagination. Most of it was a combination of both.

EVELYN VENABLE: When I went down to wardrobe to have my gowns for *Death Takes A Holiday* fitted, one of the ladies said, "I'll go get the slip you're to wear." I got very alarmed and said, "But I'm not supposed to appear in a slip in any scene of this picture!" She said, "Mr. Leisen told us to get you the most beautiful slip to wear even though it will always be under the dress and will never be seen in the picture. He wants you to feel just like a princess."

They brought it out and it was gorgeous, like something from a trousseau. It was cream colored silk with handmade lace and hand rolled hems. I couldn't believe anybody could go to so much trouble on a fine detail, but Mitch knew what he was doing. From that moment on, I knew just what Grazia felt. Travis Banton designed a beautiful gown of heavy blue grey silk for the final scenes. It was lovely but I told him I wanted something ethereal in white lace with a silver thread to catch the light. He said "Fine" and did it.

Acting with Fredric March was a pleasure until we got to the love scene. We rehearsed and did a couple of takes and when Mitch said print it, I was expecting to get up from the couch. March kept making love to me, under the lights and with everybody watching! He touched my bosom. I was so shocked I hauled off and slugged him. He ran to his dressing room and I ran to mine and neither of us would come out. Mitch ran back and forth, trying to make peace. I said I wouldn't come out until he apologized and eventually Mitch got him over and he mumbled something. I said, "That doesn't sound like you really mean it." So he said it again and we went back to work.

After I had married Hal Mohr, he was photographing *Anthony Adverse* and I visited him one day on the set. I saw Olivia de Havilland who I knew from the play of *A Midsummer Night's Dream*. I said, "Is Freddy giving you any trouble?" And she rolled her eyes and said, "Oh yes."

MITCHELL LEISEN: The effect this film had on people was quite amazing. We were Paramount's second highest grosser of the year, right behind Mae West, so a lot of people saw it. We had seven or eight thousand letters come in from people all over the country, saying that they no longer feared death. It had been explained to them in such a way that they could understand the beauty of it.

The son of a very dear friend of mine had committed suicide, and she was terribly broken up over it. I took a flying chance one day. I took her to the projection room and left her there alone and had *Death Takes A Holiday* run for her. She came out a completely different person. She said, "You've explained death, you've made it beautiful to me. I no longer feel the way I did." This was worth a great deal to me, and made the effort of doing it worthwhile if you could affect that many people and explain something they have been horrified of. As Death himself says, "Why do men fear me?"

BOLERO - 1934

MITCHELL LEISEN: That wasn't my picture, somebody else directed it, but after it was finished, they weren't satisfied with Carole Lombard and George Raft's dance number at the end, so they brought me in to shoot it over and we did it in two days. I think it was Carole who suggested that I direct the retake.

Was she a good dancer?

MITCHELL LEISEN: She certainly was. Everything she did was exquisite.

MURDER AT THE VANITIES - 1934

Leisen's next picture was as unlike *Death Takes A Holiday* as anything could possibly be. Based on a popular play, *Murder At The Vanities* was a combination murder mystery and spectacular musical which pushed the limits of bawdiness and nudity farther than they would go in any American film until the '60s.

In it, Ann Ware (Kitty Carlisle) and Eric Lander (Carl Brisson) are co-starring in a new edition of *Earl Carroll Vanities,* and plan to get married after the opening night performance. Lander's old flame, the bitchy Rita Ross (Gertrude Michael) makes him postpone the marriage by threatening to expose the fact that the wardrobe woman is actually Lander's mother who is wanted for a thirty year old murder in Vienna. Lights and sandbags start falling from the catwalks, barely missing Ann Ware, and stage manager Jack Oakie calls gruff police sergeant Victor MacLaglen in to investigate.

The show begins, and sharp eyes will notice that the orchestra leader in the pit is none other than Mitchell Leisen. Kitty Carlisle belts out the opening number, "Where Do They Come From and Where Do They Go?" and a fantastic spectacle unfolds, though with Leisen's insistence on realism, it is limited in scope to what could really be staged within the confines of a proscenium arch. A series of tableaux depict "Where do they come from," each utilizing some sly blue joke. To show "Where do they go?" the stage is transformed into a giant dressing table decorated with nudes. The lids of the powder boxes open and the mirrors reflect more nudes reposing inside. Suddenly one of the girls notices several drops of blood on her bare shoulder. Above her in the catwalk is the first murder victim.

The rest of the film alternates clues with numbers. Clad in the skimpiest of rags, Carlisle and Brisson seductively duet "Live and Love Tonight" on a desert island, surrounded by scores of girls who lie on their backs and undulate enormous ostrich feather fans to simulate the motion of the waves.

The film's most famous number, "Sweet Marijuana" is the least

Kitty Carlisle sings the finale to "Where Do They Come From and Where Do They Go?"

impressively staged, with Gertrude Michael simply moaning a lament about a lost lover and the marijuana that will "bring him back to me although it's just a fantasy," in front of a line of chorus boys in sombreros. Then comes "The Rape of the Rhapsody" in which Kitty Carlisle inspires Brisson to compose Lizst's "Hungarian Rhapsody." An orchestra tries to play it, but is drowned out by Duke Ellington's hepcats. Then comes the revenge in which the orchestra leader mows them all down with a machine gun. When the curtain closes, the terrified cast discovers there was one real bullet among the blanks, and another murder has been committed.

"Cocktails for Two" (the only tune in the film to become a standard) is simply staged, with Brisson crooning to various showgirls in a bar. As he is a suspect, he walks down the marble stairs of the massive finale wearing handcuffs which are concealed by Carlisle's muff, but a quick confession solves the mystery, and the film ends with a joke. In the greatest role of her career, Toby Wing plays a scantily clad showgirl named Nancy, who comes up to Jack Oakie over and over and says, "Oh Mr. Ellery," only to be rebuffed with "Not now, Nancy." Finally allowed

Carl Brisson and Kitty Carlisle in "The Rape of the Rhapsody" number from *Murder At The Vanities*.

to speak, she innocently reports a bit of gossip which could have prevented the murders from happening, and then, with her inimitable mischievous look, Wing departs with MacLaglen and the film ends.

MITCHELL LEISEN: Earl Carroll had nothing to do with it. He had written the play, and it was about the *Earl Carroll Vanities*, but I made it clear from the start that I would not allow him on the set. One day I saw him walking around behind some flats, trying to stay hidden, and I walked off the set and didn't return until they got him out.

We shot at least two numbers, "Cocktails for Two," and "Sweet Marijuana" using Hollywood chorus girls. Mr. Carroll decided they weren't elaborate enough to live up to the reputation of his *Vanities*, so he insisted we put some bigger numbers in, and use some of his girls. The producer called me in and said I would get $70,000 more to make the other numbers bigger.

We shot the whole thing in Stage 10, which was tiny, and used a 25mm lens to get the spread and the height. We were right up against the back wall. I conducted the orchestra. The music was prerecorded, but you had to show real musicians playing it because of the union

Victor MacLaglen, Gertrude Michael and Jesse Ralph ponder the strange goings on backstage in *Murder At The Vanities*.

Leisen gave the bride away in this wedding on the set of *Murder At The Vanities.*

rule. I didn't know what a downbeat was, but they told me in the Music Department.

For "Where Do They Come From and Where Do They Go" we moved the proscenium arch instead of moving the scenery. It was one very long set that ran the full length of the stage. There was a platform on railroad tracks that held the camera and Kitty Carlisle as she walked back and forth and sang. We just moved the platform down to the next tableaux, but it gave the appearance that the scenes were passing behind Kitty and going on into the wings.

I think I stole the wild wave idea in "Live and Love Tonight" from Sally Rand. Those fans were six feet across, green tipped with white. They were beautiful, but they must have cost a fortune. That number was the only thing that was inconsistent with the stage, because it went too far back. I think if you are showing a stage show that's supposed to be in a theater, you should stay within the bounds of the proscenium arch, and not do a Buzz Berkeley routine with a stage set that's acres big.

Don't you think Berkeley's spectacular effects justified taking this liberty?

MITCHELL LEISEN: Apparently they did because they're reviving all of his pictures and none of mine, but personally I don't like it. *Lady In The Dark* was something else again, because it was a fantasy and fantasies have no bounds. But *Murder At The Vanities* takes place in a theater. The realism of the mystery is helped by keeping the numbers on a realistic scale.

The girls wore the same costumes they had onstage, one layer of the most transparent flesh colored soufflé, a few rhinestones or beads and that was it. For the wild wave number, they only wore about six strings of fringe, and they wouldn't take their robes off and get under the fans until all the men were off the stage. The second day, I looked around; they were all sitting down, talking to the carpenters with no robes on and paying no attention at all.

We had a chorus of real Negro girls for "The Rape of the Rhapsody" which was one of the first times they did that instead of using white girls in black face. I found out that one of the girls was going to get married to a boy in the company, so we decided to have the wedding right on the set. We stopped shooting for awhile one day; I gave the bride away and we went back to work.*

There were two scripts. The left page had the show onstage, the right page told what was happening backstage at the same time. We had to keep track of everybody so that nobody would be seen backstage and then cut to the stage and have the same person doing a number. Many numbers were all scored and planned even though you never saw them. Certain members of the cast were in those unseen numbers, so they weren't present to witness what happened backstage.

Carl Brisson was the Bing Crosby of Sweden, and he wanted to be a perennial juvenile. He kept his wife hidden because she was a lot older than he would admit to being. His son Freddy, who later married Roz Russell, was full grown, and Brisson pretended that Freddy was his brother!

In one scene, he was supposed to say "She'll" and he kept pronouncing it "Seel." I thought he was having language problems, so I enunciated it very carefully for him. He said, "Oh, I know how to say it, but don't you think it's cuter the other way?"

Kitty Carlisle was delightful, very flexible and easy to work with. She overplayed a bit at times because of her stage experience, but we

---

*The wedding was filmed and included as a novelty in one of Paramount's *Hollywood On Parade* short subjects.

overcame that. Jack Oakie couldn't have been more fun. I just cast Gail Patrick because her option was coming up and the studio wasn't going to pick it up. When I put her in the picture, they had to renew her for another three months.

BEHOLD MY WIFE - 1935

Leisen's winning streak ended with *Behold My Wife*. Not that it flopped — it was produced inexpensively and made a tidy profit — but for the first time, Leisen had to contend with very ordinary material and all of his best efforts to put some life into it met with only moderate success.

Based on a play called *Translation of a Savage* that had already been filmed at Paramount as a silent, the plot resembled DeMille's perennial *Squaw Man* but was even more farfetched. Playboy Gene Raymond marries Navajo princess Sylvia Sidney on the rebound and has a hard time getting his snobbish family to accept her. The stars acquit themselves well within their one-dimensional roles (Sidney seems to have been cast mainly because of her Eurasian appearance) and there are mild moments of humor and pathos before the wholly expected conclusion.

Best of all is a brief but telling scene by Ann Sheridan, cast as Raymond's wrong-side-of-the-tracks fiance who learns of his family's plan to ditch her and commits suicide. Leisen was much enamored of Sheridan at the time; he had used her as a chorus girl in *Murder At The Vanities* and insisted on casting her in *Behold My Wife*. It was her best role in her brief tenure at Paramount, and although she played her scene with uncertainty, her talent was unmistakable: a real harbinger of what she was to achieve several years later at Warner Brothers.

MITCHELL LEISEN: I don't remember anything about it except that we went on location for awhile.

ELEANOR BRODER: It was with *Behold My Wife* that I started working for Mr. Leisen. I was out in California for a vacation, and a girl friend of mine, who was Mr. Leisen's secretary, wanted to take a vacation and asked if I would fill in for a few weeks. She never came back and I've been working for him ever since.

She gave me a long list of people Mr. Leisen would see, and ones he

Sylvia Sidney, Gene Raymond, H.B. Warner and Laura Hope Crews in *Behold My Wife.*

wouldn't, those who always wanted to borrow money, etc. She said, "B.P. Shulberg's the producer of the picture, and if Mr. Shulberg wants to see him, you get Mr. Leisen no matter where he is."

I was in the office at the studio one day when Shulberg's secretary called and said to send Mr. Leisen up. I called his house and he was nowhere to be found. I finally learned that he was up looking over the house of a friend of his to do the interior decoration. The house was still being built, so there was no phone up there, but I sent a telegram and Mr. Leisen came running. He said, "I've heard of efficient secretaries before, but this is too much."

When I took the job, I told him I wasn't very fast at shorthand and he said that was all right. Paramount had a school for all the young contract players which was taught by Phyllis Loughton. She asked Mr. Leisen to give a talk to the actors, and he told me to come along and take it down. He talked so quickly and disjointedly I could hardly get it; I missed a lot, but I managed to put it together and I typed it up. He read it and said he wanted me to edit it a bit and retype it. I thought to myself, "Brother, you don't know how edited it is already."

That was the first time I met Phyllis Loughton. We saw a lot of her because when we used somebody from her class in a bit part, she came down to the set to coach him. She married George Seaton, went to M-G-M for awhile, but came back to Paramount to work with Veronica Lake on *I Wanted Wings*. We used to have a table for lunch everyday at the commissary comprised of myself, Phyllis, Natalie Visart and Alma Macrorie who was Mr. Leisen's cutter on many pictures. If we could get away, we'd all have lunch together, even though sometimes we were all working on different pictures.

Mr. Leisen kept the same production team on all his pictures as much as he could, and we were like a big family. Mr. Leisen had an extraordinary gift for organization. He knew what each person could do, he told them to do it, and he didn't check up further. His staff was so anxious to please him that they always had whatever we needed ready on time and perfectly done. They knew he knew all about whatever jobs they performed, and praise from him meant a lot.

His powers of concentration were astounding. On pictures like *Frenchman's Creek* and *Kitty*, we had teams of researchers pouring out hundreds of pages of notes. He could read them over once and know them, and when we had to go back later and check something over, he knew right where it was.

His discipline about his work was very strict, and yet his staff always enjoyed working on his pictures because he kept a pleasant climate on the set. Whenever we had a little time to wait, or he sensed things were getting a bit strained, he would crack a joke and the tension would melt; then we'd go back to work.

FOUR HOURS TO KILL - 1935

Leisen returned to top form with *Four Hours To Kill*. Based on Norman Krasna's successful Broadway play, *Small Miracle*, the plot was a veritable *Grand Hotel* of intertwined lives whose paths all cross one night at a musical revue.

A small-time hood is on his way to prison craving revenge (movingly portrayed by Richard Barthelmess). He is hand-cuffed to a police detective who says, "We've got four hours to kill so I decided to see a show." The title soon takes on another meaning. Joe Morrison and Helen

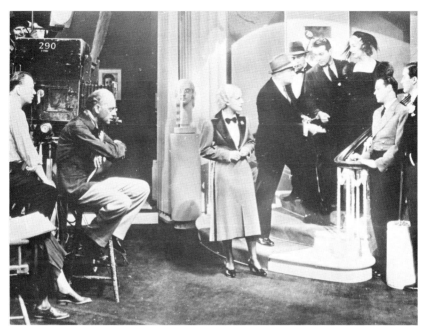

Leisen watches as Dorothy Tree, Roscoe Karns, Richard Barthelmess, Gertrude Michael, Joe Morrison and Ray Milland rehearse a scene for *Four Hours To Kill.*

Mack are a pair of innocent sweethearts trapped by circumstance and a pregnant gangster's moll, (Dorothy Tree) who works with Morrison as an usher in the theater. Interspersed are many amusing vignettes: Roscoe Karns as an expectant father, Gertrude Michael as a bitch who keeps Ray Milland (his first role with Leisen), Olive Tell as a white-haired matron married to a much younger man, and Lee Kohlman and Bodil Rosing as an elderly couple enjoying an annual night on the town.

Four Hours To Kill had a sound text and Leisen executed it with great skill and style. Aside from a brief shot of Leisen conducting the overture (an outtake from *Murder At The Vanities*) we never see any of the show, we only hear it as the drama unfolds in the audience and the lobbies. Leisen's management of space for his dramatic purposes is extremely effective. Starting with crowded areas, he moves his characters into smaller and smaller spaces as the dramatic conflicts build, playing the tensest scenes right in the audience, a tiny men's restroom, within the confines of a telephone stand and in the cloakroom of the theater. The most moving moment, in which Barthelmess reviews his sordid life to the sympathetic detective, is staged with them sitting on the fire escape, the few steps becoming their whole world.

The timing is perfect, the cutting razor sharp. Again there is the juxtaposition of comedy and melodrama, and although the film is wholly a melodrama, Leisen's deft injections of humor sharpen the melodrama by relieving the tension momentarily while not allowing the audience's attention to lag. *Four Hours To Kill* is a perfectly constructed thriller.

MITCHELL LEISEN: Robin and Rainger, like all successful composers, had a whole trunk full of songs they had written for various shows that were never used, so we used them for this. We had unknown singers come in and record them; you heard them throughout the picture but never saw them. And I've had people come up and say how much they enjoyed the numbers in the show. I'd insist they hadn't seen any numbers, but they were just as sure they had. The songs were quite good. One of them was called "Walking The Floor At Night," I remember.

Richard Barthelmess was extremely shy and wouldn't shoot the big

Richard Barthelmess in the climax of *Four Hours To Kill.*

confession scene except at night, after everybody had gone home except a skeleton crew. I took him to dinner, got a few drinks in him and worked with him a long while until he was ready. We did one take and he was absolutely sensational, and completely exhausted from it. I told them to print it, and then the sound man said, "We didn't get it." I could have killed him. There was no point in trying to get it again that night, so we all went home and I repeated the whole process with Richard the next night. No matter how much we worked, he could not get back to the level of emotion he'd had the night before. We finally got a take that was very good, but it was just not as brilliant as he'd been the night before.

RAY MILLAND: The first time I ever met Mitch was when I had just come from England in 1931 and was briefly under contract to M-G-M. In fact, the first foot of film ever shot of me in the U.S. was directed by Mitch. DeMille wanted to test me for *The Squaw Man* and he had Mitch direct the test. I was scared to death and so was he.

Then I went back to England and I saw a picture in London called *The Eagle And The Hawk*. Mitch's name was in the credits and I was glad to see he'd made it. I came back to California, did a couple of small parts at Paramount, and was put under contract. My first full picture with Mitch was *Four Hours To Kill*.

I was so shy. There was one scene where Gertrude Michael and I were having a spat at the bar of the theater after everybody else had gone upstairs for the next act. Gertrude was supposed to say, "Aren't you going to kiss me goodbye?" and I walked over to her, kissed her very slightly and walked out of the scene. Mitch yells, "Gertrude, come over here." They had a few words, then she came back and we started in again. When we got to the kiss, Gertrude stuck her tongue so far down my throat I thought my collar button would rip off. I was terribly shocked. I ran off to Mitch and said, "Do you realize what she did?" "Realize it," he said, "I told her to do it. We've got to do something to get some life in this thing."

Gertrude was a brilliant woman and had been a concert pianist before she started acting, but she was already on the sauce, even then. One day when we quit at five, she offered me a Coke. I took it — it was half gin. Years later I gave her a part in a television picture I was producing. She was flat on her back and it was a nothing part, but she was so fussy about everything she was more trouble than anybody else I ever cast.

Ray Milland and Gertrude Michael.

Mitch and I grew to be very close friends over the years. He had so much talent in all artistic directions: he could direct; he could write; he did marvelous interior decoration; he could dress people beautifully, both male and female; he staged nightclub acts; he painted, sketched and sculpted. He never stopped and I think one thing kept dissipating the other. He was always enthused about a new project to the point that he never stopped trembling with excitement.

Whatever he did, he went into it wholeheartedly. During the war, his business manager heard of a sailboat up for grabs at an unbelievably low price, and Mitch agreed to buy it sight unseen. He and I went down together to look it over, and the minute we removed the white canvas covering, he began to envision how he'd refurbish it. It was in fine shape, but he went over and redid everything. He even had special outfits made up for the crew. All of which cost him several times more than the boat had.

He asked me who my business manager was, and I said, "He's not for you." Mitch insisted, "You've got a yacht, don't you?" I said, "Yes, and I bought it with my hard earned cash." I finally had to give him the guy's name, and the fellow told Mitch he should invest in some property. So, typically Mitch, he went out and bought the Shoreham Apartments, which was the biggest building in town at the time. It had at least forty units. They were all quite nicely furnished, but he had to redecorate each one in the most stunning manner possible with antiques—the whole bit. He could never charge enough rent to make up what he'd laid out. Billy Daniels and Mary Parker, who starred in his nightclub shows, both lived there rent free. Then some has-been semi-star would be living there, and she'd come up and say, "Mitch, I can't quite pay the rent this month," and he'd say, "Oh, that's all right, we'll see how you're fixed next month." You can see why he got into trouble financially.

Mitch's wife was a horror. Why he married her I'll never know. She had aspirations to be an opera singer, but she was lousy. I heard her sing once and that was enough.

An opera company was in town and Mitch threw an enormous party for them and Sol Hurok. He had two top dance orchestras, Ray Noble and somebody else, alternating so the music was continuous, it never stopped. There were azaleas, tulips and roses everywhere, tied to the bushes and trees. Every star in town was there. Those were the days when we were young and beautiful and the world was ours. In the middle of all this, Mitch's wife got up to sing. What a letdown!

They lived across the street from us on Elm in Beverly Hills, and he was always coming over on weekends to get away from her. One day he was making a salad and he said he had a great part for me in *Hands Across The Table*. I said fine, but when I learned it would be with Carole Lombard, I didn't want any part of it. I loved Carole like everybody else, but I had had a small part with her in *We're Not Dressing* and she was so highly strung she made me very nervous. I asked Mitch if he could possibly find somebody else. He said "Sure" and went out to cast Fred MacMurray.

HANDS ACROSS THE TABLE - 1935

Hands Across The Table was a programmer that turned out to be something special. The plot is standard boy-meets-girl, but the dialogue by Norman Krasna, Vincent Lawrence and Herbert Fields is above average and the teaming of Carole Lombard with the then-obscure Fred Mac-Murray was a stroke of fortune.

Hands was the first star vehicle to be tailored expressly for the talents of Carole Lombard, who had built up a wide following in a variety of roles, none of which (with the exception of Lily Garland in Howard Hawks' *Twentieth Century*) were quite so well suited to her individual qualities as that of Regi Allen in *Hands*. Regi is a very complex girl, at once breezy and depressed, ambitious but scared, out to marry money and yet unable to ignore her sexual impulses. Untrained as he was, Fred MacMurray was the perfect foil for Lombard. Her intensity, hyperactivity and complexity contrasted well with his simple, relaxed masculinity.

The complexity of the female character gives the picture a strength beyond its plot and is also the first important evidence of a new complexity in Leisen's style. The bright comedy in *Hands* is well tempered with many serious, introspective moments which give the characters unusual dimension for a comedy and almost transform the picture into a melodrama toward the end until it culminates with a gag.

Hands Across The Table was also the first time Leisen used a reversal of the male and female roles as a thematic basis for his comedy, a construction he employed again and again. Usually the woman is self-sufficient and well-disciplined. She is aggressive and successful in a man's world. The man becomes the sexual object, valued more often for his looks and charm than for intellect or ability. (The MacMurray character in *Hands* apparently has no abilities at all, but in the later pictures it was usually revealed—albeit quite late into the picture—that MacMurray was really a clever fellow and the heroine was just too wrapped up in her own activities to notice.)

The use of role-reversal in the comedies of that era was hardly unique to Leisen: *Honeymoon In Bali, June Bride* and a whole string of Rosalind Russell vehicles were among many films that used it too. However, no other director employed it as constantly as Leisen or with such continual success. The reversal of role and the integration of melodrama into comedy became Leisen's stock in trade for most of his successful comedies.

MITCHELL LEISEN: At first I wanted Ray Milland for the part; I had worked with him in *Four Hours To Kill,* and I thought he could do it. He was just beginning, however, and he begged me, "Please don't ask me to do it because I know I can't play comedy." So I took a flying leap and put Fred MacMurray in, and I was terribly worried since it was only his third picture. There was never any consideration of using George Raft in *Hands Across The Table* that I can remember.

Leisen with Fred MacMurray and Carole Lombard during the production of *Hands Across The Table.*

Light comedy is a state of mind. You can't really direct it, the actors just have to feel it. Fred had a natural flair for comedy, but he was terribly shy in those days and he was afraid to try anything. We really had to draw it out of him, and Carole was a great help there. She worked as hard as I did to get that performance out of him. She had none of what you might call the "star temperament." She felt that all the others had to be good or it wouldn't matter how good she was. She got right in there and pitched. One day I caught her sitting on top of Fred, pounding his chest with her fists and saying, "Now Uncle Fred, you be funny or I'll pluck your eyebrows out."

Fred had been a sax player with some band—where he got all this talent from I have no idea, but sooner or later, he came through on everything. Once in awhile something would bog him down, but change the line a little, or change the movement, and you could get him around the problem. Fred knew instinctively how scenes should be played, and once he was sure of himself, he started to suggest things. When he would say, "What if I do such and such," and then he went out and did it. Then I knew we were in business.

Fred had another director, I forget who it was, who drove him crazy telling him every little movement to make. He tried to do it like that and all of the naturalness went right out of it. If the director had let him work it out by himself, Fred would have turned in a great job with no problems.

The director must free the actor with the movements he gives them. The actors must feel comfortable and not be inhibited. There are lines they can walk on, and others they can't possibly make any move on.

The main problem with Fred in those days was that he didn't project much sex, aside from being very good looking. In the scene when he says "Aren't you going to kiss me goodnight?", Carole was supposed to walk in and kiss him, then walk out of the frame. Well, she came out past the camera, just looked at me and shrugged her shoulders as if to say, "So what?" Poor Fred!

I'm sure Fred has the first dollar he ever made. In those days, the men were supposed to wear their own clothes in the modern dress pictures, but Fred didn't seem to have much of a wardrobe. He and I were exactly the same size, so I let him use my clothes in several of the pictures we did. When I asked him why he didn't get some of his own, I found out that he hadn't even cashed his payroll checks. He was certain he wouldn't last as a movie actor and he wanted to be some money ahead.

To me, an actor is hopeless if he hasn't got a sense of timing. There's just no way you can give it to him if he doesn't already have it; I've even tried to have them count, "One, two, three" and say the line, but it never worked. Lombard was superb; she could time it to a breath. Jean Arthur had a fantastic sense of timing, so did Colbert. MacMurray developed a wonderful sense of timing and Milland did too, once he did comedy.

Timing is a feeling of rhythm; you know how long to wait to come in with the next line, or when to cut into the other person's line. You never hear two people speaking without one of them cutting in on the other because he's already caught the thought. The sound men and the cutters always wanted you to give them a pause between sentences so they'd have a place to make a cut. I'd say, "Wait a minute fellows, somewhere in that sentence there is a little pause and you can make the cut there. You don't have to cut at the end of the sentence, and you don't always have to be on the person that's talking. You can hear their voices off screen and then cut back after they've said a few words."

You have to know how to use business too. When I say business, I mean action that fits the scene, or plays against the scene, but keeps it alive. They're doing something, they're not just standing there talking. There was one scene in *Hands Across The Table* that was just plot information and nothing else. It went on page after page and we needed it all to tell the story. So what can we do to disguise it a little? As it starts, I have Carole carrying in a bag of groceries. The sack of sugar drops and breaks, and she's cleaning up a mess of sugar on the floor as they're talking. Meanwhile, he's lying down in the other room eating chocolates. It suggests quietly that she's vulnerable and he's unconcerned. That was a plot scene and plot can get deadly dull unless you disguise it somehow. Let the audience catch the points of the story, but don't throw them in their faces.

You have to use the actors' spontaneous reactions too. I think the long distance telephone scene was one of the funniest things, where Carole pretends to be the nasal Bermuda operator. Her constant interruption "Bermuda calling, Bermuda calling" establishes a rhythm in that scene. When they finished the take, Carole and Fred collapsed on the floor in laughter; they laughed until they couldn't laugh any more. It wasn't in the script, but I made sure the cameras kept turning and I used it in the picture. It is so hard to make actors laugh naturally—I wasn't about to throw that bit out.

Hands Across The Table is a good example of another important point: you must create the right atmosphere to bring a sense of reality to the mind of the audience. That barber shop where Carole works was a tremendous set with seven barbers going. The lobby outside was constant action; it was all real. Her apartment wasn't really plush; I just wanted to show she had a certain amount of taste. As a manicurist, with the tips she was getting, she could afford a place like that. Ralph Bellamy's suite in the hotel, with the map and the model plane, shows right away that he's interested in aviation. You don't hit the audience over the head with it, but it's there.

FRED MACMURRAY: I never set out to be an actor at all. I was a sax player with a few lines in *Roberta* on Broadway when Paramount tested me and sent me out on a stock contract. I sat around for months doing nothing and finally RKO borrowed me for *Grand Old Gal* with May Robson. Then I did *The Gilded Lily* for Wes Ruggles and I had no idea of what I was supposed to be doing at all. Before *Hands Across The Table* started shooting, I was called into the still gallery to do the usual poses with Carole Lombard, whom I'd never met. I felt very awkward embracing this woman I didn't know, but she did everything she could to make me feel more at ease.

That evening I went to see Lilly, who later became my wife, and she said, "Well, how did it go with Carole Lombard?" I said, "I had never heard such profanity from anybody, man or woman." Lilly said, "Other than that, what's she like?" I said, "She's wonderful." Carole and Lilly later became very good friends.

Carole always said her language was a holdover from her days with Mack Sennett. After awhile you got so used to it that it sounded perfectly normal. I owe so much of that performance and my subsequent career to her. She worked with me on every scene. The first scene we shot had me playing hopscotch on the linoleum of the hotel as Carole walks by. Now that's something I would never do myself in a million years, but Carole coached me and somehow I got through it.

Hands Across The Table was a big hit and the studio wanted to reteam me with Carole in *The Princess Comes Across*. My name was in star billing right after Carole's, but I was still being paid a pittance from my stock contract. Carole advised me to go on strike, just not show up at the studio. I was living with my mother in a little apartment on Franklin Avenue, and every day I went out to spend the day with Lilly. Every evening I came back to find notes from the studio saying I would be fired if I didn't come back the next day. I called Carole up every night and said I was sure that they meant it this time and I'd better get back, and she always said, "Listen, I know how to handle them. Don't go back

Ad art of Lombard and MacMurray.

until they offer you a lot more money. You're worth it, they know it and sooner or later they'll have to give it to you. Besides, I'll tell them I won't make *The Princess Comes Across* with anybody else."

So I went down to Palm Springs and the threats kept coming. Finally the studio told me it was willing to renegotiate the contract and I came back. The new deal was for four pictures a year and they loaned me out all over town when there was nothing for me on the lot, but the money was a lot better, and I think they respected me a little more. I owe all of that to Carole.

THIRTEEN HOURS BY AIR - 1936

In another complete change of pace characteristic of his early career, Leisen next turned to a thriller. Based on another story by Bogart Roberts, who had written *The Eagle And The Hawk, Thirteen Hours By Air* again made good use of Leisen's aviation experience, and provided an interesting record of the earliest days of commercial flying.

Retaining Fred MacMurray from *Hands Across The Table,* Leisen cast him to good advantage as the devil-may-care pilot of an airplane which is hijacked. Joan Bennett has a nothing role as an heiress trying to prevent her sister from marrying the wrong man, but she is charming and ZaSu Pitts gives her usual characterization as a nurse charged with the care of a bratty little boy. There are bits of humor and interesting character vignettes throughout, but Leisen knew that speed was of the essence, and he kept it going at a lightening pace. *Thirteen Hours By Air* remains as exciting today as when it was first released, and indeed compares very favorably with such contemporary aviation thrillers such as *Airport* and *Skyjacked.*

MITCHELL LEISEN: Actually it took at least fifteen hours to fly across the continent in those days, but I knew that sooner or later they would get the time down, so I decided to call it *Thirteen Hours By Air* and get the jump on them. We flew all the way to New York, then came back and photographed the whole trip, so that whenever you see some terrain out one of the windows, it's actually the place they're passing in that part of the story. I had my own crew with me from Hollywood, and the New York unions weren't about to let somebody else photograph in their jurisdiction, so we had to be very careful to avoid being seen and tipping them off. They found out anyway, and we just barely got out in

Fred MacMurray and Joan Bennett in *Thirteen Hours By Air*.

time. As we were taking off, from Newark, I think it was, we saw a whole bunch of detectives in derby hats chasing down the runway, trying to get on the plane to confiscate the film. We had to shoot everything from the co-pilot's seat, which was fine for the shots in the cabin, but it was wrong for the ones with the passengers; there should have been a bit of the wing in the corner of the frame. Those windows were too small to shoot out of, however, and when we tried knocking one out, we lost all our air pressure.

ZaSu Pitts was a dear friend of mine of many years standing, and Joan Bennett was a doll to work with. She was very near-sighted and she refused to wear glasses. Between scenes, she'd sit on the set doing *petit point* and she'd stick the thing about an inch from her eye to see what she was doing. I was scared to death she'd poke her eye out with the needle sometimes, but she never did.

THE BIG BROADCAST OF 1937 (1936)

Leisen then made *The Big Broadcast Of 1937,* the first of a trio of pictures which might be best referred to as "the banal musicals." This isn't to say that the series, which continued with *The Big Broadcast Of 1938* and *Artists And Models Abroad* wasn't enjoyable; indeed, the films were highly entertaining, but there was little of Leisen in any of them. For the most part, they were cast with highly talented radio performers who repeated on the screen the characterizations they had perfected through thousands of broadcasts, and thus had little need for a film director. There were production numbers, but they were geared more to the performers' personalities than to spectacle for its own sake, and Leisen seldom had a chance to stage the sort of fantastic creation he had done in *Murder At The Vanities.*

Sharp eyes will catch Leisen himself in a brief gag routine with Bob Burns; the perspicacious will also notice that when Ray Milland and Shirley Ross go out on the town, most of the footage in the montage is lifted from various numbers of *Murder At The Vanities.* These bits and the interesting execution of Leopold Stokowski's number are the only parts of *The Big Broadcast Of 1937* that relate to the rest of Leisen's career.

MITCHELL LEISEN: I went to New York to talk to Stokowski and ask him to do the picture. He was very interested in recording sound so he was delighted and we chose "Impregnable Fortress" for his number. I

Gracie Allen, Jack Benny and George Burns in *The Big Broadcast Of 1937.*

signed him at a salary of $10,000 for the whole picture. When I went back to the front office and told them I had Stoki for $10,000, they blew their stacks and said, "How dare you offer him as little as that?"

We brought the whole Philadelphia Philharmonic Orchestra out here; they used a little recording studio for ninety pieces, so the sound was not very good. Stoki was disgusted when he heard the tracks, so he went in and recorded all the instruments singly, mixed them, and brought the thing to life.

He gave me his conductor's score to shoot it, and while I couldn't read music to save my life, I studied it until I knew every note. The melody goes from choir to choir within the orchestra. I decided to not show the whole orchestra, just spotlight whichever choir was playing, until the very end when the whole thing was going full blast, and then I pulled back and showed the full orchestra.

I loved working with Jack Benny and George Burns and Gracie Allen. Burns and Allen supplied a lot of their own gags, and I just let them go. I couldn't say, "No Gracie, you're not reading that right" because she knew damn well what she was doing all the time. She was nothing like

Jack Benny and Ray Milland film a scene for *The Big Broadcast Of 1937* as Leisen watches.

the character she played. She was a quiet person, charming, very delightful. She was thrilled with her dress for the wedding scene because it was the first time she'd ever been so glamorous. It was covered with bugle beads, and as she came down the aisle in the wedding procession, she ad-libbed a line, "Don't I look pretty?" It was not in the script, but I used it anyway.

SWING HIGH, SWING LOW - 1936

Most major film artists of the '30s have made one or two films, which for various reasons, are generally unavailable for screening today. In Leisen's case, there have been three, *Cradle Song* (for which the screen rights have apparently reverted to the authors), *Murder At The Vanities* (long off television because of its vulgarity, but recently made available on 16mm) and *Swing High, Swing Low* (unseen since the mid-'40s when the rights to the source play, *Burlesque* were sold to 20th Century-Fox). Of the three, the loss of *Swing High, Swing Low* is the most serious, for it is probably Leisen's finest work.

A vehicle more perfectly suited to all the varied talents of Carole Lombard cannot be imagined, and *Swing High, Swing Low* contains Lombard's greatest performance.*

Photoplay in reviewing the film for the April, 1937 issue said:

> That vivid climb toward stardom started by Carole Lombard in *Twentieth Century* three years ago here reaches glory, for, while this photoplay is the smoothest possible blend of laughter and tears, of torch numbers, fine production, direction and camera work, it is Lombard's art that makes this a great emotional experience. Carole, by turns beautiful, comic, drab, heart-stirring dominates every scene of the story of a girl who marries a lazy charming boy, gives him ambition, makes a star of him and gets her heart broken for it. Fred MacMurray who did such a beautiful job teamed with her in *Hands Across The Table* again troupes masterfully. Arthur Hornblow has given it a superlative production; Mitchell Leisen's direction is positively poetic; the song hits will haunt your memory. It's all perfect and it's all Carole's.

Swing High, Swing Low represents Lombard at her zenith, both as an actress and as a star. For her performance, Paramount paid Lombard an astronomical salary not equaled by any other star until the '50s. She proved to be worth every penny of it, for *Swing High, Swing Low* was Paramount's most profitable picture of 1937, a year of generally dismal box office.

In every aspect it is a rich work. It demonstrates, more than any of his other films, Leisen's complete mastery of every phase of the cinematic craft. His handling of the actors is sublime and the script by Virginia Van Upp and Oscar Hammerstein, Jr. is flawlessly constructed. Ted Tetzlaff's photography of Lombard makes her screen image the most beautiful of all her films, and the dresses and hats Travis Banton made for Lombard in *Swing High* are the best he ever did in their long association.

The title accurately reflects the careful comedic-dramatic balance of the film, but the silly title song and none too original format of the

---

*Actually Barbara Stanwyck who had played *Burlesque* on Broadway and Irene Dunne were both announced for the role before it was assigned to Lombard.

credits (neon lights on a Manhattan skyline) give the initial impression of a routine backstage musical. The first sequence, however (several shots showing the opening of the locks of the Panama Canal), has a certain grandeur which is intensified by Victor Young's lushly orchestrated score. A great ship is passing through the locks; on board is a most inexpert hairdresser (Lombard) who is distracted by a smart-aleck sentry (MacMurray) guarding the canal zone. The exchange between them is sarcastic and amusing, and the next few scenes continue light-heartedly as Lombard and her wise-cracking girl friend (Jean Dixon) go ashore and are picked up by MacMurray and his hypochondriac friend, Charles Butterworth.

They go into a cabaret and suddenly the film becomes serious. MacMurray picks up a trumpet and starts to play. Lombard is so entranced, she hardly notices a Spaniard making a pass at her (Anthony Quinn in an early film role.) MacMurray notices, however, a barroom brawl results, and he and Lombard are jailed.

His weaknesses are all evident, yet she is inextricably drawn to him, and when her ship sails away, she moves into the messy bungalow the two men share. When MacMurray pawns his trumpet to bet on a cockfight, she gets him a job playing in a nightclub by telling the tough proprietress (Cecil Cunningham) that they have been secretly married.

They do a strange and fascinating number together; her head nestled in the crook of her husband's elbow as he plays the trumpet, Lombard sings:

> "When you blow that horn you thrill me,
> To the marrow of my bones you chill me,
> There it goes,
> I feel a call to arms."

In the play, *Burlesque* and its first film version, *The Dance Of Life*, the MacMurray character had been a dancer who threw himself all over the stage and was appropriately called Skid Johnson. The scenarists of *Swing High, Swing Low* made him a trumpeter, but the name, Skid Johnson, was retained. There is a feeling of inevitable tragedy about the name Skid, and from the start even in the midst of all the humor, there is the feeling that within him are forces which will cause him to destroy himself. He is defenseless against them, and despite all of her love, so is his wife. Into their lives comes Anita Alvarez, a raven-haired seductress extremely well portrayed by Dorothy Lamour. He leaves his wife Maggie behind in Panama and takes Anita with him when he gets a chance at the big time in New York. Maggie arrives on the scene, decides on

Fred MacMurray and Carole Lombard on the jungle set Leisen created on a soundstage for *Swing High, Swing Low.*

divorce, and Skid pretends he doesn't care. He goes on a perpetual bender until he is washed up professionally and near death. Even the army won't take him back. His last chance is a broadcast where he can barely stand up to rehearse.

Though they are long since divorced, Lombard appears to try to pull him through. He tries to be nonchalant; leaning on her, his legs give way, and he falls to the ground. Her efforts to revive him, bordering on hysteria, are heartbreaking. He feebly starts to play "I Feel a Call To Arms." Propping him up and watching his every breath, she sings her verse. Somehow he gets out the final note, it is pale and faint, just a shadow of Skid's former glory and yet, somehow, there is a vague hope. Leisen, ever optimistic, ends the film on that note.

MITCHELL LEISEN: We used to call Carole "the profane angel" because she looked like an angel, but she swore like a sailor. Especially with the front office. We'd be on the set and she'd call up Y. Frank

Freeman and give him hell. She was the only woman I ever knew who could tell a dirty story without losing her feminity.

Clark Gable didn't go for all this profanity, and one day after they were married, he said in his calm, matter of fact way, "I'm the man of this household and if there's going to be any swearing done, I will do it." Carole never uttered another four letter word again.

I had dated her before she married Bill Powell, and the three of us were very good friends. She used to call him Pop and call me Junior. As well as I knew her, I never knew why they were divorced.

She was so very much in love with Clark. I don't know why that was either, but she was utterly devoted. Come hell or high water, she left the set at six. She had to get home to her man. They were always playing the silliest jokes on each other. One time before they were married, she got a photo of him sitting on a rocking horse, had it blown up life size and cut out and sent it over to him with some real horse manure to put around the bottom. Then he sent something equally silly back to her. She was always a lot of fun.

If there is any word that describes Carole, it is generous. She was generous to a fault, always helping somebody and never taking any credit. Her pet electrician was flying across the country and the plane crashed somewhere in the vicinity of Kansas City. He was badly injured and lost both his legs. Lombard heard about it and immediately caught a train for Kansas City. She personally hired a baggage car and had a bed set up for him sprung on springs to cushion the shocks and make him as comfortable as possible. She got a folding chair and sat up with him all the way back to Los Angeles.

Word went around town about this and when the train pulled into Union Station downtown, the place was crawling with reporters. Carole took one look from the platform of the train and went into a rage. She called them everything in the book and said if any one of them printed the story she'd never give another interview or let another reporter on any of her sets. "If one word is printed," she said, "God help you all." She meant it and not one word was printed.

Working with Carole was always marvelous. We were both Libras, both happened to be born on the same day, October 6, though several years apart. We had a peculiar rapport that was amazing. We each knew what the other was thinking half the time without even speaking. She'd do a take and when it was over, I'd say, "Carole . . ." and she'd say, "Yeah, I know, we were wrong, weren't we? I know what you want." I'd say, "Don't you want to rehearse?" She'd say, "No, come on, let's shoot it."

She'd go in and give the scene a completely different interpretation, which happened to be just the interpretation I wanted.

She was usually at her best on the first take, after that she got bored with it and it would lose spontaneity. Since Fred MacMurray often needed the first couple of takes to get into the swing of it, I'd give her a new bit of business or something each time and they'd both be great on the third or fourth take.

Sometimes she would stop a perfectly good take right in the middle, and I'd say, "For heaven's sake, what's the matter with that?" She'd say, "I turned my face too far, didn't you see what that light was doing to my nose?" But she was so beautiful it didn't matter how you photographed her; any angle, any kind of lighting was fine. Ted Tetzlaff was our cameraman on both *Hands Across The Table* and *Swing High, Swing Low.* She loved the way he photographed her and never questioned anything he wanted to do. She had been in a car accident and there was a little scar on her cheek which we always tried to wash out with fill light. It was quite visible in some of the big, dramatic close-ups in *Swing High, Swing Low,* but she didn't complain, for she had complete faith in Ted.

Swing High, Swing Low was the heaviest dramatic role Fred had played up to that point and he was worried that he couldn't do it. In the original play, *Burlesque,* Skid Johnson was a dancer, but Fred has two left feet when it comes to dancing, so we made Skid a trumpet player. Between takes, Fred walked up and down the set practicing on that trumpet until you thought you would go out of your mind, but he got the lip movements just right. We had the two best trumpet players in town make the tracks. They could both hold their notes longer than anybody else, but to make the final note of "I Feel a Call To Arms" even longer, we had the first one play it as long as he could, and as he was finally beginning to fade out, the other one came in softly on the same note and gradually increased to full volume so that two notes were perfectly joined together.

I loved my idea of having Carole inside Fred's arms as he played the trumpet and she sang with him. I insisted that Carole do her own singing. She didn't think she could do it and she begged me to have somebody dub her numbers, but I said that nobody could have the same quality of voice and it would be unbelievable. So she did it and it came out beautifully.

In the scene where Fred proposes to Carole, the line read, "I love you, will you marry me?" and I knew we were in for trouble, he'd never get

Leisen directs Carole Lombard and Fred MacMurray, cinematographer Ted Tetzlaff next to Leisen. *(Photo courtesy Photofest)*

that out. He was alibiing all over the place, saying, "I just don't think Skid Johnson would say that." I said, "Well, what do you think Skid would say?" He said, Well, I don't know, but I know Skid Johnson and that character would never say that to her."

So I said, "Well, let's just run through it and see what happens." I told Carole, "Look out, I don't know what he's gonna say, so be prepared for anything." Fred thought it was a rehearsal, but I quietly waved my hand behind my back to get the camera going and they started. All of a sudden, out of him came this fabulously wonderful line for Skid Johnson, "Gee I'm kinda sick to my stomach, but will you marry me?" It was perfectly in character for Skid. Carole threw her arms around Fred and said, "Bless you, that was wonderful."

Towards the end there was a scene where Skid is so sick he cannot stand up straight. He nonchalantly tries to hold himself up by holding onto Carole but his legs give in and he slowly slides down her body and collapses. This again was hard for Fred, but we worked on it and he did one take that was fantastic. I knew we'd never get another like that, so we just went on. Then Carole came up to me and said, "We've got to shoot it over. I wasn't expecting him to fall like that and I waved my hand and ruined it." I said, "Just wait until we see the rushes tomorrow."

We went to the projection booth the next morning and ran it. It was one of the greatest things I'd ever seen and Carole came out sobbing. She said, "I was watching as closely as I could, but when Fred collapsed, I couldn't see myself anymore. Nobody will ever notice what I did."

Actors have to know how to use their bodies. Backs are vitally important; make an actor turn his back to the camera and play the whole scene that way. Carole was great at that. We had a scene in *Swing High, Swing Low* where she had to talk to Cecil Cunningham. Cecil had to be very tough with Carole and we just couldn't get it out of him. Cecil said, "She's so beautiful and so pathetic, I just can't be tough with her." We were trying to do this in a two shot and Carole said, "Look, you've got to come around and take a close-up of me anyway, let me turn my back to the camera for this take and we'll get it out of him."

Carole, with her back to the camera, bit the dialogue out at Cecil in the nastiest way she could say it and Cecil was nasty right back, but Carole's back in the over the shoulder shot was the most pathetic thing. Then I came around and took a close-up of Carole saying the same lines, but pathetically, and we cut all of Carole's nasty dialogue out of the other take and put in the pathetic reading. Since we were on her back and didn't see her say it, we didn't have to worry about matching it and it all went together perfectly.

The scene where Skid comes to see Carole and pretends he doesn't care she's divorcing him was very hard to set up. He keeps asking her to sing, and she doesn't want to, and when she finally does, she breaks down and starts to cry. It was played in a penthouse looking out on an enormous panorama of the New York skyline. When he comes in, it's late afternoon but still light outside. It slowly gets darker as the emotions get sadder. The lights begin to go on outside, somebody turns on a lamp in the room, then another. When the scene ends in desperation it's total night outside.

When we saw the rushes the next day, the skyline backdrop didn't work. The effect was there if you really looked for it, but it wasn't too clear. Since the performances were so good, I didn't do it over.

This was one of the first pictures Dottie Lamour ever did. She was a singer with Herbie Kay's orchestra, and a luscious, luscious beauty. They made a test of her, I saw it and said, "She's fine, let me use her."

*Swing High,
Swing Low* was
the beginning of
Dorothy Lamour's
lifelong friendship
with Leisen.

"We used to call
Carole 'the
profane angel'
because she
looked like an
angel and swore
like a sailor."

DOROTHY LAMOUR: *Swing High, Swing Low* was my second picture and they had been shooting awhile when I joined the company. The moment I stepped on the set, Carole Lombard took one look at me and said, "This poor girl's eyebrows are too thin. Get Wally Westmore." She refused to shoot anything until Westmore came down to the set and fixed my eyebrows.

I was still very new in the game, and being such a big fan of Carole's, I was completely in awe. On our first scene together, I blew my lines over and over. Carole always knew her lines perfectly, but she began to blow them on purpose just so I wouldn't feel bad! Any star who will do that for a newcomer has got to be the greatest, and Carole really was wonderful. She made me feel right at home. She called Mitch "Popsy" and that's what I've called him ever since.

Eventually I inherited Carole's dressing room after she left Paramount and the next year at Easter, she sent me an azalea plant to "cheer up the place." I have never known anybody to be as kind and generous as Carole. Her death was a terrible loss to me.

NATALIE VISART: Mitchell invited me to the preview of *Swing High, Swing Low* which was held in some grimy theater in the most run down section of Long Beach you can imagine. We drove down with Carole and Clark and Eda Warren who cut the picture. The word about Carole and Clark's romance was just beginning to spread, and the sight of them together drove the fans wild. We were mobbed by the fans but somehow we got inside the theater and the picture finally started.

The audience was very restless and didn't pay very close attention. Mitch had done a beautiful, quiet, little scene where Carole sits down on her bed and slowly takes off her stockings, and starts to cry. The audience laughed and Mitch decided the scene had to come out.

On the way home, Carole and Mitch were close to tears because the audience had laughed at that scene. They both loved it, but they were determined to remove it. Eda insisted that it was just a reaction to the fact that Carole and Clark were there. Any other audience would have found it beautiful. Clark and I were the only cool, logical ones, and we agreed with Eda, but Mitch kept saying, "If they get too tense and you don't give them a legitimate laugh, they'll laugh at anything." Carole agreed with him and he cut the scene out. I have always thought it was a pity, because that scene showed the exquisite quality Carole had just a little bit better than anything else she ever did.

MITCHELL LEISEN: It was uncanny the way Carole always knew she would die by fire. We tried to kid her out of it, but she was certain.

I was still in bed one morning when my wife came in with the news that Carole's plane had crashed. I called up their secretary, Madalynne Fields and she said that Clark was already on his way to the scene of the crash. When he got there and started to climb the hill, such a mob of fans followed him that he had to turn back. It was such an incredibly horrible thing to happen to him and to all of us. If there was any justice, it was the fact that Carole's mother was in the plane with her and died too. They were always so close that I don't think Mrs. Peters could have gone on without Carole.

I went into a state of shock when I heard the news. We were doing post production on *Take A Letter, Darling* and I went down to the studio in a daze. The only person I talked to all day was Claudette Colbert. She was devastated too. Finally she led me behind a flat on some sound stage and said, "Nobody's looking. You can let go." I cried.

I had to leave the studio. I spent the whole day at the beach, walking up and down, looking at the waves. I could not make myself believe that Carole wasn't there anymore. I haven't gotten over it yet, and I never will.

Author's note: When Fox bought the rights to *Burlesque*, Paramount may have sent over the original camera negative, as was often done. In the late '60s, The American Film Institute asked both studios to search for the film and all that turned up was an incomplete nitrate release print at Paramount. Leisen's 16mm print was borrowed from the friend to whom he had willed it and the missing three reels were blown up to 35mm. Thus the film exists now but hardly in a condition to showcase Leisen's beautiful imagry. It is also available on home video.

EASY LIVING - 1937

Easy Living, which came in the midst of the three banal musicals, was, of course, much superior to them, and clearly ranks with *Midnight* as the best of Leisen's comedies. Yet the material, in genre, is closer to the *Big Broadcast* than it is to any of Leisen's other successful comedies. *Easy Living*'s comedy comes from situations rather than the characters, and characterization, whether in a comedy or a drama was always Leisen's dramatic focus. *Midnight* and *Arise My Love* have almost equally extraordinary situations, but these situations are created by the characters and

Leisen and cinematographer Ted Tetzlaff watch as Edward Arnold and Mary Nash act a scene for *Easy Living*. (*Courtesy of Academy of Motion Picture Arts and Sciences*)

are consistent with them. The situations in *Easy Living*, however, are all externally created and the stereotype characters only react to them.

Easy Living works beautifully nonetheless because Leisen's talent was great enough to deal with material to which he was basically unsuited, if the material was good enough, and in this case it was. Preston Sturges' script was marvelous, full of well contrived situations and very clever dialogue. Leisen's decision to interpolate slapstick also made the film stronger, because it gave him a visual element to work with in what was otherwise an all-talk script. Never having used slapstick before, he was challenged by it, and enjoyed himself to the hilt.

Although *Easy Living* is now regarded as one of the classic social comedies of the '30s and is one of the few Leisen films to have a wide reputation today, it was not received as anything special at the time of its release. Paramount gave it a big advertising budget; Jean Arthur's popularity in the Capra films was fully exploited, and yet the picture gathered only modest returns at the box office. *Swing High, Swing Low* and all three banal musicals were Paramount's box office block-busters for their respective seasons, but *Easy Living* just earned back its costs and slipped away unnoticed.

MITCHELL LEISEN: I was getting just a little bored with the polite drawing room comedies I had been doing, and I decided to cut loose and do a lot of slapstick. It starts right at the beginning when Edward Arnold goes tumbling down the stairs and lands with a crash at the bottom. His butler says, "I see you're down early today, sir." I set it up from the very beginning.

All the dialogue between Jean Arthur and Ray Milland in the Automat was just plot points, and in Preston Sturges' script, they said it all in the doorway when he's entering and she's leaving. Then I thought, what would happen if all the doors in an Automat opened at once and all the bums in New York rushed in to get free food. I took it from there, and it was the biggest mess you've ever seen in your life. Floors were swimming in food, and it was real food. I had every stuntman in

Arnold and Jean Arthur with the fur coat that started all the trouble. (*Courtesy of Academy of Motion Picture Arts and Sciences*)

Hollywood in there taking pratfalls. There was a man named Murphy, who had a restaurant here called Murphy's and he kept stuffing himself until it made me sick to my stomach. Then another guy put some pepper in the fan and everybody started sneezing. And Jean just sat there, calmly eating her chicken pie through the whole mess.

When Jean's being shown her hotel suite, the obvious thing would be to have her react to every little thing. So I did just the opposite. She didn't react at all until Luis Alberni left her and then she just sat down and said, "Golly." That was an enormous set, it took an entire stage to build. The hotel was based on the Waldorf Towers, which when it was first built during the Depression, was a financial failure. Preston took the idea from that hotel and the owner says, "How could such a phenomenon be such a flop?"

Ray Milland actually got stuck in that plunge while we were filming the shot and it was the funniest thing watching him trying to crawl out, so we kept the cameras grinding and we used it. Then he put a terry cloth robe on that had "Stolen from such and such hotel" on it, that was one of Preston's best gags. We had to play the love scene with them both lying on this long couch in opposite directions and their heads meeting in the middle because that was the only way we could get it past the censors. There could be no physical contact outside of a kiss. After he kisses her goodnight there is a delayed reaction. She suddenly realizes what has happened and she says "Hey" because she realizes she kind of liked it, so. . .

I cast Esther Dale as the secretary because she looked just like Eleanor Broder. We dressed her just like Eleanor, and fixed her hair like Eleanor, and Esther watched Eleanor very closely to get some pointers about how to play her character. That business where Esther gets the various telephones all mixed up, that was definitely Eleanor; we stole that right from under her nose. As a matter of fact, when we came back from the screening the other day, Eleanor asked me, "Did they laugh about the telephone bit?" and I said, "They howled over that." Eleanor had several telephones on her desk and she always answered the wrong one and got them all tangled up, so of course we had Esther do that too. I made Esther even more dead pan and matter of fact than Eleanor, if that's possible.

ELEANOR BRODER: Everybody in Hollywood was always talking about how difficult Jean Arthur was to work with, but we didn't have any trouble with her at all. She was on the set on time every morning

Easy Living was filmed during a hairdressers strike and when non-union people were brought in to pinch hit, the results were not always satisfactory. Here Leisen reassures Jean Arthur by combing her hair out himself. (*Courtesy of Academy of Motion Picture Arts and Sciences*)

and she knew all her lines. She was painfully nervous and she stuttered terribly through the rehearsals. But the minute the camera turned, she was fine, she became a completely different person, brash and sure of herself.

She was terribly concerned with the way she looked on the screen. Mr. Leisen came in the week before and personally directed all her wardrobe and hair tests, he even styled her hair himself. She was very pleased when she saw the results, and from that moment, she had complete trust in Mr. Leisen. Mr. Leisen always said, "If an actress is satisfied with the way she looks on the screen, she'll devote all other attention to her acting," and he was right.

THE BIG BROADCAST OF 1938 (1938)

Leisen returned reluctantly to the genre of banal musicals with *The Big Broadcast Of 1938,* the fourth, last and most successful of the *Big Broadcast* series. Although it was Paramount's top grosser of the Winter 1938 season, the studio elected to make no more, producing instead banal musicals that were college rather than radio oriented, and eventually abandoning the omnibus vehicles with massive casts for musical comedies built around certain personalities such as Bob Hope and later, Betty Hutton.

There is little about *The Big Broadcast of 1938* that is characteristic of Leisen. The scene of Kirsten Flagstad singing "To Jo To Ho" from *Die Walkure* was shot by an unknown director in Paramount's Astoria studio, and the Rippling Rhythm cartoon that accompanied Shep Fields' Orchestra was the work of Leon Schlesinger. The film's one big production number, "The Waltz Goes On" was stylishly staged by LeRoy Prinz, although Leisen created the visual concept, all glossy blacks and glaring whites. Leisen handled the slapstick interludes between the numbers competently but could do little more.

The Big Broadcast of 1938 is remembered today chiefly because it was Bob Hope's debut in feature films and also introduced "Thanks For The Memory," the song with which Hope has been indelibly associated ever since. Hope had not yet perfected his personal style, but his performance in a conventional juvenile lead is pleasing. With his direction of "Thanks For The Memory" Leisen managed to interpolate his customary touching moment into a comedy script which provided absolutely no other chance for pathos.

Leisen with Tito Guizar on the set of *The Big Broadcast of 1938.*

MITCHELL LEISEN: It was my most embarrassing moment when they ran that one at Greystone. The only part that was any good was "Thanks For The Memory." I went to see Robin and Rainger to choose a tune for Bob Hope and Shirley Ross to sing together. They played several things, and I said, "No, that's not what I want, I want something like the Isle de France with all the gulls on it."

I went up a couple of days later and they played "Thanks For The Memory" for me. The words were all different and they played it so fast, like polka tempo. I said, "O.K. fine, fellows. Now give me your word you won't come down on the set until I send for you." They agreed and then I went to the production office and said I wanted to make a direct recording, which meant having a 90 piece orchestra on the stage. I also said I needed three cameras because there was a lot of emotion in the number and we had to get all the angles we needed in one take. They raised hell, but in the end I got what I wanted.

I forget now who rewrote the lyrics; maybe I did it, but we established

Lionel Pape, W.C. Fields and Russell Hicks in *The Big Broadcast of 1938.*

a sentimental, wistful feeling right from the beginning. I slowed the tempo way down, and then I rehearsed Bob and Shirley over and over, until they could give it just the mood I was trying to get across. We had three cameras, one on Shirley, one on Bob and one covering them both in a two shot. When we were all ready, I sent for the composers and everybody else came down to watch the take. At the end, when Shirley walked away from Bob, she could hardly hold the tears back. The composers came out crying too. They said, "We didn't know we wrote that song!" I said, "I know you didn't, that's why I didn't want you to hear us rehearse." What a letdown it was afterwards to go back to directing Martha Raye looking at mirrors and having them break.

The trick department should have done that by hitting the mirror from behind with mallets, but there was some new guy running the department and he built a compressed air chamber behind the mirror. It didn't just break, it exploded and pieces of glass flew everywhere. I had visions of everybody's eyes being put out, but nobody got hurt except W.C. Fields. He got cut on his head, and he went speeding down the alley saying, "Gonna sue, get me my lawyer, gonna sue."

He was the most obstinate, ornery son of a bitch I ever tried to work with. Really. He used to say, "Waal, I think I'd better go down and rehearse my dialogue." We'd sit around waiting for him to come back, and he'd finally come back, two hours later, very well soused and say, "I've decided I'm not going to do that routine after all," just to louse you up.

One time I said, "Bill, you did exactly the same routine in your last picture." He said, "I did not. This one is different." I said, "What's different in it?" He said, "In the other one it's a bottle of whiskey, in this one, it's a bottle of gin."

I think he charged the studio $25,000 every time he did one of his routines. That pool routine was in every picture he did. And that interminable golf routine of his. My God! It goes on for 45 minutes! Finally I couldn't take it any longer, so they got Ted Reed to shoot the pool routine and the golf routine, but I shot anything that had to do with the rest of the cast and Fields. I needed to know the last line of his routine so we could dovetail it somehow into the story. I said, "Give me a cue line, Bill. Anything." He said, "Sure, sure, I'll give it to you." Do you think he did? Never!

Ted Reed and I were having dinner at Lucey's with Fields one night. Ted had won $17,000 at the racetrack that afternoon, and was bragging about it. Fields said, "Oh, you think that's a lot of money, do you?" He reached in his wallet and pulled out cashiers' checks for $250,000. Anybody who got hold of them could have cashed them. He said, "Think that's a lot of money, how about this?"

He always acted the same as he did in his pictures. William LeBaron, who ran Paramount, thought W.C. Fields was the most fascinating person in the world. I was shocked yesterday when I saw that he was starred, that the billing read "W.C. Fields in . . ." I didn't remember that. He even went to the front office and said that Ted Reed should get sole credit for directing the film. I don't know how they talked him out of that.

The only time I got around him was with Kirsten Flagstad. We had this footage of Kirsten Flagstad singing from *Die Walkure* that somebody had shot in New York. Fields had to get in on that act. He wrote a scene where he walked in as she was singing and said, "Who's that?" They said, "That's Madame Flagstad," and he said, " Oh, I thought it was a screeching parrot." I wouldn't direct it, so they must have gotten Ted to do it. I went down to see Bill LeBaron and he said, "Oh, we'll just put it in for the preview to make the old man happy." I said, "Oh no, it's not even going to the preview."

Leisen pondering a problem with Fields.

So I went down to the legal department, and I said, "Well boys, we've just got a suit for a million dollars. Bill Fields just called Kirsten Flagstad a screeching parrot and only one performance is necessary to get a libel suit." Twenty minutes later, the order came out and the negative was burned!

There's a cute story Dottie Lamour loves to tell on herself. I, loving lots of business as usual, told Dotty to get out of her deck chair on a certain lyric, then walk to the rail, then do something else. Anyway, there were three things. Dottie looked at me and said, "Three things! Popsy, I'm not smart, I'm dumb. I can't sing and do three things!" I fell over laughing and simplified it.

DOROTHY LAMOUR: And then you cut to 30 years later, I'm doing *Hello, Dolly* at the Santa Monica Civic Auditorium with Mitch sitting right in the front row. When it was over, he sprang to his feet and led the audience in a standing ovation that went on and on. So I made a little speech and I said, "Ladies and gentlemen, there's a man here who helped me get my start. In those days, I couldn't sing and act at the same time, but since then I've learned." I looked down at Mitch and he was grinning from ear to ear. He was so proud.

ELEANOR BRODER: W.C. FIELDS made that picture an absolute nightmare. The night we finished shooting, Mr. Leisen went home and had his first heart attack.

ARTISTS AND MODELS ABROAD - 1938

Leisen's heart attack was severe and he was forced to spend six restless weeks in bed recuperating. He used his time considering various projects which were never realized. He was very interested in filming Zoe Akin's play *The Old Maid* and drafted treatments, but had to abandon it when Paramount was unable to borrow the players he needed from other studios. It was subsequently made at Warners with Bette Davis and Miriam Hopkins.

Paramount then proposed that he direct *French Without Tears* as a vehicle for Marlene Dietrich. The prospect of working with the already legendary Dietrich intrigued him and he met with writers, but eventually rejected it as a one-joke story. The story, he explained, was one which depicted Americans committing unintentional malapropisms in

Jack Benny and Joyce Compton, among others, in *Artists And Models Abroad.*

their efforts to speak French, and the humor in the situation would be oblivious to anybody who didn't speak both languages.

Paramount let Leisen bow out of *French Without Tears* even though he was not guaranteed script approval in his contract, but he was therefore more or less obligated to take whatever came along next. It turned out to be another banal musical, but Hornblow was the producer, and he agreed to do it. Although it seems unremarkable today, it was one of Paramount's most important productions of the year, and the $1,157,000 budget Leisen got was his highest to date (all of his subsequent films until *Lady In The Dark* cost much less).

The practically nonexistent plot line had Jack Benny in his familiar characterization of Buck Benny as the head of a very untalented bunch of performers stranded in Europe. Leisen opens with the troupe giving a painful rendition of a number called "That's how they do the Buckaroo" and follows them through various scrapes until the finale, an elaborate fashion show production number lasting over twenty minutes.

Excepting the fashion show, there is no more evidence of Leisen's touch in *Artists And Models Abroad* than in the preceding musicals, but it is all competently done, and it became one of Paramount's highest grossers that year. Paramount continued this genre of musical comedy well into the '40s, but Leisen never made another.

MITCHELL LEISEN: Jack Benny had a character called Buck Benny, and he was making all those Buck Benny pictures, so I wanted to call the picture *Buck Benny Rides Abroad,* but the studio wouldn't let me do it.

I think they wanted me to do it because of the fashion show. Somewhere I got the idea of having the clothes made in Paris by all the famous couturiers of the period, Patou, Chanel, Mainboucher, Molineux and so on. I sent a woman to Paris; she supervised the dresses and made sure they worked in pictures. She brought them over and we chose models that fit the dresses as closely as possible. The only one we had trouble with was the Elix white jersey. A girl called Kansas was the only one skinny enough to get into it, and just barely!

I designed Mary Parker's dress; it was white satin with white birds on it. Later we copied it in black for her nightclub shows at the St. Regis in New York. She'd wear the white one for one show, and the black one for the other show.

Joan Bennett was just furious when she saw her dress. I think it was Chanel's and Joan had hysterics when she learned she had to wear it. It was trimmed with silver Christmas tree ornaments.

That bubble bath scene was something else again. The girls broke out because we had real soap in it, and compressed air to keep the bubbles coming up.

ELEANOR BRODER: That picture may not seem like much today, but the public sure liked it then.

The doctor only let Mr. Leisen work half days preparing it, and I had to give him orange juice with sugar in it to keep his strength up. One of the first things we shot was a scene where they're all climbing from one balcony to another and Jack Benny was supposed to hang from his knees. Mr. Leisen always said he wouldn't let the actors do anything he wouldn't do himself, so he went in and demonstrated and we were scared to death he'd have a relapse. Then Jack decided he'd be able to do it.

Jack Benny was a very nice man to work with. He did his radio show Sunday night, and Monday and Tuesday he was very relaxed on the set. By Wednesday, his writers would start coming in with the material for

John Barrymore sat alone as Leisen entertained Don Ameche, Rex O'Malley, Mary Astor and Claudette Colbert on the set of *Midnight*.

the new show, and every spare minute he had to confer with them. It was murder to tear him away to rehearse the next scene. When the shooting was over, he gave everybody on the crew a check.

MIDNIGHT - 1939

Leisen's happy partnership with Arthur Hornblow, Jr. was made even more productive with the addition of the screenwriting team of Charles Brackett and Billy Wilder for *Midnight*. Their superb dialogue gave Leisen his best comedy script ever, and his reunion with Claudette Colbert was most advantageous. Carole Lombard had turned it down because she thought it was similar to pictures she had already done. Then Barbara Stanwyck was cast (but she had to withdraw due to commitments at another studio), and Marlene Dietrich was announced for awhile until her position on the infamous box office poison list caused Paramount to buy out her contract. In the six years since *Tonight Is Ours,* Colbert had become Paramount's biggest box office draw, and her participation suddenly made *Midnight* a much more important project. The $1,025,000 budget was a full $300,000 higher than that of *Easy Living,* and at Colbert's request, Leisen was assigned the masterful cinematographer Charles Lang for the first time since *Death Takes A Holiday.* All of this talent, as well as an extraordinarily rich supporting cast including Don Ameche, John Barrymore, Mary Astor and Hedda Hopper, made *Midnight* one of the great comedies of the '30s.

The plot Brackett and Wilder concocted is one of the most delightfully complex and unpredictable yarns ever spun. The story opens in Paris, where the scheming Eve Peabody (Colbert) is seen leaving the hard wooden benches of a third class coach, clad in a gold lame evening gown. She meets her match in Tibor Czerny (Ameche) a wise-cracking cab driver who takes her to dinner and drives her across town. Seeing a crowd entering a mansion, she decides that this will be as good a place as any to revive her fortunes, and lacking an invitation, she hands the doorman a pawn ticket and goes in.

Hostess Hedda Hopper is giving a dreadfully dull soirée featuring a painful recital by a coloratura soprano. Eve fears she will be ap-

Francis Lederer, John Barrymore, Rex O'Malley, Don Ameche, Hedda Hopper, Claudette Colbert and Mary Astor (holding her pregnancy-concealing scarf) in *Midnight.*

Claudette Colbert in a most moderne millinery shop (designed by Robert Usher) complete with *trompe l'oeil* mural, with Elaine Barrie, in *Midnight*.

prehended and John Barrymore notices her squirming, the tension mounting as the singer vocalizes higher and higher. The party moves to the bridge tables where Barrymore notices that his wife's lover (Francis Lederer) has his eye on Eve too.

Barrymore decides to set Eve up in society to lure Lederer away from the wife (Mary Astor). Borrowing the cab driver's name, Eve installs herself on Barrymore's country estate, much to the annoyance of Astor who plots an exposé of Eve's chorus girl origins with her swishy confidante (Rex O'Malley). At the crucial moment, the cab-driving Ameche arrives and announces that he is Count Czerny, Eve's husband. The escapades continue as Czerny tries to force Eve to leave the villa with him and she counters with a "confession" that he is insane. Finally, the principals are seen in a Paris courtroom in which "Countess Czerny" stages a phony divorce for the benefit of Judge Monty Woolley. Eve eventually realizes, however, that she loves Tibor Czerny (who really is a count and drives cabs because he likes to) and in the final fadeout, they go off to really get married.

Midnight is Leisen's best known work today, and some conclusions have been drawn about his attitudes in general from this single film. With a vague feeling of cruelty and deceit sugar-coated by wit and the conventions of a genteel society, *Midnight* makes Leisen seem a master of sly cynicism. The cynicism, however, comes from the Brackett-Wilder script. Leisen contributed to the project by instinctively toning down its harsher aspects enough to allow it to be funny. He made Eve human and sympathetic despite her avarice and hostility. That Leisen's deftness in handling the material was necessary to the film's success can be seen by comparing it to *Bluebeard's Eighth Wife* made the year before. Written also by Brackett and Wilder and directed by Ernst Lubitsch, it had Colbert playing a mercenary woman quite similar to Eve. Despite the bright lines and amusing situations, the ugliness in the woman's character drowned out the comedy. Instead of being entertaining, *Bluebeard's Eighth Wife* is a distasteful experience.

Leisen managed to avoid this pitfall, retaining the basic concept of Eve, but making the film funny nonetheless. Eve has a lot of bad qualities and few good ones aside from her beauty and charm. Fascinated by Eve, Leisen treated her sympathetically, admitting her faults but without quite making her a heavy. Lombard had had a few lines in *Hands Across The Table* to explain that her motives were the result of a deprived childhood, and Colbert got a minute of justification in *Midnight* too. The darker side of Eve's nature lends a feeling of credibility to *Midnight* that complements the screwball comedy and strengthens the film.

From its inception, *Midnight* had every ingredient necessary to make a successful film: the script, the cast, and the budget were all top drawer. The most vital factor, however, was Leisen. His comedic instincts, tempered by taste and discretion made *Midnight* the most delectable of screwball comedies.

MITCHELL LEISEN: Arthur Hornblow wanted to make this a very special picture. He loved the script and we threw money at it like drunken sailors. The sets were something else again, really enormous.

Writing a script with Charles Brackett and Billy was very hard work but we got results. We had daily meetings in Arthur Hornblow's office, and built the thing up slowly, sequence by sequence, arguing all the way. Billy Wilder was a middle European fresh from the old country, and most of my fights were with him. Having done eight years of psychoanalysis, I knew that a character had to follow a certain emotional pattern. I'd say, "Billy, you have this guy doing something that is completely inconsistent. You suddenly introduce a completely different emotional setup for this character, and it can't be. It has to follow a definite emotional pattern."

Well, Billy couldn't figure this one out, but Brackett could. Brackett was sort of a leveling influence. He would referee my quarrels with Billy. As a team they were the greatest. Billy would scream if you changed one line of his dialogue. I used to say, "Listen, this isn't Racine, it's not Shakespeare. If the actors we have can't say it, we must give them something they can say." Later, I went on the set one day when Billy was directing one of his own scripts and it was very funny. He was having to rewrite the whole thing!

When it was absolutely necessary, we sent for Brackett and Wilder to come down to the stage and we would explain the problem, but we tried to avoid doing that because it's always an expensive delay if you have to stop shooting and sit around while they rewrite a scene. We did as much as we could to get the script in order before shooting started. I would have readings in my office, if I had the cast, but there would be an awful lot of parts that were one, two or three day parts. We couldn't bring these people in ahead of time to read the script because then we'd have to carry them on the payroll until we got around to using them. The readings were usually just with the principals. Nowadays, I understand they have everybody sit around and read the whole bloody thing. We didn't do that.

I thought that Eve Peabody was a very interesting character. You see, there's a little bit of good and a little bit of bad in all of us. A lot of poor girls want to get rich. Eve wants money more than anything else, but in the end, she admits that she's in love with Czerny and is willing to go in and wash his spare shirt and scrub floors if necessary.

Claudette Colbert was wonderful to work with. You had to respect her wishes as to how she would appear on the screen. She had excellent taste and I never fought with her about her wardrobe because I'd known directors who tried to impose a costume on her, and boy, all hell would break loose then. I just let her loose, and if some costume turned out bad, she wore one of her own dresses in the picture.

Claudette swore by Irene, who made all of her wardrobe. Irene was a genius, but there was one suit she did for *Midnight* that Claudette didn't like. She said, "It's my fault, I just don't like it." She calmly came with her own suit on, which had a beautiful jeweled pin on the shoulder. She wore it in the picture and didn't charge us anything.

You'll notice, if you sit down and analyze it, that there's hardly a shot where you see the right side of her face. She had a crazy idea that her nose was crooked on that side, and she used to shade her nose with green and put a highlight down the center to straighten it up. I never could see the difference, but she was adamant about it and there was nothing we could do with the lighting or anything else that would make her let us use that side.

We had to keep Claudette's angle in mind when we built the sets. Every scene I would start with her at the right hand side of the set, and I'd take her across the stage, angle after angle. Then when she turned back and walked the other way, I'd take a very long shot so you wouldn't get a chance to see that side. You could get a left profile or a three quarter shot, she was fine on three quarter shots. Once in awhile she let you do a full face, but not too often. I didn't fight with her about it. I always said that if an actress is satisfied with the way she looks in a picture, she can give her full attention to her acting. Claudette always watched her rushes with a very critical eye. She'd see something she didn't like and she'd say, "Well, I'm not going to do that anymore!"

The first shot of the picture, as the train pulls into the Gare de L'Est, was really taken at the Gare de L'Est in Paris. We sent Hornblow's assistant over to make it and then we duplicated two or three cars of the train. We did all of that sequence at night because you can't block out the sunlight enough during the day. Even if you throw black diffusers over the entire street, you'll still have one of them flapping up there every once in awhile, letting in a ray of light. Claudette had sinus problems and was afraid of catching cold, so we had to make gold galoshes and rubber stockings to keep her feet dry. She wanted to cover her head too, when she ran through the rain, so I let her use a piece of newspaper, which kept her dry but was funny too, to see her in that gold lame gown with a piece of newspaper on her head.

Don Ameche was great to work with also. We were out on the backlot one night and Ameche and I pulled the oldest gag in the world on Claudette. We found the oldest extra you've ever seen in your life and sent him over to her dressing room. He knocked on the door, and when she opened it, he said, "Miss Colbert, I've adored you ever since I was a little boy." Claudette chased Ameche all over the lot!

How did Midnight *rate such a good cast? At that time, John Barrymore, Francis Lederer and Mary Astor were getting leads in other pictures, but here they played small parts.*

MITCHELL LEISEN: You make me sound very egotistical, but everybody wanted to work with me. I never had any trouble, people would play small parts to get in a picture with me directing, and Hornblow was willing to spend more money to get them.

Working with John Barrymore was sheer heaven, just fantastic. We had all of his dialogue written on big cards which were held up just out of camera range. He'd read one speech over Claudette's left shoulder, then she'd say her lines, and he'd get the next speech over Claudette's right shoulder. It was always funny the ways he could find to stall in a scene while he was trying to find the cards with his next speech.

We had one scene where he takes Claudette down a long narrow corridor. There was no room for the idiot cards, with the lights and the camera, so I told John, "I'm terribly sorry, but you're going to have to memorize this." He said, "My dear fellow, do you want me to recite the the soliloquy from *Hamlet?*" And he proceeded to recite it right then and there. I said, "You can remember the lines, why the idiot card, John?" He said, "Why should I fill my mind up with this shit just to forget it the next morning!" We managed to get his cards in there somehow.

He was quite a character. I had to give his wife, Elaine Barrie a part in the picture just to keep him sober. She was on the set every minute and watched him like a hawk. The set where they had breakfast outdoors was full of bushes and as far as John was concerned, the whole thing was a toilet. There was no stopping him. Then when he decided to use the restroom, he got into the Ladies' Room by mistake. He was urinating when some woman came in and exclaimed, "But this is for ladies!" John turned around and said, "So is this."

Barrymore's reactions were great. Every time Rex O'Malley said a line, Barrymore gave him a look that was something else again. It was a great loss when Rex O'Malley died because he was a wonderful comedian. There is another actor in town who has that same quality, and in serial television shows I tried to get him to do a Rex O'Malley. He fought me every inch of the way because he didn't want to get established as that kind of faggotty character. I made Rex play his part in *Midnight* as straight as he could; it's about the straightest part he ever did.

Mary Astor was pregnant, and she kept getting more pregnant as the thing went on. Finally, she was really beginning to show, and we'd let the seams of her dress out as far as they could possibly go, so we gave her a black chiffon scarf. If you remember, she's out in the middle of the dance floor and the scarf suddenly appears in her hand; it hadn't been there in the last shot. We were in that ballroom set a long time, with the big party and the conga dance. Later on, in the breakfast scene, we hid her behind the chafing dish, or had somebody stand right next to her. Oh, we had to put all sorts of tricks.

I think you once quoted Hedda Hopper as saying that Mitch Leisen had taken a bolt of jersey and just thrown it at her? Well, it's true. She was standing in the wardrobe department in her slip; I found this red and white jersey, threw yards and yards of it at her and stuck pins in where it landed. They made it up, and it was a difficult thing to wear, but she handled it fine; she sailed right through it.

ELEANOR BRODER: Francis Lederer was a gentleman of the old school. Every morning he kissed my hand when he came on the set, and I'd always get so flustered I'd drop something. We were shooting the scenes at the bridge tables late one afternoon. Claudette had it in her contract that she didn't have to do any close-ups after 5:00, so we did her close-ups first, and she went home. We started to shoot the reverse shots of Francis sitting at the table, and he said, "I can't do this, talking to nobody and looking into air. Please have your lovely and charming secretary sit across from me when I do the scene."

So I sat down at the table, out of camera range, of course, and he played the scenes looking straight into my eyes. The word went around like wildfire and Doane Harrison, our cutter, and everybody else came over to see this. I didn't know whether to try to act or what. They played back Claudette's tracks, so I didn't have to read the lines.

CLAUDETTE COLBERT: I was very fond of Mitch Leisen and loved working with him. I adored Mitch as a person and admired his talent as an artist. He was a fine artist as you undoubtedly know—which was of great help to his cameramen and gave an extra dimension to any script he directed. He was not a "Svengali" director, ever. He never imposed his will on any player that I can recall. He left the acting to the actors who presumably knew their job—obviously he would suggest perhaps "A little more of that" or "a little less" and he knew exactly when it was right. Many film directors of that era (when time and film were cheap) shot scenes *over* and *over* and *over* then chose the second or third take. I always felt it was either sadism or insecurity. Mitch was never guilty of either! He was also willing to allow plenty of rehearsal time, which any good director will tell you is imperative.

REMEMBER THE NIGHT - 1940

Mitchell Leisen collaborated with screenwriter Preston Sturges for the second and last time on *Remember The Night*, a warmly sentimental comedy-drama which well demonstrated Leisen's ability to work with actors, and to convincingly create a milieu. It was the first of several perceptive Leisen films which contrasted the characters, lifestyles and values of New York City with those of rural America.

The story opens humorously in a Manhattan courtroom where we find Assistant District Attorney Fred MacMurray prosecuting Barbara Stanwyck for shoplifting. It is just before Christmas and Stanwyck's lawyer drones on so long MacMurray is able to get the case continued until after the holidays. MacMurray feels sorry for the defendant having to spend Christmas in jail, so he bails her out. Realizing that they are both from Indiana, he offers to drop her off at her home on his way to his mother's farm.

They get lost en route and are forced to spend the night parked in a farmer's field. The farmer drags them in to the local justice of the peace for trespassing, but Stanwyck starts a fire and in the confusion they manage to sneak out.

The film eases into a serious mood as night falls and they drive through the barren little town where Stanwyck grew up. Stanwyck's mother (Georgia Caine) proves to be bitter and hostile and MacMurray offers to let her spend Christmas with his family, which consists of his mother (Beulah Bondi) a spinster aunt (Elizabeth Patterson) and their hired hand, Sterling Holloway. Leisen slackens the pace as Stanwyck finds in the family an atmosphere of warmth and affection she has never known. Humor is used to prevent certain scenes from becoming cloyingly sentimental, but it is a mild, gentle humor. Holloway announces that he can sing "The End of a Perfect Day" and there is a short laugh when Bondi snaps back, "Well so can everybody else," but then Leisen lets Holloway sing it, and he sings it beautifully.

MacMurray and Stanwyck inevitably fall in love, and passing through the Canadian side of Niagara Falls, he offers to let her escape. Stanwyck, however, has been impressed by his family's honesty and has promised his mother she will not let their love ruin his career, so she refuses. Back in the courtroom, she realizes he is trying to lose the case and she pleads guilty. The film ends in the jail, where she promises to marry him after she has paid her debt to society.

Two scenes which were cut from *Remember The Night;* MacMurray, Stanwyck and Beula Bondi after they've bobbed for apples at a Christmas Party (above); and a love scene between Stanwyck and MacMurray (opposite).

Since the reputation of Preston Sturges currently eclipses that of Mitchell Leisen, it might be assumed that Sturges and not Leisen was the main creative force behind *Remember The Night.* Such an assumption is unwarranted. Certainly Sturges' screenplay is excellent, one of the best Leisen ever directed. The screenplay, however, was very different from the final film, and in modifying it to suit his own tastes, Leisen markedly changed the concepts of the characters and the whole emotional tone of the piece.

Sturges' screenplay was overwritten in every possible way. At 130 pages, it was much too long for Paramount's usual maximum running time of 100 minutes. Leisen produced the film as well as directed it, and lacking Hornblow's assistance, the decision to not film several long sequences included in the screenplay was Leisen's alone. One of these sequences had Stanwyck going to church with MacMurray's family and being profoundly moved by the sermon. Several other sequences were shot but eliminated by Leisen from the final cut. They included a scene

In each case, Leisen decided, "The point had been made." Keeping these scenes would have meant trimming some others and Leisen decided he wanted to have a slow pace for the "down home" section of the film.

in the prison where a surprised Stanwyck is informed she has been bailed out, a party at the farm in which everybody bobs for apples and gets soaking wet, and a love scene between Stanwyck and MacMurray after Stanwyck has told Bondi that she will not allow their love to ruin his career. Leisen could have kept at least some of this material by speeding up the cutting on some of the sequences he used, particularly the one in which the family sits around the parlor and sings " Swanee River" and "The End of a Perfect Day." Leisen decided, however, that all the necessary plot points were covered in the footage he kept, and that a deliberately slow pace in editing was necessary to communicate the exact emotional climate of the farm life. More than a half hour of Sturges' most brilliant writing therefore never saw the light of day.

Leisen also shortened and simplified all of the scenes he shot. Sturges often had a tendency to overdevelop his scenes and characterizations, a tendency which made the films he later directed difficult to edit. Leisen, however, instinctively knew exactly what lines he needed and he ignored all the rest. Sturges wrote a very funny exchange between Mac-Murray and his black valet that was long enough to serve as a vaudeville routine. Leisen cut out pages of dialogue, using only the last few sentences with which the valet announces the arrival of Stanwyck and the bail bondsman.

The farmer who hauls Stanwyck and MacMurray into court snorts, "And they ain't even married." MacMurray replies, "You talk about marriage as if it's the least thing people could be." Sturges had continued that speech with a rather profound discourse on the subject of marriage which Leisen didn't use.

Leisen softened the dramatic moments too. Sturges had Stanwyck's mother refer to another daughter who went bad as well. Leisen excised the line because it made the mother unrealistically heavy.

Tailoring the script to fit the personalities of Fred MacMurray and Barbara Stanwyck drastically changed Sturges' original concept of the characters. Reading the script, one gets the impression that it is the attorney who dominated the story. Sturges gave him many lengthy and clever speeches which made him assume almost heroic stature. Leisen felt that this was a bit theatrical, and the wordiness of the dialogue demanded a certain articulate quality on the part of the actor that MacMurray simply didn't have. Cutting MacMurray's lines down to the minimum, Leisen played up the feeling of gentle strength MacMurray could project so well. It was a far cry from Sturges' highly articulate hero.

Since Stanwyck retained most of the lines Sturges wrote, her character automatically got a larger percentage of screen time than Sturges had intended when MacMurray's lines were cut. As usual, MacMurray quietly underplayed his role and turned in a most satisfactory performance. Stanwyck is less intense here than in many of her roles, but even so, her characteristic interpretation, when contrasted with MacMurray's style, seems to shift the greater weight of the film onto the female character.

Although Leisen greatly changed Sturges' intentions in his direction of *Remember The Night,* virtually all the dialogue in the film remains the work of Sturges. Leisen selected what he wanted from the script, but he did not rewrite anything himself. There was little need for revision during production, and since Sturges was on the Paramount lot, Leisen always sent for him when it was necessary to write a few lines to bridge major gaps or add a gag. Although the two men were not close friends

Stanwyck, Leisen and
MacMurray discuss the
script.

personally, each respected the other's talent. Despite all of Leisen's pruning, Sturges seems to have been pleased with *Remember The Night*. Of all the films he wrote but did not direct at Paramount, *Easy Living* and *Remember The Night* are the only ones Sturges liked enough to buy 16mm prints.

In the final analysis, *Remember The Night* is a very fine work, and most of the credit belongs to Leisen. Had the same script been filmed by some other director or even Sturges himself, it might have been just as good, but it certainly would have been different.

Remember The Night *was scheduled for 42 days and you shot it in 34 days, at a saving of over $50,000. How did you do it?*

MITCHELL LEISEN: Barbara Stanwyck was the greatest. She never blew one line through the whole picture. She set that kind of pace and everybody worked harder, trying to outdo her.

ELEANOR BRODER: Before we started shooting, she knew her part completely and everybody else's, so she could prompt them. She had this uncanny way of knowing what she did with her props. If she had to do the scene over, she put everything back before the prop man could get there. She had a scene in *Remember The Night* where she had to pack a suitcase, and in every take, she put things in the suitcase exactly the same way.

The scene where they're out milking the cow was shot out at the Paramount ranch, and it was the hottest time in summer. She had on a wool suit, a sweater, a fur coat, galoshes and a scarf while everybody else was walking around with practically nothing on. She would never take any of it off between scenes because she said it took her too long to get it back on when we were ready to start again.

MITCHELL LEISEN: Barbara had a bad back, and when we were shooting the barn dance sequence, the corset she had to wear under the old fashioned dress was very painful for her. I'd say, "Look, you've got two hours until your next scene, why don't you just take it off and relax?" and she'd say, "Oh no, you might need me," and she sat on the set the whole time. She was always right at my elbow when I needed her. We never once had to wait for her to finish with the hairdresser or the make-up man.

CHICO DAY: One day Mitch told Barbara he was finished with her for the day and she left. He worked with other actors and suddenly, about an hour later, he said, "Oh my God, I need another shot of Barbara to wrap up this set. Go see if she's still on the lot." I ran to her dressing room, and there she was, still in costume and still with her make-up on. She said, "I knew you would need me again." It turned out she had been waiting around every time she was dismissed early, just in case.

MITCHELL LEISEN: The crews always loved her. I came in one morning and a voice came down from the electrician's gallery saying, "Come on, let's get this show on the road." It was Barbara, she was up there on the catwalks, talking with the electricians.

ELEANOR BRODER: Another time Barbara was up there while the cameraman was telling the electricians how he wanted the lights. He'd say, "Down a little, turn it to the left, turn that one to the right," over and over. Barbara finally put her hands on her hips and said, "For God's

Mitchell Leisen and Elizabeth Patterson help Barbara Stanwyck get into her painful corset for *Remember The Night.*

sake, make up your mind," and I'm sure every electrician has wanted to say that all his life.

Both Barbara and Fred had it in their contracts that they didn't have to work after 6:00 p.m., but they almost always stayed later. We were doing the scene in the taxi cab, and between set-ups, Mr. Leisen and his assistant went over to the courtroom set where we were supposed to begin shooting the next day. When they came back, it was after 6:00 p.m. and Barbara and Fred had gone home. Everybody was madder than a hornet because it meant we couldn't wrap up the taxi scenes that day and move to the courtroom right away the next morning.

If they had stayed just a few minutes, we would have been able to strike the set that night, but this way we lost several hours the next day. I couldn't see how Mr. Leisen could put over his point without giving them hell, and he was such a good friend of theirs. When he came in the next morning, he had an alarm clock set at 6 o'clock hanging from his lapel. Barbara took one look and came up and threw her arms around him. Fred apologized to. But the whole crew was not going to let it go at that. We moved over to the courtroom set. They were deep in

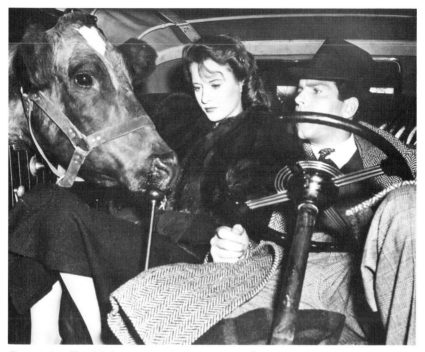

Remember The Night was shot in the summer. Stanwyck's fur coat was uncomfortable but she refused to take it off for fear she'd waste time putting it on again when Leisen was ready.

rehearsal at 6 o'clock when the alarm went off, and everybody, the sound man, the boom man, the cameraman and the whole crew turned and walked off and left them sitting there.

Marjorie Main was supposed to play Stanwyck's mother. Why was the scene reshot with Georgia Caine?

ELEANOR BRODER: She played it just like a crazy woman. She went into the scene and she lost all control. She threw herself down on a bench and it just wasn't real. After one take, I can remember going up and asking her if she needed some smelling salts.

We all dreaded having to shoot the love scene at the end of the picture, because Fred was terribly shy and love scenes were the hardest thing for him to do. But Barbara knew how to handle that. For days before we did it, she kept saying, "This is really going to be something, doing a love scene with Fred" to everybody on the crew and even to Fred. All this ribbing really got his dander up and he decided he'd get it right in spite of himself. The day came, Fred gritted his teeth and he did it perfectly.

ARISE MY LOVE - 1940

Midnight was released late in 1939 and was earning a small fortune as Leisen put the finishing touches on *Remember The Night*. The latter looked like another hit, and considering that it had come in eight days under schedule and $50,000 under budget, Leisen was Paramount's fair haired boy of the moment. There followed, nonetheless, a long and disheartening period of unrealized projects, and it was almost a year before he set foot on a sound stage again.

Dalton Trumbo's *Johnny Got His Gun* was published in 1939 and immediately attracted great attention. Leisen read it and took a 90 day option on the screen rights, intending to film it with William Holden in the title role. Insiders predicted it would be impossible to adapt, and after writing several treatments—all of which he ultimately rejected—Leisen left *Johnny* temporarily and began working on an adaptation of a popular Broadway play, *The Night Of January 16*. Leisen's option on *Johnny Got His Gun* subsequently lapsed.

The Night Of January 16 had been written by a wardrobe department worker at RKO named Ayn Rand. RKO initially turned it down, but eventually it was produced on Broadway and became a staple for little theater groups. RKO bought the screen rights, but could not adapt it, so it was sold to Paramount where it remained unfilmed for several years. The gimmick of this courtroom drama worked fine in the play—twelve members of the audience were chosen to sit onstage in the jury box and vote whether the heroine was guilty or not—but obviously, it couldn't be filmed that way. Without the gimmick, the whole story seemed to fall apart.

Leisen had never done a courtroomer before and his fresh approach resulted in a script the studio felt could be produced. On February 14, 1940, Hedda Hopper's column in the *Los Angeles Times* related: "They were having a tough time with *The Night Of January 16*. Try as they might, they just couldn't seem to solve the murder. In desperation, Leisen suggested they find themselves a murderer, apprehend him at the end of the script and then move back through the yarn, tossing in clues and red herrings as they go. The method worked."

Claudette Colbert had been mentioned in the trade papers for the lead, but the studio eventually gave the part to Barbara Stanwyck. Unable to get Joel McCrea from Walter Wanger, Paramount again arranged to borrow Don Ameche from 20th Century-Fox. At the last minute, Ameche refused to play the role unless it was rewritten. Fox suspended Ameche and Paramount searched in vain for another actor. Stanwyck's next commitment was due to start immediately after the original closing date of *The Night Of January 16,* and as the delays piled up, Paramount finally had to release Stanwyck and postpone the picture. (Paramount then announced that Ray Milland and Patricia Morison would assume the leads under the direction of Charles Vidor, but nothing came of it. Finally William Clemens directed a version starring Robert Preston and Ellen Drew which was released late in 1941.)

Paramount had purchased Samuel Raphaelson's popular stage play *Skylark* as a vehicle for Colbert. It was speculated in the press that the project would be assigned to Leisen; it eventually went to Mark Sandrich. Leisen turned instead to another collaboration with Arthur Hornblow Jr., Charles Brackett and Billy Wilder. Another original, the script was entitled *La Polonaise,* inspired by the Warsaw radio station which kept broadcasting Chopin's "Polonaise" as Nazi troops were capturing the city. In the story, an American athlete goes to Warsaw to find his grandmother. She refuses to leave, and he becomes embroiled in the war. Maria Ouspenskaya was cast as the grandmother, and when Joel McCrea again proved unavailable, Paramount tried to cast William Holden. Columbia, however, shared Holden's contract with Paramount, and when Columbia demanded Holden's services at the same time for *Arizona, La Polonaise* had to be postponed.

Leisen and Hornblow had been preparing another script called *Arise My Love* with Brackett and Wilder with the intention of starring Claudette Colbert in it after *La Polonaise.* On April 8, 1940, the *Hollywood Reporter* announced that *Arise My Love* would be shot first. Walter Wanger still refused to loan out Joel McCrea, so the male lead went to Ray Milland.

When *Arise My Love* finally started shooting on June 24, 1940, it was over ten months since Leisen's last work on a soundstage. Despite the delays, the production had everything going for it. Arthur Hornblow Jr. was again producer, and the Brackett-Wilder script was brilliant, giving Leisen his best opportunity to vacillate between comedy and melodrama since *Swing High, Swing Low.* It was the kind of story Leisen could bring off better than anybody else, and he triumphed with it.

The title *Arise My Love* does not particularly suggest either comedy or

Leisen shows Claudette Colbert what to do with her pencil as Ray Milland watches on.

drama. The credits are shown, white lettering against a dark background with a burst of light, and the title music, neither cheerful not somber, is a stirring march. The low key motif is continued in the first scene where we find Ray Milland in a Spanish jail, playing cards with a priest as he awaits the firing squad. The moment comes, he bids the priest farewell, and numbly follows the guard down the hall to the warden's office where he is confronted by a vivacious Claudette Colbert who embraces him as her long lost husband!

In the space of ten seconds, Leisen had swung the picture into high comedy. Colbert, naturally, isn't his wife; he doesn't even know her. The prison officials become comical, the grim situation is suddenly absurdly funny and once she has him in her custody, Colbert explains that she is a girl reporter who used the wife routine to spring Milland so she could get a story.

Leisen maintains the funny repartee for the next half hour of the film. Colbert is that staple of '40s movies, a career girl determined not to fall in love. Milland, of course changes all that as he pursues Colbert all over Paris. She tries to sneak away when her fast-talking editor (Walter Abel) sends her to Berlin, only to find Milland waiting for her on the train. As Leisen fades out, then fades in on the same scene several hours later, the film becomes serious again. The dreamy poet of the Milland character emerges when Colbert asks him what he sees out the window and he replies, "Stately trees practicing their curtsies in the breeze because they think Louis XIV is still king." As they stop in a little village near the German border, Leisen produces his most lyrically beautiful images since *Tonight Is Ours.*

Their idyll is suddenly ended by the invasion of the Germans and although their idealism tempts them, they decide to ignore European politics and return to the United States. Their ship, the Athenia, is torpedoed and the film ends as they are washed ashore and vow to put aside personal feelings and fight the war.

Leisen and Hornblow knew that *Arise My Love* skated on thin ice politically, since the United States had not yet entered the war and any film dealing with the war would certainly offend some segment of the public, as well as affect the foreign market. To protect themselves as much as possible, all of the scenes with anti-Nazi dialogue had alternate takes which were toned down, and Leisen told the press that he was holding off shooting the end of the film until the last day, and the conclusion would be dictated by the newspaper headlines that morning. Paramount hurriedly previewed and cut *Arise My Love* and rushed it into release as soon as possible.

MITCHELL LEISEN: Claudette had a clause in her contract that said she didn't have to work after 6:00 p.m., but she was always a good sport about it. If she had one scene remaining to do on a certain set, she would stay until it was done so that we could start on the new set the first thing in the morning. One evening we were doing a long speech near the end of the picture. It was one of Charlie Brackett's best efforts and she finally began to cry and said, "I just can't convey all the beauty of Charlie's lines." It was after 6:00 p.m. so I suggested we break for the day and try it again in the morning. She said, "No, I'm not going to let this lick me." We kept taking it over and over. It was nearly midnight and she was wringing wet before we finished, but she was satisfied that she had given it everything she had.

On another scene, we got a take that satisfied me, so I said, "Print it." Claudette said she wanted another take. Now I never denied any performer the right to another take, so I said, "Fine, we'll do it again."

Claudette cut loose and cried all over the place. When she finished, she said, "That's the one I want." I said, "All right, I'll order special rushes the first thing tomorrow morning and you can see for yourself which one is better.‘

We went into the projection room the next morning at 8:00 a.m. and ran both takes. When it was over, Claudette looked at me and said, "Well, you were right." I said, "Once you lose control of the scene and it begins to control you, you're nowhere.‘

Claudette speaks French magnificently, of course, since she is French and was born in France. But whenever she was called upon to speak French in *Arise My Love,* she spoke it with an American accent, which I think is a hell of a clever characterization on her part.

Arise My Love was Charlie Brackett at his best. He had a facility with words that was fantastic and I think his poetic sense came through particularly well in this picture. Billy Wilder was very emotional and would argue every time I objected to something in a scene. But then he and Charlie would go out and put their heads together and come up with a superb scene. It wouldn't be the scene we decided upon at all, but something much better.

My philosophy regarding changing the dialogue was simply this, there was no tradition behind it and if it had to be changed, all right. But some of Charlie's lines were so beautiful you just couldn't tamper with them. Where Ray says he sees "Stately trees practicing their curtsies in the wind because they think Louis XIV is still king," you just couldn't cut a line like that! Ray had trouble saying all that, but we just went over it until he got it.

Then there was the love scene where his head was in her lap and she leaned against the tree. You know exactly what has happened when she says, "There's an ant crawling on your cheek" and she reaches over and kisses him. He says, "That's an awfully small kiss" and she says, "It was a small ant." He says, "I wish it had been an elephant." I think those kind of love scenes are much more vital than any *I Am Curious Yellow* thing you could do today. You don't have to have them naked or in bed to put over the fact that a very romantic affair has gone on.

Of course we had our problems with the censors. If I was afraid something in a scene might not pass, I'd insert another line in the same scene that was absolutely outrageous. Then the censor would start screaming bloody murder that the line had to come out, never noticing the thing I wanted to keep. In *Arise My Love* when Ray is taking a bath, I had one of his buddies look into the bathtub and say, "I didn't know you were Jewish." Of course they made me cut it out, but they never noticed the line I was trying to keep in.

ELEANOR BRODER: It was often very funny. We sent the script to the Hays Office and some of the lines we were sure they would pass were rejected. The writers went away moaning but then they came back with another line that was ten times funnier.

I heard you talking about how you never notice the camera work. Mr. Leisen always said the minute the audience is conscious of the camera moving, you have destroyed the illusion. If you left the choice of the camera angles to the main cameraman, you'd never have anything. They had to set up tracks and do all kinds of tricky things.

MITCHELL LEISEN: If you have noticed, the camera never moves arbitrarily in any of my films. It follows somebody across the room or some kind of action; therefore you are not particularly conscious of the camera moving. Unnecessary camera movement destroys the concentration of the audience. The amount of movement depends on the

Ray Milland and Claudette Colbert in a love scene from *Arise My Love*.

picture. There are some pictures where the camera never stops, always on the move. And other pictures where the camera remains quite static.

The scene at the bar of Maxim's was ten pages long and it was shot in one take all the way through. Usually they shot three lines and cut, then shot three more lines but I felt they needed the whole thing to build the scene. We broke it down when we did the close-ups, but I still had them lap back three or four lines from the place where I really intended to start, so they could get going. I always tried to do over the shoulder shots rather than single close-ups.

The set was an exact duplicate of the real Maxim's. Even the headwaiter was as close to the real Charles as we could get, because Charles was quite famous. I didn't concoct that terrible drink; it was in the script. I asked Charlie, "Where did you get the idea for that drink?" He said, "I just made it up." God, it was horrible! Champagne and creme de menthe. Green creme de menthe to boot! We used real booze and they all got loaded.

RAY MILLAND: Mitch reconstructed Maxim's down to the tiniest detail, which was very nostalgic for me because I spent a lot of time there during my youth in Europe. Mitch, in his perfectionism, insisted we use real booze in that scene at the bar where I'm trying to get Claudette drunk. Creme de menthe and champagne, what a ghastly mixture. We did three bad takes, kept drinking through each one, and on the fourth take we got it right. Mitch said, "Just one more to be sure." Claudette looked at me and said, "I don't think I can stand any more." We did it and I managed to stagger away when it was over, but Claudette and Walter Abel turned around and fell flat on their faces, dead drunk. Mitch had to call the studio ambulance to take them home. He was laughing so hard, nobody enjoyed it more than he did, even if he did lose half a day's shooting.

MITCHELL LEISEN: I think something that would be interesting to explain is that when the Athenia is torpedoed, it seems to roll back with the shock. The set was absolutely solid on the floor of the soundstage, the whole rolling back and the explosion was all done with camera work on the boom. We set off a gross of flashbulbs for the explosion. Then, another little trick I always used was to cut in two pure white frames in the height of the burst so the screen was absolutely white. The water was all from firehoses. We just opened them up and hit the side of the boat. We had to train the actors to fall around like they'd

Esther Dale, again impersonating Eleanor Broder, with Walter Abel in *Arise My Love*.

been hit. One thing I noticed, much to my disappointment, was that the deck chairs didn't move. They should have slid forward.

The long shot of the lifeboats coming into the shore of Ireland was really done at Laguna. The reverse shot of the boats actually landing on the shore was done in a big tank at Paramount. At the edge of the tank was a gigantic process screen showing the other side of the quai. We built a real quai which ran all along the edge covering up the line of demarcation. To get the effect of sand, without really using sand which would wash away and wreck up the tank, we used heavy textured gold cloth which sparkled just enough. After every take, you had to wait for the pumps to fill the hoppers up again with thousands of gallons of water. Then they let go and all the water flowed down runways and splashed up on the shore like waves. And there was Claudette with her rubber stockings on.

RAY MILLAND: I loved it! It was a beautiful script and Mitch did a beautiful job. I thought Claudette hated my guts because we had done *The Gilded Lily* together several years before and I couldn't act at all then. After every scene, I just walked away—didn't say anything. After several days, Claudette came over and said, "Why don't you ever say anything?" I said, "I thought you hated my guts." She said, "And I thought you hated me!" and after that we were the best of pals.

Claudette is a very nice person to know. She's always immaculate; she'd never go to the grocery store in blue jeans! It is a joy to see a woman so well turned out and elegant as Claudette is. I never understood the phobia she had about the right side of her face. There is nothing the matter with it that I could ever see. Always using the left side of her face meant I always had to use the right side of mine, and that's the side I don't like!

Charlie Lang photographed it beautifully. He was the top man at Paramount and also the slowest. Between takes he'd make very fine adjustments of the lights, always trying to improve. Mitch would say, "Fine, print it," Charlie would be so busy he didn't hear, and he'd still be up there moving the lights.

Arthur Hornblow Jr. was a fine producer. He put together a marvelous package and then he let us shoot it and didn't interfere. He seldom came to the set, and when he did it was just to get out of his office for awhile. When you employed a director with the competence and creativity of Mitch Leisen, the producer didn't need to come to the set. Hornblow always watched the rushes with us and sometimes he suggested something or said, "I like the way you did that scene, try to get that feeling again." That was about all.

Brackett and Wilder didn't hang around either. When we ran into an impasse and couldn't shoot a scene, we called them up and they came down to the set. Then they went back to their office where they could fix it, no matter what the problem was. Billy was wild and flamboyant, while Charles was the quiet one. He had a calming influence on Billy. They were inseparable.

Claudette was always great to work with; between scenes we got together and talked over the next scenes. Then we showed Mitch how we wanted to do it. He would correct it for the camera and tell us his ideas. He was very adventurous and always tried to find new ways of doing standard things. He let me play the part myself as much as I could and a lot of things were mine. When the fellows asked me if I'd gotten a date with Claudette and I just grinned and nodded, that was business I thought up myself. But boy, when I needed help, he was right there. Once I said, "I don't know how to get through this door," and Mitch showed me how he thought I should do it. He never let an actor down. Don't think that he didn't care about the performances just because he was so involved with the camera work and the sets. He cared about every aspect of picture making very deeply and what's more, he knew how to get it all up on the screen.

The night I saw the first rough cut of *Arise My Love,* Mitch and I were on location in Texas on *I Wanted Wings.* It was towards the end of the location work and one day Mitch came over between takes and said, "Well baby," (he always called everybody baby) "What do you say if we run it tonight for the boys here on the field?" I said it was all right with me as long as he didn't mind my sitting near the back so I could get out fast.

We ran it, and before it ended, I had to leave because I was so sure it had flopped. I thought I was too young for the part and a lot of other things. It was after midnight, but I called up my wife long distance and said, "Mal honey, when this picture comes out I'm finished. Sell everything we've got and we'll try to start a new life somewhere else." Then it came out and was an enormous hit which really boosted my career— that shows you how much I knew in those days.

I WANTED WINGS - 1941

Charles Brackett and Billy Wilder continued to work on *La Polonaise* while Leisen shot *Arise My Love.* It was retitled *Birth Of A Hero,* and the *Hollywood Reporter* of July 2, 1940 carried an announcement that *Birth Of A Hero* would follow *Arise My Love* on the schedules of Mitchell Leisen and Arthur Hornblow Jr., with William Holden, Maria Ouspenskaya and Albert Dekker in the leading roles. However, on July 10, 1940, the trade papers carried news that the film had been shelved, due, as *Daily Variety* put it, to "Unhealthy market for films dealing with the war sector. . . ." In addition, Eleanor Broder remembers that Brackett and Wilder had not been able to complete a satisfactory script.

Louella Parsons' column of August 2, 1940 stated that Mitch Leisen would next direct Mary Martin in *New York Town,* an original by Jo Swerling to be produced by Anthony Veiller. Preliminary plans indicated an unknown leading man, and Leisen planned a trip to New York to screen prospective candidates, but Paramount eventually decided to use Fred MacMurray and set October 1 as the first day of shooting.

On Saturday, September 7, however, Paramount informed Leisen that J. Theodore Reed had resigned as director on *I Wanted Wings,* and that Leisen was to report to the location in Texas immediately. Reed,

Ray Milland, Wayne Morris and William Holden in *Wanted Wings*.

who had started shooting August 26, returned to Hollywood for a Henry Aldrich picture and Charles Vidor took over *New York Town*.

I Wanted Wings is an epic tale of three Air Force recruits (Ray Milland, William Holden and Wayne Morris) with Brian Donlevy as the tough commanding officer who trains them, and with Veronica Lake and Constance Moore on hand for love interest. The script by Richard Maibaum, Sid Herzog and Lieutenant Bierne Lay Jr. (who also wrote the story on which it was based) had a very involved storyline which followed the destinies of the three flyers, individually and collectively. It was all plot, with little time for characterization. Leisen always preferred to work with stronger character studies in simpler plots, but he managed to develop the Holden and Lake characterizations fully in the brief time allotted. He kept the cumbersome plot moving along rapidly, filled the screen with magnificent aerial photography and in the end, turned out an adventure, which was uncharacteristic of him but nonetheless exciting and entertaining. Released in May, 1941, *I Wanted Wings* delighted the American public, which was again preoccupied with war, and became Paramount's top grossing film of the year.

The box office take was also aided by the presence of Veronica Lake in her first major role. Lake's eye-concealing coiffure had already made her a household word by the time *I Wanted Wings* opened, and although her position in the billing (sixth) could not be changed, Lake's image dominated all the ad layouts. Lake's scenes were few in number, but Leisen made the most of them, and from her first appearance, singing in a nightclub, to the final hysterical scene when she hides in a plane and finds she's trapped as it takes off, she steals every scene she's in. With all of its thrilling episodes and beautiful aerial photography, *I Wanted Wings* is nonetheless best remembered today for the debut of Veronica Lake, and with this treatment of an incidental and secondary female character, Leisen put his personal stamp on what was otherwise as well done but conventional actioner.

ARTHUR HORNBLOW JR.: In that picture, Mitch literally saved me from disaster. *I Wanted Wings* was falling apart on location at the hands of an inept director. As I was in the hospital, there was nothing I could do except send Mitch down to the location (in Texas) to take over. Mitch soon mastered the mess, and we wound up with a tremendous hit. The day we finished shooting, Mitch presented me with a money clip which he had designed and had had made. It said, "You wanted wings."

MITCHELL LEISEN: I never would have picked that one myself, but Ted Reed who was doing it wasn't making it spectacular enough to suit the front office. They had sent the company all the way to Randolph Field in Texas and they said, "We could get that much production right here on the back lot." I knew all about aviation, so I was called in and told to leave immediately for Randolph Field. That was that. I left within the hour for San Antonio and was on the set the next morning at 11 a.m. In the meantime, I watched the film that had already been shot. There were about four reels and I decided that none of it could be used, so we started all over.

We started at Randolph Field and then went down to Kelly Field. I had all three boys, Ray Milland, Bill Holden and Wayne Morris take flying lessons when we got to Kelly. They didn't solo, but they went up and learned how to handle the controls. Of course we rigged the whole plane up in front of a huge transparency screen for all the close shots. It was on a ball and socket joint and we could maneuver it any way we wanted. We were on a twenty foot platform, so we could get the whole plane in, but you'll notice that you never see the bottom of the plane or any space under it.

It was the only time I ever worked with Bill Holden. He is a very gentle, kind person, an excellent actor and very easy to work with. He was very timid about looking at the camera during a take, but we worked with him and got him over that.

It was Veronica Lake's first picture, and she was impossible. Hornblow had seen her in the commissary, and he was fascinated by her hair and her cool sort of beauty. Later on she became a very good actress but she was lost on this one. Every suggestion you made, she fought; you fought with her all day long. I kept her scenes as simple as possible. I gave her very few movements and hoped the other actors and her appearance would carry the scene. For her number in the nightclub, I dressed her in one of Carole Lombard's old gowns: a beautiful thing covered with bugle beads. She was a lot smaller than Carole, and we had to pin it all the way up the back. I gave her only one movement, to gently rub her thigh, like Dietrich did, as she sang. The voice was dubbed, I don't know whose it was.

Her autobiography is the most vicious thing I've ever seen. I don't care what she says about me, but to talk like that about Constance Moore is unforgivable, and every word of it is untrue. Connie and I were not old friends when I took it over. I don't think I'd ever met her, though I'd known her husband Johnny Mascio slightly because he was with us on the DeMille pictures at M-G-M.

It's absurd that Connie could have kept Lake up with all night parties. They did not room together and hardly ever came in contact. Connie was pregnant, and she had almost finished her part when I took over, and then she had to stay down there in the most blistering heat and start all over. The heat was really getting to her and we were all afraid she'd lose the child, which ultimately happened. So you can be sure, under those circumstances, that Connie wasn't fooling around while we were on location.

What Lake says about her car accident is all quite true, however. When we got back to Hollywood, she asked me if she could have the day after Thanksgiving off so she'd have a four day weekend. I said I was very sorry, but she was in every shot all day long and we couldn't shoot around her because we'd done every scene she wasn't in. When we got on the stage Friday morning, Miss Lake was nowhere to be found. We called all over town but nobody knew where she was. Finally I took my assistant Chico Alonzo aside and said, "I've got a hunch. Her husband

Constance Moore and William Holden in *Wanted Wings.*

works for M-G-M, and I think he's on location somewhere in Arizona. Call them up and see." He called them up and she was there. We told her to get the hell back.

They were speeding to catch the next plane back to Los Angeles, when the car crashed, turned over and her leg was broken. She finally arrived on the set Monday morning and I was in a rage. You know I almost never lose my temper, but this was too much. She says in her book that I cursed her out and that much of it is true. I said, "I don't give a damn how you feel, we're going to shoot this scene. Cry, damn you, cry!" It was the scene where she gets trapped in the airplane and gets hysterical. She really broke loose and cried and cried and the scene was perfect.

RAY MILLAND: Fred MacMurray and I were the juveniles on the Paramount lot. I had no confidence in whatever talent I may have had, so I just took what they gave me and didn't argue. As I recall, we finished our last scene of *Arise My Love* at 3:00 on a Saturday afternoon and by 5:00 I was on the plane for San Antonio.

It wasn't long before they sacked the other director and told Mitch he had to take over. He was in the middle of re-recording the sound track of *Arise My Love* and he had to drop everything and come. He always prepared every film very thoroughly but he had no time to prepare this. It was an odd sort of picture for him to be doing, to say the least, but he was a pro and did as much with it as he could.

HOLD BACK THE DAWN - 1941

Leisen eagerly began work on his next assignment, *Hold Back The Dawn,* which ultimately proved to be one of his all time personal favorites. The Brackett-Wilder script had all of his favorite ingredients; it was rich in characterizations, complexly plotted, and set in an unusual locale. It was his last collaboration with Brackett and Wilder as a team and also with Arthur Hornblow Jr. who soon relocated at M-G-M. In every way, *Hold Back The Dawn* was a most auspicious conclusion to a very productive creative relationship.

The plot was derived from a short story by Ketti Frings which was reminiscent of the author's own marriage to Kurt Frings. Brackett and Wilder added a prologue in which Georges Iscovescu (Charles Boyer) sneaks into the Paramount studio and finds Leisen directing Veronica Lake in a scene from *I Wanted Wings* as Brian Donlevy and Richard Webb look on. Leisen breaks for lunch, but Iscovescu persuades him to stay and listen to his story, which is shown in flashback.

Iscovescu had been a highly successful ballroom dancer and gigolo in Europe, but the Second World War made him decide to emigrate to the United States. Stranded in a Mexican border town, he becomes desperate when the immigration authorities inform him that his quota has a long waiting list, but then he encounters his old partner, Anita (Paulette Goddard), who tells him that marrying an American citizen will get him across the border. His eye falls on Emmy Brown (Olivia de Havilland) a virginal schoolteacher who has crossed the border to give her busload of screaming little boys a taste of Mexican culture. "I wanted them to see a real fiesta and learn about pottery making and hand weaving" says Emmy, as Leisen cuts to a very tight close-up of de Havilland wearing a facial expression that shows Emmy to be a bit foolish and naive.

Iscovescu's clever scheme forces Emmy and her students to spend the night in the lobby of his hotel, and at dawn, Iscovescu wakens her, says he loves her deeply and persuades her to marry him. Leisen shot a

Two scenes shot for *Hold Back The Dawn* that were not used: The marriage of
Emmy and Georges; and Georges and Emmy crossing the border at the end,
this time legally.

wedding scene in the office of the Justice of the Peace, but he decided not to use it in the final cut; weddings cause profound emotional responses in audiences and this wedding created a climax too early in the story. Boyer's voice-over narration informs us that they were married, and we see a long shot of the couple entering the building, fading into another long shot of them leaving after the ceremony.

Emmy returns to her hometown of Azusa, California and Iscovescu proceeds with his immigration, telling Anita that he cannot hurt Emmy. Emmy suddenly reappears in Mexico, intent on going on a honeymoon. Sexually awakened, Emmy is a radiantly beautiful creature, but Georges finds a ruse to avoid consummating the marriage during their week-long trip. Returning to the bordertown, Emmy is confronted by Anita, who spells out the lurid details of her husband's past. When the wise immigration official (Walter Abel) tries to shock her with a similar account, Emmy says she knew about Georges' past all along, but afterwards leaves in tears, denouncing her husband with one of Charles Brackett's most poetic speeches, "I live in a small town, and we eat at the drugstore, but we leave a tip just the same. The lies I told were not too much to pay for one week's happiness, but let me go."

Hysterically driving home, Emmy crashes her car and is very seriously injured. Iscovescu learns of his wife's accident, and crossing the border illegally, he rushes to her bedside and gives her the will to live. The immigration officials arrive at Paramount to arrest Iscovescu just as he finishes telling the story to Leisen.

Weeks pass and we find Iscovescu back in the bordertown with no hope of ever immigrating to the United States. The immigration officer, however, tells him that he will overlook the earlier illegal entry, and looking up, Iscovescu sees Emmy waving from the American side of the border. The film ends with a fadeout of Boyer as he runs through the crowd to meet her. Leisen also filmed a more conventional happy ending, in which Emmy shows the border guard her husband's credentials and then the husband and wife embrace, but Leisen and Hornblow both fought for the ambivalent ending and Paramount allowed them to keep it.

Hold Back The Dawn is one of the few Leisen films to contain a perceptible amount of social comment. Leisen has always said, "If I want to send a message, I'll call Western Union," and *The Eagle And The Hawk* (as it was originally released) is the only real message film of Leisen's whole career. *Arise My Love* and *I Wanted Wings* have certain political orientations, but they reflect only their eras, not Leisen's attitude; the social satire of *Easy Living* and *The Mating Season* was put in by the screenwriters, and Leisen retained it because the scenes well served his other purposes (to build characterizations or provide humor).

Nonetheless, *Hold Back The Dawn* is a most poignant statement of the plight of the European immigrants who came to America to escape the tyranny of fascism, only to be refused entry under the archaic quota laws. Forced to live in a dreary bordertown hotel called the Esperanza ("I did a stretch at the Esperanza" remarks Paulette Goddard), they look for loopholes in the immigration laws that may allow them to cross the border; they study American history and observe American traditions. Leisen did not construct this powerful statement just to prove a point; rather, his love for realism made him depict an actual situation as accurately as possible, and his sympathy for each of the immigrant characters as individuals made them doubly sympathetic as a group.

Each resident of the Esperanza has a brief vignette that is a complete characterization in itself. There is a Belgian history professor (Victor Francen) with two pretty daughters (Micheline Cheirel and Madeline LeBeau) and a French hairdresser (Curt Bois). Most poignant of all is the pregnant Mrs. Kurz (Rosemary DeCamp) who is informed by the immigration officer that her husband's tuberculosis will probably prevent their immigration forever. In a beautifully touching scene, Mrs. Kurz insists that she is not yet in labor, and struggles out of her room and down the stairs. Using a ruse, she crosses to the American side of the border. There her child is born, an American citizen, thus enabling Mrs. Kurz and her husband to cross as well.

Leisen was very careful to avoid showing the Mexico that houses the emigrants in an unflattering light, and no Mexicans appear in the story except for the hotelkeeper and an obese maid. One scene shot for comic relief, showing the French hairdresser styling the maid's hair into a ludicrous '40s pompadour, was cut out entirely to avoid poking fun at the maid, although Leisen used the same business again, almost imperceptibly, as comic relief in a very dramatic scene.

In the brief vignette of Mrs. Kurz, Leisen knew that the first of the two scenes, in which she painfully leaves the room, carried too much dramatic impact. He had to save the punch for the next scene when she gets over the border, so he undermined the drama with a tiny detail of comedy. The hairdresser and the obese maid are part of the crowd standing by as Mrs. Kurz tells her husband she's going out. As she laboriously crosses the room, the hairdresser sticks the rat tail of his comb into the maid's pompadour and starts lifting it up. While the attention remains on Mrs. Kurz, this barely perceptible bit of business subliminally lightens the mood so that the audience is receptive to the full impact of the woman crossing the border and giving birth.

Hold Back The Dawn is flawlessly cast, from the smallest bit parts right up to the leads. Rosemary DeCamp's portrayal of Mrs. Kurz fairly glows with warmth and tenderness and Walter Abel displays just the right balance of gruffness and sympathy as the immigration officer. None of the painful nervousness Paulette Goddard displayed in her other early films, such as *Nothing But The Truth*, is evident in *Hold Back The Dawn*. Leisen concealed it or made it work for her tough-as-nails characterization.

Of Charles Boyer's performance in a most difficult role, Bosley Crowther commented in the *New York Times*, ". . . never, we venture to remark, has the bounty of the fellow's masculine charm been so neatly and tastefully distributed through a story of timely consequence—never has his cool sophistication been so well exposed to warm simplicity—as it is in *Hold Back The Dawn.*"

Olivia de Havilland was equally fine in the pivotal and taxing role of Emmy Brown. She had been starred for several years at Warner Brothers, but because of her great beauty, was often cast as the bland heroines of Errol Flynn's epics and was given few challenging parts, even after her triumph in *Gone With The Wind*. On the face of it, it might have seemed that she was too beautiful to be Emmy, that a plainer actress would have made a more convincing spinster schoolteacher. With his usual careful understatement, Leisen did not attempt to change de Havilland's good looks. The hairstyle chosen for Emmy was severe but stylish at the time and her clothes were simple but not unattractive. Leisen, moreover, filled the picture with lyrically beautiful close-ups of de Havilland. The particularly lovely shot introducing Emmy as she expounds on the virtues of pottery making and hand weaving, established from the beginning that Emmy is beautiful as well as naive and inexperienced.

That Emmy was so beautiful and intelligent, yet had reached her mid-twenties apparently unaware of sex, implied a very protected rural upbringing and created an ambiguity which made the part more complex and difficult for de Havilland than it would have been for another actress. Ida Lupino, for instance, in her *Ladies In Retirement* make-up, might have seemed more obvious casting, but de Havilland rose to the challenge. Her conviction in the part, with all its inherent ambiguities, is the film's greatest strength. *Hold Back The Dawn* confirmed de Havilland's success in *Gone With The Wind* and prompted her second Oscar nomination.

ARTHUR HORNBLOW JR.: It is interesting to learn that you are planning to do a book on my dear friend and colleague Mitchell Leisen. My professional and personal relations with him were happy and rewarding ones.

Leisen was a brilliant and hard worker in all fields of film making. As a designer for DeMille and others, he was tops in his day. Through that he became expert in his handling of the camera and all the best cameramen at Paramount learned a lot from him. He was a sensitive and strong director, with a fine ability to deal with the artists he had to handle on many, many films. Even in the field of writing he had an

Leisen got into the habit of coming to the gallery himself to pose the ad stills, including this one of Paulette Goddard, Charles Boyer and Olivia de Havilland in *Hold Back The Dawn.*

Emmy's dip into the ocean on her honeymoon had to be handled with extreme care; this publicity shot of Olivia de Havilland relaxing on the beach was rejected by the Hays Office on May 21, 1941.

excellent sense of values and his opinion in story conferences always made a valuable contribution.

The time finally came for the members of the team to break up and pass along to the development of their various careers. But we all profited from our long relation with Mitch and look back on it with fondness and gratitude.

I see this film as a variation on the Flying Dutchman *theme, the love of a pure woman redeeming the soul of a sinful man.*

MITCHELL LEISEN: I can't say that I ever noticed that before. Perhaps, if you want to go into it that deeply.

Weren't you trying to make a point about the immigration laws?

MITCHELL LEISEN: I wasn't trying to make a case for anything. I did it because it was a damn good story. I think some of the immigrants I showed were sympathetic characters. Victor Franeen was sympathetic; Rosemary DeCamp as the pregnant lady was a very sympathetic character. It is one of the best things Rosemary ever did. But I don't think the hairdresser was particularly worthy.

I did not want to create any sympathy for the heel in the beginning. His business has been women all his life. He's made a living off of being fractious. Borrowing his ex-mistress' wedding ring, is that sympathetic? I didn't intend to make him sympathetic until the very end when it gets down to the nitty-gritty, when she's had the accident and he jumps the border to get to her. He goes to the hospital and gives her the will to live. Then you realize this man is really in love with the woman.

But before that, little things show he has a good side to his nature. He doesn't consummate his marriage to Emmy, and he tells his mistress to get out, that he can't dump Emmy so fast.

MITCHELL LEISEN: Well, nobody's all good, or all bad, not in my movies at least. There's a little bad in the best of us and a little good in the worst of us.

OLIVIA DE HAVILLAND: It was a miracle I ever got to do *Hold Back The Dawn* at all, because I was under contract to Warner Brothers and Jack Warner hated to loan anybody out, especially if it was a role you were well-suited for that might help your career. I had just had my appendix removed and because extended bedrest after surgery was the rule in those days, it was taking me a long while to recover, so Geraldine Fitzgerald and her husband, Edward Lindsey-Hogg, invited me to stay with them. Charles Brackett called up Geraldine to invite them to his house for a Sunday luncheon, but she said they couldn't come because she had to look after me. He said, "Oh, you must bring Olivia, I've been trying to find her for days. Promise me that you'll bring her no matter what happens."

I was so weak, I'd been in bed ever since the operation. But Geraldine got me up and dressed. I raised my arm to arrange my hair and I nearly blacked out. Somehow they got me over to Brackett's, and somebody carried me in from the car. They sat me down in an armchair and Charlie Brackett came over and said, "I've just written the most fantastic part for you. If you like it, just call me up and say 'yes.' Don't say anything else, and don't tell *anybody* not even your agent.'

I read it and I loved it, so I called and said "Yes." Then the long days of waiting began. Of course they couldn't come right out and tell Jack why they wanted me; he would have refused point blank or demanded a million dollars. But it so happened that Jack wanted to borrow Fred MacMurray from Paramount. Charlie Brackett had the front office all ready. When Jack asked for Fred, Paramount said, "Who do we get in return?" Jack named several people he had under contract who weren't busy, and when he came to my name, Paramount didn't show any particular interest. Some time passed and finally Paramount very grudgingly agreed to take me in exchange for Fred. Jack had no idea they'd wanted me all along, so he was sure he'd gotten the better of the deal. My agent called me and said, "You're going to be loaned to Paramount, but it's all right, I've seen the script."

I was still very weak when we started shooting, but I tried very hard not to let it show because if they know you are ill, they make such a fuss over you that it's worse than suffering in silence. I only told the make-up man and when I got tense, he massaged my neck between scenes. I had gained weight in the hospital, eating the jello which was the post-operative diet then. I could see that I was heavier in the rushes, and this troubled me greatly, although I now think Emmy's plumpness is an advantage to the characterization. Edith Head made me some marvelous clothes that helped a lot. She was very careful that the surfaces of the fabrics had no shine and the lines were all quite good.

ELEANOR BRODER: *Hold Back The Dawn* was Olivia's first encounter with Phyllis Seaton. Phyllis was on the picture to help Paulette Goddard along; Paulette couldn't make a move without her. I don't know how much they worked together ahead of time in Paulette's dressing room. Then Phyllis would get all of the cast together and they would do the scene together. Phyllis was officially only the dialogue director, but she gave so much more than any other dialogue director ever did. She went over the characters and their motivations and what should be going through their minds when they played a certain scene.

Phyllis had no compunction about saying exactly what she thought. One day Olivia was chewing some gum and she spit it out. Phyllis said, "Olivia de Havilland, you know that isn't nice. You pick up that gum." And Olivia went over and picked it up.

Olivia was always a very pliant actress. She responded well to suggestions and gave them a lot of thought. If there was a break in the afternoon, she was already thinking about the next day's scenes and she would ask Phyllis how we saw them.

Leisen rehearses Olivia de Havilland and Paulette Goddard in the confrontation scene between Emmy and Anita for *Hold Back The Dawn*.

OLIVIA DE HAVILLAND: It was hard for me to get used to working with Phyllis at first. I hadn't had such detailed direction since Max Reinhardt on *A Midsummer Night's Dream,* and I resented it a bit. We had dialogue directors at Warners but they just listened to you read the lines to check the pronunciation of the words. They didn't get into the characterization much. Indeed, a lot of directors didn't get into the characterization either. They blocked out the action and from then on, you were on your own, for better or worse. That was what I was used to, but I knew I could learn something from Phyllis, so I kept still. She did help me; Emmy Brown is a good performance and I'm proud of it. But Mitch was the director of the picture. Phyllis didn't usurp his function, she just complemented it, helping us to find more depth and dimension.

Paulette was so very nervous I felt sorry for her. I was nervous too, but nothing like this. When we did our scene together, Polly's upper lip was trembling so badly I was afraid it would show on the film.

It was a pleasure to work with Charles Boyer. I always felt such a rapport with him.

Mitch says that in the initial scene between Emmy and Georges, Emmy is supposed to be indifferent to him but that your affection for Boyer showed in your eyes to such an extent that he had to go back several days later and retake the scene.

OLIVIA DE HAVILLAND: So that's why we had to do it over again. It was one of the first scenes we shot, and then at the end of the week, we had to go back and do it again and nobody told me why. I got very worried about my characterization. I thought perhaps that something was wrong with my whole performance and that they regretted casting me in the role. And now, after all these years, I find that was not the reason at all! How curious. I do remember that the next time I played that scene, I played it differently, much more contained, and they said it was fine, so I tried to keep that in mind through the rest of the picture.

The screenplay came from a story by Ketti Frings. It was much like her own marriage to Kurt Frings, who had been trying to get into the country from Mexico when she met him. I knew Ketti already and I always liked her. The first time I met her was when she was a fan magazine writer named Katherine Hartley, and she came out to Warners to interview me over lunch. Kurt Frings later became my agent. I thought a lot about Emmy Brown and Georges Iscovescu and wondered what would become of them after our story about them ended. I eventually came to the feeling that they would separate in the end. Ketti and Kurt were perfectly happy then, and yet after twenty odd years, they split up.

THE LADY IS WILLING - 1942

With a stable management team producing soundly commercial pictures, and a marked improvement in the American economy, the early '40s began Paramount's most profitable period since the coming of sound. Modest projects were becoming big hits and studio officials were concerned with the growing number of unreleased pictures. One consequence of the backlog was the outright sale of several Paramount features to product-hungry United Artists, and another was the loaning out of contractees, no matter how valuable, in an effort to keep them busy at a time when Paramount's decreased production would have otherwise kept them idle.

Mitchell Leisen had considered several projects after the completion of *Hold Back The Dawn,* but none had come to fruition, and Paramount assented to agent Charles Feldman's proposal that Leisen and Fred MacMurray be loaned to Columbia, apparently for a simple payment of money instead of the usual exchange of talent of equal value. Marlene Dietrich had signed a one picture contract with Columbia to play George Sand in a film that had been called off (that film eventually became *A Song To Remember* with Merle Oberon as George Sand) and as Dietrich was also a Feldman client, and wanted to do a picture to raise money for her upcoming USO tour, Feldman arranged for her to play the female lead even though it was not exactly the kind of part she was identified with.

The plot had stage star Dietrich trying to persuade physician MacMurray to marry her so she could adopt a baby. Typical of Columbia fare, most of it took place in one set (Dietrich's apartment.) The romantic comedy with one song was so different from what Dietrich usually did that it actually helped to make this predictable little tale a little more interesting. Dietrich proved herself facile at handling rapid-fire dialogue, and moving around with an unexpected animation (despite her injured foot), she proved to be a good sport in her unaccustomed surroundings. Admitting that he was unhappy and had been to see a psychiatrist, the MacMurray character was a little more complex than the passive, happy-go-lucky guy MacMurray was usually asked to play in Leisen's films. This brief mention of psychiatry was probably Leisen's idea as he tried to inject a bit of reality into the fluff. This was the first of Leisen's films to have a tangible feeling of homosexuality, mostly evident in the relationship between the ever-patient secretary played by Aline MacMahon and Dietrich's Elizabeth Madden. Like Esther Dale (albeit with a bit more youth and style) MacMahon was directed to copy the ever-patient Eleanor Broder but there is the suggestion (on the secretary's side at least) that there is more than the desire to keep a good job. She has her own pet name for her employer (Lise) and seems to take particular pleasure in locking MacMurray out of Dietrich's apartment. Then also are the extraordinary costumes (white tights, and white head scarves topped with tilted sombreros) that Roger Carroll and the chorus boys wear in the not-very-spectacular production number, "I Find Love." It is doubtful that Leisen would have been permitted to exercise his personal taste to this extent if *The Lady Is Willing* had been made at Paramount.

MITCHELL LEISEN: Columbia was always short of top name stars and directors, and Harry Cohn had to look far and wide to get good people

Fred MacMurray and Marlene Dietrich in *The Lady is Willing.*

on the lot. Charlie Feldman was a good friend of Harry Cohn, and he had already arranged with Paramount to let me make an extra picture at Columbia some time earlier. I forget what the picture was, but I signed a contract and then Columbia tried to break it. I was not going to be pushed around by those bastards at Columbia. Feldman said, "Just sit it out," so I went there every day and sat all day in the outer office. They finally paid me off with $20,000 and I went back to Paramount.

Then Charlie put another package deal together whereby Fred and I were loaned to Columbia and Marlene was included because she was one of Charlie's clients and best friends. I had known her slightly at Paramount when she was working with von Sternberg, but only to say "hi" when we passed on the lot. He spent hours lighting her and nobody was allowed to go on their sets. Later she joked about her days with him. She'd say, "All Joe ever let me say was yes and no," or "Joe photographed me through gunny sacks." But boy, she knew everything about lighting that there was to know. She knew right where to turn so the key light would pick her up, just how the shadows should fall.

I wish you could have known her then, David. She was the most fascinating woman who ever lived. She was also one of the most sincere, hardworking people in the picture business. She was very humble, always perfectly willing to do exactly what you wanted her to do, and tried her darnedest to do it too. I wasn't in awe of her, but I adored her.

The Lady Is Willing is one of Marlene's best performances. You see her sitting on a couch in a suit covered with black bugle beads and a bugle bead hat with paradise feathers. She sits there crying with the little baby in her arms, and you see a real actress. That script wasn't the greatest in the world either. She could cry hysterically on cue, but she didn't think that was enough. She said she had been up all night too, so she sprayed this horrible fluid into her eyes until they were all red and puffed up, and then she really let go and sobbed.

Every time Marlene cried, the baby would cry too. There was some wise reporter on the set while we were doing that scene, and the next day, there were big headlines, "SO MARLENE LIKES KIDS, OH YEAH?" and it went on to say how she had made the baby cry. How dare anybody say things like that! It could not have been more malicious

Mrs. Leisen (Sandra) visits the set of *The Lady is Willing.*

MacMurray and Leisen inspect Dietrich's plaster cast.

and untrue. After that, the press was barred from the set unless they had my express permission and Marlene's. That reporter never got on another set of mine again.

We had only been shooting a few days when she hurt her foot. She was very late that morning because she said her astrologer, Carroll Righter, had predicted that she'd have an accident that day. She made her chauffeur drive very slowly to the studio just to be on the safe side. We started in, and she picked up one of the twins who were being used for the baby. I didn't see exactly what happened, but she was walking behind the couch, and tripped on a little red wagon. As she fell, she turned herself over so she landed on her back with the baby on top of her, and in doing so, she cracked the little bone of her ankle. It must have been very painful for her, but there was never any question of recasting. She got some orthopedic shoes and we went right on.

We had to trick it up a little so that the audience wouldn't see her limp. The set had a mirrored wall, so every time she had to cross the room, we'd start her out with one step on her good foot, then cut to a reaction shot of Fred sitting on the couch with the reflection of her double in the mirror behind him crossing the room. Then we cut back

With Dietrich hiding her bad foot behind her other leg, Leisen made another cameo appearance for one of his films. Once again, he removed it from the final cut.

to Marlene as she was arriving and she took one step into the scene with her good foot. We could always angle the camera so it wouldn't photograph itself in the mirror, but putting the lights where Marlene wanted them and not picking them up in the mirror was sometimes very hard. Eleanor always sat right under the camera, and Ted Tetzlaff had to say to her, "Get down, we can see you in the mirror." For awhile, she was practically lying on the floor.

We kept it right on schedule, even did the production number, although that didn't require her to dance much. She wore a big head-dress in the number covered with bugle beads, and she spent so much time in front of a mirror arranging the beads I finally had to tell her to get on the set. She was a good sport about it all, but the one thing she couldn't understand was why Fred MacMurray didn't fall madly in love with her. I said, "Listen Marlene, Fred's so much in love with his wife Lilly, he couldn't care less about any other woman, so you lay off. Just make the picture; forget about making Fred."

FRED MACMURRAY: I had never had anything like this happen on a picture before and it was very embarrassing.

CHICO DAY: Mitch insisted that Ted Tetzlaff and I come over from Paramount with him for this although that wasn't usually done. Dietrich was always telling Ted Tetzlaff how to light her. He was patient with her, but he could also be assertive in his own quiet way. One day he asked her to stay behind after the rest of the company went home. He wanted to make tests, one lighting her exactly according to her instructions and another doing it the way he thought was right. She stayed and when she looked at both tests the next day, she liked his better. She agreed not to make any more suggestions.

MITCHELL LEISEN: Marlene knew that my proteges, Mary Parker and Billy Daniels, were going to open on Broadway in Let's Face It and that the opening coincided with our last day of shooting. She offered to work nights to get ahead of schedule, and that way we saved about five days. We took the train across the country together, and when I got off at Chicago, she said, "You just watch. Mama's going to make all the front pages when she gets to New York." When she got there, she was wearing her famous pants for the first time in years, and sure enough, she made every front page.

I arrived in New York the next day, and I invited Marlene to attend the opening night of Let's Face It with me. The word went around that she was in the theater, and at the end, when they opened the doors to let the audience leave, hordes of kids came in from the street and went racing down the aisles, to get to Marlene. We had to call the police and finally managed to get her out the back and into a cab, but the fool

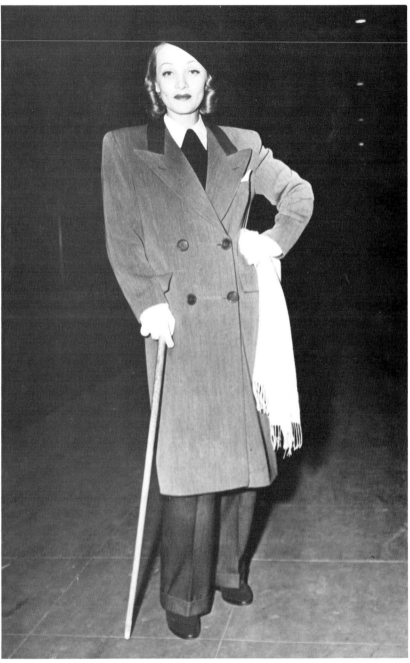

Dietrich arrived in New York wearing her pants and made all the front pages as she had predicted.

driver stopped for a light and the kids caught up with us. They actually tore one of the doors of the cab off and jammed themselves in, just to get a look at Marlene. She wasn't the least bit perturbed, she talked to them and signed their autograph books.

TAKE A LETTER, DARLING - 1942

After the great success of *Arise My Love,* it was not surprising when Paramount assigned Claudette Colbert to Mitchell Leisen for *Take A Letter, Darling,* his first picture on the lot after his loan out to Columbia. Claude Binyon's screenplay was amusing, and Fred MacMurray, who had already proved an ideal partner for Colbert, got the male lead. Frances Farmer was assigned the secondary female part. MacDonald Carey, recently the psychiatrist on Broadway in *Lady In The Dark,* was to make his debut in the secondary male part.

Then, complications developed. Preston Sturges, about to begin *The Palm Beach Story,* couldn't come to an agreement with the front office on casting the female lead. His choice was Carole Lombard, who had signed a non-exclusive deal with Paramount stating that she would receive upwards of $150,000 for any subsequent Paramount picture. She had not made any pictures under this deal, since she had rejected all the scripts Paramount had submitted, and had made instead moderately successful films at RKO. The front office claimed that these films had lowered her box office value, but she refused to lower her price accordingly, and in a final attempt at compromise, the front office proposed Claudette Colbert, who was due to begin *Take A Letter, Darling* at the same time *Palm Beach Story* was scheduled to start. Colbert agreed to the change in assignment, and Leisen, who was acting as his own producer on *Take A Letter, Darling,* magnanimously let her go, allowing her to star in what became one of the classic comedies of all time. Suddenly finding herself without assignment, Carole Lombard embarked on the war bond tour that eventually cost her her life.

In the meantime, *Take A Letter, Darling* was postponed indefinitely until it could be recast. Barbara Stanwyck, under non-exclusive contract to Paramount, turned it down and other possibilities were either unavailable or not interested. Finally it was accepted by the free-lancing Rosalind Russell, and scheduled to begin at the end of her current

Leisen with MacMurray and Rosalind Russell in a country store set for *Take A Letter, Darling.*

commitment. When problems developed with Frances Farmer, she was replaced by Constance Moore.

Take A Letter, Darling could not have been more perfectly tailored to Rosalind Russell's talents and popular screen image had it been written for her in the first place. The Claude Binyon script's premise also fit Fred MacMurray perfectly. Woman executive Russell hires MacMurray to serve as her secretary, or more specifically as an escort who will keep serious suitors away. Warning him that all his predecessors had been fired when they obeyed their natural male instincts, Russell then does a slow burn when MacMurray gets romantically involved with the seductive sister (Constance Moore) of Russell's wealthy client (Macdonald Carey).

All ends happily, and in the meantime, there is a lot of clever business. In an effort to add interest to the routine presentation of the credits, the film opens as Leisen picks up a stack of title sketches, then slowly leafs through them, signifying his approval by initialing each card before passing to the next. There are several amusing interludes with Robert Benchley, who had been the head of the company until his ambitious secretary Roz took it over, and who now spends his time playing with sophisticated toys. Best of all, there is Rosalind Russell, unique and inimitable.

MITCHELL LEISEN: I don't think any of the comedies I made in the '40s were as good as the ones I'd done earlier, and the reason is very simple; I didn't have Arthur Hornblow with me and I needed him. But they were still fun to do, and I guess *Take A Letter, Darling* is about the best. It made a lot of money, at least.

Roz Russell has to be one of the funniest women ever, both on the screen and off. She played the role her way, which was very different from what Claudette would have done if she had stayed on the picture, but I just let her go right ahead and she was wonderful.

I loved the scene in the restaurant, where Fred and Connie Moore just keep dancing by and Roz does a slow burn. Fred always had two left feet when it came to dancing, but Connie was so good, she could lead and make it look like he was leading. She's a very talented gal and she should have been a much bigger star, but she was more interested in her husband and their kids. Then at the end of the scene, Fred had to take a pratfall and he really took it. Gin rummy was the big craze at that time so I got that in too. And I used real food in the scene, even if the war was on. I never went for this beebee-shot-in-axle-grease-for caviar routine.

FRED MACMURRAY: The one thing I remember about that picture was how considerate Mitch was of the extras. He always made a point of directing each and every one of them himself, even in the big scene in the restaurant, because he said he was an extra once and he knew how disconcerting it was to have the assistant director give some vague instructions to the whole company and that would be it. Mitch gave every single one of them some kind of business even if they were way in the back.

CONSTANCE MOORE: I loved every minute working on that, because Mitch loved doing it and his enthusiasm spread through the whole company.

Mitch designed all of my clothes for the picture. When I tried on one of the gowns, I called him up and asked what kind of jewelry he had in mind to go with the dress. He said, "Just what's on my desk." I went to

Constance Moore and MacMurray in *Take a Letter, Darling.*

his office and saw the most fantastic things he had designed and had made up for his wife, which he let me wear in the picture. They were of diamonds, emeralds and crysobals. There was a bracelet, the center of which could be detached and worn as a pendant or as a pin. The earrings were actually three little loops, one of each stone. They could all be worn together or singly. Mitch also designed Roz Russell's hairdo for the picture, and she was very pleased with "Mitch's creation" as she called it.

Mitch really knew how to give us good business and he loved walking through the scenes to show it to us. The business where Fred MacMurray and I fell over the back of the couch looked like it was completely spontaneous, but it wasn't at all. Mitch knew exactly how I could suddenly fall over backwards, but do it gracefully so my skirt didn't fly over my head. I'm sure he had worked it all out the night before at home, so he knew just what to show us on the set.

There were subtle little things he had us do to show tension. Once he told me to sit down on the edge of the couch rather than lean back normally. Another time I picked up a cigarette and just held it in my hand, forgetting to light it because I was so absorbed.

Mitch always came to the set completely prepared. It is one thing for the actor to prepare by knowing his lines, but Mitch always knew how to do everything technically that would come up that day. He could handle all the physical problems very quickly and then he was free to work by instinct in directing his actors.

MACDONALD CAREY: It is a pity that Mitch got so involved with working with Phyllis Seaton. He didn't need her, he was very good at directing performances. *Take A Letter, Darling* was only my second picture, and while I had no problems with the line readings, I was ill at ease with the camera. Mitch helped me get used to the medium. When I was stiff, he'd give me a bit of business to ease my way through a scene. One thing he thought of was to never have me touch a door with my hand. I'd kick it to close it. This sounds like a little thing but he'd gone to the heart of the character. This was a man who had so much money that material things had no meaning to him.

All of Mitch's pictures started with a couple of days of meetings in his office where we'd read over the script and talk about it. He served tea from a rococo tea set that was so heavy that it took two prop men to move it! Then each day on the set he'd block the action and ask us what we thought. The other actors were very kind to me too. Fred MacMurray really went out of his way to help and encourage me. He didn't look upon me as competition. After the big love scene, Roz Russell said to Mitch, in my presence, "You don't have to worry about this one!" I had always had a connection to Connie Moore; as a teenager I acted with her cousins in Gilbert and Sullivan and I'm sure I met her at least once in my home town.

NO TIME FOR LOVE - 1943

Take A Letter, Darling finished shooting January 16, 1942, and on June 8, Leisen was back on the soundstage shooting another Claude Binyon script starring Fred MacMurray, and this time, Claudette Colbert. Viewing the two films together reveals that Colbert, at least, was fortunate in not having done both of them, for the characterizations (assertive female and passive male) and the plot (career girl meets *homme fatal*) were virtually the same in both films. What differences there are between the films are not in their scripts but arise rather from the contrast between Russell's stylized and emphatic method of playing comedy as opposed to the more natural and realistic style of Colbert. There are an astounding number of shots of the wrong side of Colbert's face and at one point, Leisen even got her to allow a close (though brief) full face two-shot.

Even if there was nothing new in a story about a strictly-business lady photographer who falls for the muscular foreman of a crew digging a tunnel under the Hudson River, Binyon's lines were bright and well tailored to his stars. The performances were fine, Leisen kept it going at a good pace and although it was entirely predictable, wartime audiences must have found it highly entertaining. The Quigley Publications *Fame* poll listed *No Time For Love* as one of the six top grossing pictures for its month of release, April 1943.

A couple of factors lift *No Time For Love* out of the ordinary. First, much of the action takes place in the tunnel, which suddenly caves in and drenches everybody with mud. When MacMurray invents a means to counteract the flow of mud, they all go in to try it out. Colbert has slipped into the tunnel to take pictures, and when it seems that MacMurray's theory wasn't working, her pictures save the day. The mud gave Leisen a great opportunity for physical comedy and *No Time For Love* has more slapstick than any of his comedies since *Easy Living*.

It also has an amazing number of blithely uncloseted homosexuals as Leisen gleefully compares the effete, witty men in Colbert's social circle (including Paul McGrath, who she plans to marry even though she doesn't love him) with the brawling mudhogs that MacMurray works and hangs out with. Richard Haydn is on hand in many scenes, peering over his glasses (a dead giveaway) and takes no offense when June Havoc addresses him as "pantywaist." In another scene, when Mac-

Murray barges uninvited into Colbert's swank party, Haydn's lover (Robert Herrick) instinctively grabs Haydn's shoulders and says, "My dear, do you think we could harm this Viking?" Colbert constantly addresses and refers to MacMurrary as "ape", "gorilla" and "King Kong."

As in *Take A Letter, Darling*, *No Time For Love*'s main titles were cleverly worked out. After the Paramount logo, we see a close-up of a woman's hand agitating a photograph in a developing bath. Slowly the words of the first title appear, then the next until the series is completed. Finally, *No Time For Love* has a brief dream sequence. Colbert dreams of Superman, who is MacMurray, of course, his shoulders made even more massive with padding. They go sailing through the air and MacMurray slugs the appropriately costumed villain. As dream sequences go, this one was very modest. Lasting only a few minutes, it seemed to have been inserted to pep up a dull spot in the picture. It is interesting today only because it was Leisen's first dream sequence. Already he was interested in Freudian psychology as expressed in dreams. Immediately after *No Time For Love*, Leisen began work on *Lady In The Dark*.

MITCHELL LEISEN: That was a real fun picture to do. Fred and Claudette worked so wonderfully together. Many times when I was setting up the next scene, they'd go off in a corner and work it up themselves. They'd show me how they wanted to do it and it would be just right. I might edit it a bit, but they were talented natural performers and I wanted them to do it in a way that was comfortable for them. When we blocked the scene, I always said, "This is how I see it. You move over her while you say this line and then you pick up the cigarette while she's talking. If you don't feel natural with these movements, tell me and we'll do what is natural for you."

In the story, Fred is working on a tunnel under the Hudson when the river bottom breaks through and there's a sea of mud. We set the tunnel up in Stage 18, which was Paramount's largest stage. It was about twenty-five feet long, although it was blocked off about ten feet ahead of the actors, so the whole thing didn't have to be filled up all the time. We tried everything we could think of to avoid using real mud, even mixing sawdust and water, but nothing looked real. We had to get adobe and water and mix them in cement mixers on the stage all day long. We must have been in there at least two weeks; you couldn't work very fast.

Leisen and MacMurray on the muddy set of *No Time For Love.*

I never asked my actors to do anything I wouldn't do, so on our first day in the tunnel, I dove right into the mud, head first. I came up and said, "All right, let's go." I doubt Claudette knew it would be as bad as this when she agreed to make the picture, but she was a good sport about it. We mixed the mud with baby oil and soaked her costumes with that, so they wouldn't dry out between takes. In one take, she dragged herself through mud up to her neck, but when she got to the other side there wasn't a speck on her face or her hair. I said, "Come here, honey," and took a handful of the mud and slapped it on her face. She went right back and did it again.

We had showers set up all over the stage for the extras to rinse off between scenes. One day Claudette walked over and announced, "I'm coming in, boys" and she went right in! You never saw so many naked men in your life. They ran out in all directions and hid behind the flats.

Fred MacMurray breaks Claudette Colbert's flimsy chair when he tries to sit in it in *No Time For Love*. The sets were reused from *The Palm Beach Story*.

Another time we heard this very faint voice crying out, "Let me out, I'm the star." It was Fred; he'd been buried under several feet of mud.

ELEANOR BRODER: During the war, the government set a $5000 ceiling on the amount of new materials which could be used for sets and costumes on any one film. We found that this meant an average of $5000 per film, and if we used less than the maximum on one film, we could go over $5000 on another. So we decided to use virtually no new materials on *No Time For Love*.

The sets for *The Palm Beach Story* were still standing, and since they had all been built with Claudette's angle in mind, we simply painted them white, made a few minor changes and used them again. Then Mr. Leisen got all sorts of Victorian furniture from the prop department, painted it white, and it was lovely.

There was also a big drive on to conserve raw film stock, and we set some kind of record by only exposing 6500 feet on *No Time For Love* which is about a quarter of the usual amount. Mr. Leisen managed this by having such extensive rehearsals before the first take that, in most cases, we could print the first take and that was all the film we used.

FRED MACMURRAY: It was always a pleasure to make a picture with Claudette. She was in the second picture I did, *The Gilded Lily* and I'll never forget how kind she was. I didn't have the slightest idea what I was doing, but she was so patient with me. She worked and worked with me and got me through it.

Whenever we did a script by Claude Binyon, we didn't need much direction. We just knew what to do. Several years later, we did *Family Honeymoon,* which Binyon wrote and directed as well. All of the other actors were complaining that Binyon didn't direct them enough, but Claudette and I just went right ahead and did it by ourselves. We knew instinctively how it should be played. I might say, "Give me a couple more beats before you come in with your line," or she'd say, "Try reading that a little faster, Fred," and we'd keep working on it together until we had it just right.

LADY IN THE DARK - 1944

Leisen's next picture, *Lady In The Dark,* was the climax of his career. It is his most ambitious work, and probably the highest grossing film of his career, but it also contains the first signs of his decline as an artist.

As a play, *Lady In The Dark* had revolutionized Broadway. Moss Hart's text was based on his own psychoanalytical experiences, and the score by Kurt Weill and Ira Gershwin took a great stride in the integration of music into the drama. Hollywood was impressed, but there was no great competition for the film rights, which eventually went to Alexander Korda. Filming it as it had been performed on the stage was impossible since there was a strong indication of the Electra complex in the characterization of the heroine, Liza Elliott, and the whole structure of the piece, with its constant choral music, was too theatrical for mass consumption. Casting it was impossible too. Gertrude Lawrence, who had portrayed Liza on Broadway, was not well known to movie audiences, and virtually none of the big female movie stars of the period could handle all the dramatic and musical requirements. Irene Dunne had turned down the stage version when the producers had despaired of getting Gertrude Lawrence to sign a contract; this was not due to any lack of sympathy for the material but simply because she didn't want to move her daughter to New York and dreaded the grind of eight live shows a week. Had Dunne been cast in the film role, she could have acted and sung better than Ginger Rogers (who was finally cast) and probably would have accepted the plain versus sexy dichotomy of Liza Elliott more willingly than Rogers did. However she didn't dance as well and could not have carried off the high school flashback like Rogers did.

Sympathy for the material was Ginger Rogers' problem. Garson Kanin (who directed Rogers in *Tom, Dick And Harry* also wrote *From This Day Forward* as a vehicle for Rogers) has said that Rogers could play any role if she understood it. She would have been a dark horse in the search for Liza Elliott, for in the play, Liza was apparently in her forties and Rogers was still playing ingenues. However, Rogers' RKO contract had expired soon after she won the Oscar for *Kitty Foyle,* and with every studio in town offering lucrative multiple picture deals, Rogers became very selective in her choice of scripts. Paramount offered a three picture deal, to begin with *The Major And The Minor.* Wanting to return to musicals, but with a story that would offer more dramatic opportunities than usual, Rogers accepted Paramount's offer with the stipulation that *Lady In The Dark* would be the second picture of the deal. Paramount purchased the property from Korda and then spent the next two years trying to adapt it. Mitchell Leisen finally submitted a workable treatment and the film went into production.

Ultimately Rogers' performance in *Lady In The Dark* was professional, likable but inexplicably not quite good enough. Cheerful, healthy and a practicing Christian Scientist, she did not have the insight into Freudian psychology that someone who had spent much time in analysis (as Leisen had) would bring to such a project. Nothing that Leisen could say quite got the point across and this was a case where Phyllis Seaton wasn't much help either.

Also Rogers was getting tired. She had the audacity and box office clout to make Paramount produce *Lady In The Dark,* but no longer quite the ambition needed to push herself to met its extraordinary demands. She had been working virtually nonstop since she was a teenager, but after *Lady In The Dark* she would choose to work less frequently, turning down both *To Each His Own* and *The Snake Pit* in favor of the undemanding *Weekend At The Waldorf* and *It Had To Be You.*

It was a very troubled project right from the start. Up to that time, all of Leisen's productions had been noted for congenial working conditions on the set. Conflicts among workers on any project as complex as

Leisen and Rogers work on the final scene of the film but one shot early in the production. Photo taken 2/2/43.

a motion picture are inevitable, but Leisen's organizational ability minimized these troubles, and his staff, which followed him from picture to picture, was like a large family.

The enormous size of *Lady In The Dark* as well as the addition of Technicolor necessitated additional workers in all departments which undermined the *esprit de corps*. Leisen had to bring in two extra assistant directors to supplement his perennial aide, Chico Day, who was to join the Navy before the picture finished shooting. When Leisen passed over Day to give a friend of Billy Daniels' the most prestigious job, the entire crew was furious. Although Day did not complain (and worked again with Leisen after the war), the other staff members felt this move was an affront to their seniority in the Leisen unit, and they responded by becoming as uncooperative as possible. The same people who had eagerly followed Leisen's every move now became impossible to find. On the one picture of his whole career where he most needed a dependable staff, Leisen got the least help. He said at the time that he knew it would take a long while to regain their respect, and it wasn't until several pictures later that the old ambiance was completely restored.

Eleanor Broder was among those mad at him but one day when things were going especially badly she smiled at him. Leisen, surprised, looked behind himself to see who she was smiling at.

The estrangement from his production team had a markedly deleterious effect on Leisen, and *Lady In The Dark* suffered accordingly. Leisen tried to restore his self-confidence by concentrating on what he was most confident doing, the sets and costumes, lighting and camera work, avoiding the drama of the story which he could have handled much more satisfactorily. As it became apparent that Ginger Rogers' acting was failing to capture all the nuances and ambiguities of Liza Elliott's complex psyche, the visual aspects of the film assumed greater importance in Leisen's scheme of things as he tried to convey certain points. As a result, *Lady In The Dark* is a work that is more interesting visually than dramatically and this problem would occur again in other Leisen films.

Leisen's first use of three-strip Technicolor is extremely tasteful and well worked out in terms of '40s chic. He subdues and controls the color throughout the story, allowing full saturations only in the hallucinatory dreams, and then with very limited chromatic schemes. The blue dream, which occurs first, concentrates on a medium shade of blue; the wedding dream then limits itself to golds, whites and browns. It isn't until the final, circus dream that Leisen employs the full spectrum, in one of the most delightfully garish spectacles ever conceived.

The story opens in a doctor's office where fashion magazine tycoon Liza Elliott is informed that her illness is psychosomatic. She consults a psychiatrist (Barry Sullivan) who suggests a trial psychoanalysis. Returning to her office, she confronts her insolent advertising manager, Charley Johnson (Ray Milland), her wise girl friday (Mary Philips), an eccentric photographer (Mischa Auer), and Kendall Nesbitt (Warner Baxter) her financial backer who is trying to divorce his wife to marry Liza.

A symptom of Liza's mental illness is that she can no longer make decisions. Johnson has proposed discarding the magazine's traditional Easter cover for a circus motif, and lying down in desperation, the first dream begins. She hears a strange tune and finds herself enveloped in a sea of blue. She is adored from all sides as she poses for a portrait which will be used for the new two-cent stamp. Relating the dream to her psychiatrist, she mentions that she has always detested the color blue.

The psychiatrist points out the discrepancy between the stiffly efficient Liza of the office and the entrancing creature of the dream, and

Ginger Rogers and Barry Sullivan in *Lady In The Dark.* The "pensive" nature of her eyebrows was achieved by make-up, an effect nobody could dissuade her from using.

suggests that Liza secretly longs to be feminine, an explanation she refuses to accept. Her problems compound and she has a second dream, all in gold, in which she is supposed to marry Nesbitt and realizes she doesn't really want to. The minister, sternly looking down from the wedding cake, is none other than Charley Johnson.

In the final, circus dream, an adolescent Liza dressed in a middy blouse, is at the surrealistic circus. Looking up, she discovers her adult self, glamorous in a towering pompadour and wearing a fantastic dress, with a skirt of mink, lined with red and gold brilliants. Liza is being brought to trial for refusing to make up her mind. The judge is Mischa Auer, the prosecuting attorney Ray Milland and the attorney for the defense is Warner Baxter. In her defense, Liza goes into a seductive rendition of "The Saga of Jenny":

> "There once was a girl named Jenny,
> Her virtues were varied and many,
> excepting that she was inclined,

always to make up her mind;
Jenny points a moral,
with which we cannot quarrel,
as you will find."

The dream fades into a scene of Liza on the psychiatrist's couch. She remembers a scene from her childhood, in which she overheard her father tell a friend that she wasn't as pretty as her mother. She tried to sing a little song for the guests, but froze with embarrassment. The song is "My Ship" and it is the tune that haunts her. Later her mother died and Liza tried to cheer her father up by putting on her mother's favorite blue dress. Her father angrily ordered her to take it off and that is why she hates blue.

Leisen shot another scene, in which Liza is trying out for a play at school and overhears somebody say she isn't as pretty as another little girl. The studio cut that sequence out entirely and continued Liza's account on the night of her high school prom.

Liza was not invited to the prom, so she decides to spend the evening in the town library. There she finds a popular boy who's had a fight with his girl friend, and she accepts his invitation to go with him. Pausing in a little park before entering the high school gymnasium, Liza remembers a tune that has haunted her since childhood. They sit down and she sings "My Ship." The boy's girl friend then lures him away from Liza and she is left alone.

B. G. DeSylva, the producer of *Lady In The Dark*, insisted that Ginger Rogers' rendition of "My Ship" be cut out, leaving that element of the drama resolved. Fearing just such an action, Leisen refused to shoot any covering shots that would allow a graceful excision of the song, but DeSylva took it out anyway. Just as Liza is about to begin to sing, there is a clumsy fade into the gymnasium, then a quick cut to the girlfriend coming out the door.

Liza returns to her office and tells her friends she has solved her problem. The audience remains unconvinced, however, because it has heard ghostlike choirs humming "My Ship" throughout the film and in the end is deprived of the satisfaction of hearing the lovely song sung straight. "My Ship" had become a standard by the time the film was made, and its elimination was a gross error.

Having come to an understanding of her psychological problems, Liza now sees her career ambitions as an aspect of her neurosis and while this is now unacceptable, in its day it represented the prevailing thought. Millions of women had entered the work force because of

The unkindest cut of all, Ginger Rogers sang "My Ship" to Rand Brooks a capella against faint strains of the band playing "Ain't She Sweet."

World War II, but it was considered to be only a temporary arrange-
ment. They were generally expected to return to lives of domesticity
when the war ended. The play had ended with MacDonald Carey
singing "My Ship" to Gertrude Lawrence but Leisen chose to end the
film with a gag. Quickly settling her differences with Charley Johnson
(and inferring that she is willing to give the magazine up and let him
run it), the two sit down to work on the circus number of the magazine.
Mischa Auer is astounded by this and he says, "This is the end, the
absolute end," and THE END title flashes on the screen.

Even though many of the psychological ramifications of *Lady In The
Dark* had been watered down considerably, Paramount feared public
antipathy and promoted the film very carefully, avoiding any reference
to psychology in the advertising. *Lady In The Dark* proved to be a

tremendous success at the box office. Opening finally at the New York Paramount with Xavier Cougat in February of 1944, it broke the record of *Star Spangled Rhythm* with Benny Goodman and Frank Sinatra a year earlier, grossing $123,000 the first week and in Los Angeles, at the Hollywood and Downtown Paramounts, it bettered *Dixie*'s second week record by 26%.

The New York press was uniformly positive about the production values and the spectacle although divided about Rogers' performance. Leo Mishkin of the *Morning Telegraph* commented, "Miss Rogers seems to have been overwhelmed no little by the very size of the assignment she had to do, and wanders through the film with little more than a worried frown on her face. With all due respect to Ginger Rogers, she fails singularly to come up to either the demands or the expectations." In the *New York Times* Bosley Crowther was a bit milder: " Except for her gay and raffish singing of "The Saga Of Jenny" (slightly cut) and her burst of enthusiasm at the finish, Miss Rogers moves through it all in a variety of stunning costumes but a plain brown study most of the time. Her mood is particularly depressing. Physically, however she's all right." Howard Barnes of the *Herald Tribune,* however thought, "Great credit must go to Miss Rogers for a sumptuous and satisfying show. Only a top Hollywood performer could have followed Gertrude Lawrence in a part which she had made peculiarly her own. The film star has built her own impersonation of a screw-ball career girl and it rarely falters. ..Miss Lawrence was "magnificent" as this reviewer wrote after watching her on the stage. Miss Rogers does her one better in the film."

For all its positive reviews and super box office, *Lady In The Dark* was not an all out triumph for its participants. Paramount did not exercise its option for a third film with Rogers and though she would command a record salary the next year for *Weekend At The Waldorf,* her career had peaked and her days as a top star were over. Leisen's problems with the studio's front office were just beginning.

MITCHELL LEISEN: I fought against doing that one for two years. Frances Goodrich and Albert Hackett had written a script which completely and utterly ignored Moss Hart's play. They had dreams where people were running down the streets in their underwear, hiding in doghouses and being chased by wild horses. Moss had done psychoanalysis and he wrote the play right after he finished. It's all very consistent to the theory of Freud: the people in her dreams are the same

Leisen and Rogers confer; Eleanor Broder sits behind Rogers.

people who appear in the story. In the Hackett version, the dreams had nothing to do with the plot. They just wrote a whole different story.

I was in New York after *No Time For Love* and Buddy DeSylva called me and said that he had never expected to have to make it, but part of his three picture deal with Ginger Rogers was that she play this part, and for God's sake, would I please agree to do it. I said I would not shoot the Hackett script. He said, "I don't give a damn what you shoot. Just say you'll make the picture."

So I went to Moss Hart and got his original prompt copy, and I came back to California and wrote the script of *Lady In The Dark*. I had a gal come in afterwards and do a little polishing here and there. Her name was Kearney or something like that. The Hacketts got credit but their script was thrown in the wastebasket.

I knew it was not up Ginger Rogers' alley, although seeing it the other day, I say she gave a better performance than I expected of her. It took ten years off my life, I can tell you that. In those psychoanalytical

The Blue
Dream.
Photo taken
March 6,
1943.

scenes on the couch, she didn't know what the hell she was talking
about. I'd go in quietly and try to explain to her what the thing meant
and pull it out of her. I mean I really pulled.

She was very bad at matching action. You take a master shot first and
then you go in and make your close-ups. If she lights a cigarette on a
certain line in the master take, it has to be lit on exactly that word in the
close-up, otherwise you can't cut it together. She always had a hard
time remembering how she'd done it.

She was always late coming to the set. The day we did the "Suddenly
It's Spring" number, she arrived on the set at half past three in the
afternoon. I had 165 electricians waiting all day. I told DeSylva, "I'm
not going to be a policeman; if you don't like it, you talk to her. I didn't
want her for the picture in the first place."

One day we were doing the scenes on the couch and she blew take
after take until I thought I'd go out of my mind. Finally she said, "I'm

sorry. I just can't keep my mind on this because I'm getting married tomorrow." Mr. DeSylva let her go off and get married in the middle of the picture and the entire company just sat there for two weeks. He said, "You can shoot around her." I said, "No we can't. She's been late every day and we've shot up every scene she's not in." She came back and gave us two weeks at the end of the picture free. She would have been sued if she hadn't.

The play and our picture were quite different. The picture is ten times as elaborate as any stage show could possibly be. The play had more music and relied more on the lyrics. When we were planning it, I remembered going to Napoleon's tomb at Les Invalides in Paris and I got the feeling that the very air there was blue. I looked up and discovered that all the windows in the ceiling were of ancient blue stained glass.

For the blue dream, we got the same effect by flooding the soundstage with blue light. To intensify the blue, we put in a little violet and a little green. We used tons of dry ice to get the cloudy effect, and we found some marvelous stuff you could just spray into the air and it would form a cloud that would stay right there. Unfortunately the extras complained that it was hurting their respiratory systems so we had to stop using it.

The sets were blue, the costumes were blue, the make-ups were blue on some of the women though their hair was red like Liza's mother's. The girls made everybody in the commissary sick when they came in for lunch with their blue faces, scarlet lips and red hair. In fact we flooded our eyes with blue to such an extent that we lost our ability to perceive the color blue and we'd have to leave the stage and stand in the sunlight for twenty minuets to get our eyes back to normal so we could continue. We really got blue on the screen. That Eastman color dupe we saw yesterday can't compare with the brilliance we had in our original Technicolor prints.

We shot all the dreams in the big Stage 18 where the basement was storage for furniture. We took all the furniture out and made it into a dressing room for the chorus girls. For the blue dream, the girls made up and came upstairs in blue kimonos. After we'd rehearsed and lit everything, they'd go downstairs, get dressed, and come up again in the freight elevators. Their costumes were so enormous we could only get three of them in the elevator at a time.

We had Dorothy di Frasso's Rolls Royce all covered with blue glitter and the lap robe was the blue Picasso that hung behind Liza's desk in her office. Mischa Auer became her chauffeur in the dream and he sang "Tchaikowski," the famous number Danny Kaye did in the play where he names all the Russian composers. We had quite a job cleaning Miss di Frasso's car up, and in the end, we cut that whole section out of the sequence.

We used tons of dry ice in the gold dream too. The wedding dress that Raul Pene du Bois designed for her had yards and yards of skirt. When Ginger danced with Don Loper the dry ice would make it so wet it weighed a ton and she could hardly move in it. Between takes we had sixteen wardrobe girls with ironing boards all around her trying to dry it out so she could go on and do another take.

Those chorus girls in the gold dream really had to know their stuff. They came down these little runways that were ten or fifteen feet off the floor and only a few inches wide. They twisted and turned all over. I had the girls rehearse it over and over until they knew all the little turns of the runway by heart and could come down without looking at their feet. Then they turned on the dry ice, which covered the runways and made it look like they were floating on air.

The "Tchaikowski" number had been Danny Kaye's triumph in the stage version of *Lady In The Dark,* but Mischa Auer's rendition was cut from the film.

The cathedral in the dream was all done in topiary, trees clipped to give the effect of a cathedral, which was one of du Bois' ideas which was very good. He did some good stuff, but he'd drive you nuts doing it. No telling what Raul had in mind when he did anything. The chorus boys were all in gold tail coats and Ray was preaching from the wedding cake. The choir boys were so beautiful they were like the angels in Botticelli's paintings.

Ray Rennahan was the cinematographer. I kept telling him to put some more amber gels on the lights, but he found some reason not to. Sure enough, when we got the color rushes, the thing wasn't gold enough and we had to go back and do some of it over. Rennahan annoyed me. I'd tell him where I wanted the camera and he'd say, "But don't you think it would be better over there?" I had always set my own cameras and before that I set DeMille's, and I knew what I wanted.

The circus dream was something else again. It starts out with Liza as a child, and she looks into a cage and sees herself all grown up and wearing the mink dress. Randy comes in on a horse, hi ho silver, unlocks the cage and she gets out. Mischa Auer, the photographer, is now a judge with asses ears on, and the jury box is full of clowns and a jack-in-the-box that pops up. Ray Milland is the prosecuting attorney. They bring in the proclamation to bring her to trial and Ray sings it. That was his own voice; he did it live on the set. Warner Baxter is the attorney for the defense. Billy Daniels and Mary Parker are the court stenographers and they take down what she says in "The Saga of Jenny."

When Ginger started doing her dance to "Jenny," I told her to be sexier, to do some bumps and grinds. She said she couldn't because it would hurt her image! When we came in for the closer shots, she kept covering her legs up with the skirt. So I moved the camera way back, but put a long lens on so we got a full figure of her showing the legs.

The egg heads followed everything that was going on in the trial. They were made of *papier maché* and were attached to a stick, so you could pull the stick and they all moved together. All the dresses the models wore in her office appear in the circus dream, all distorted, worn by stilt walkers. We had an apparition of the blonde sheepdog, Veronica Lake, in there too.

The saddles on the horses on the merry-go-round were tufted red velvet. There were twelve horses on it, and when they were all finished, du Bois decided the color wasn't right and he was going to have it all ripped out and done over in a sightly different shade of red. I said,

There were actually two mink dresses. The first had a mink jacket and stole and the bodice and gloves were completely encrusted with heavy red and gold glass beads. The lining of the skirt, also jeweled, was so heavy Rogers couldn't dance in it, so a whole new dress covered with red and gold sequins was substituted for the circus dream.

"Raul, there are going to be 1600 colored lights on this thing. You can't tell what color it's going to turn out." But he went down to DeSylva who said, "Go ahead and change it."

Buddy DeSylva didn't know anything about psychoanalysis. He suddenly discovered that Liza was in love with her father and he said, "I'm not going to have any incest in any picture we make around here." I said, "Buddy, that's the whole basis of the plot." He said, "I don't care what it is. You don't need to tell me about psychoanalysis. I've got a book over there and I've learned all about it." We managed to get the idea in, but it had to be slipped in very quietly.

The only thing I didn't get in was the song, "My Ship." We had made a live recording of Ginger singing it right on the set, and she sang it *a capella* in the park with the boy as the band played "Ain't She Sweet" in the gymnasium dance. But Buddy just put his foot down. He couldn't stand Kurt Weill and he couldn't stand that song. Having been a songwriter himself, he was adamant about it. It was vital to the story, the one spot where she remembers the lyrics finally, after being haunted by the tune through the whole story. The whole picture hung on that song. I said, "You'll take it out over my dead body," but I was overruled.

Ginger insisted we use Gail Russell as Barbara, the girl who steals Liza's boyfriend right after she sang "My Ship." The poor girl was gorgeous, but she had hysterics every time the camera started to turn. She only had a couple of lines, but it took us almost two days to get them shot. Ginger felt so sorry for her that she tried to work with her and help her as much as she could. She was really a neurotic character and I'm not surprised she became an alcoholic.

It was Frances Robinson's first major picture too, and I made a great mistake in casting her. She was always an hysterically funny person at a party so I thought she'd be just wonderful as the girl with Randy Curtis, but she just dried right up on the soundstage. I really had to work with her, and I don't know why, because she's a very talented actress and later did TV until it was coming out of your ears.

The costumes were out of this world. When I came back from New York, I had made deals with all the different coutouriers to have each one dress a different character. Y. Frank Freeman then told me he had signed Valentina up and she was going to come out here for one day and design all the clothes. I said, "That's great. Everybody will look the same." Valentina happened to be a very good friend of mine so I had a very difficult time. She did one jersey wedding dress for the gold dream which wasn't used. Babs Wilomez, who was the fashion editor of *Vogue,* did at least 85 drawings. I had to buy them outright from her. The rest of the costumes were done by du Bois, Edith Head and myself. I had all of Ginger's tailored suits made at Mitchell and Haigue, the tailor shop I owned. I wanted them to be as masculine as possible.

The mink dress Ginger wore in the circus dream was all mine, and it got us half a million dollars worth of free publicity. When the picture ran in London, they had a blow-up several stories high above the theater showing Ginger in that dress. You'll notice how we alibied it in the story, saying it had just come in from Hollywood. The skirt was detachable, so in the scenes where Ginger was seated behind the table with Jon Hall she didn't have to wear it. Originally the underside of the skirt was all jeweled, but when Ginger started to rehearse the "Jenny" number, it was so heavy she couldn't move at all, so we replaced the jewels with sequins.

Did you design her hairstyle too?

MITCHELL LEISEN: Don't blame me for that, it was something she and her hairdresser cooked up themselves. The pompadour with it hanging down the back soon became completely passé. *Lady In The*

Gail Russell
visits
Ginger
Rogers on
the set of
*Lady In The
Dark.*

Dark was on the shelf well over a year because Paramount had a terrible backlog of unreleased pictures during the war. The pictures that would have run two weeks earlier were now running six months and the newer films couldn't be released.

I finally went to the front office and started screaming bloody murder. "Look, this was high style when we made it, but if you don't hurry up, these gowns will be a joke." They knew that Ginger Rogers' hairstyle had changed amazingly in the meantime so that sped them up a little, I guess.

EDITH HEAD: There were three designers on *Lady In The Dark*, Raul Pene du Bois, myself and Mitch. Mitch did more of it than either Raul or I did, but he insisted that I take sole credit for the street clothes, which was extremely generous of him since many of them were his. He said he wanted a jeweled red gown with a mink skirt that would open up and be lined with brilliants, and that's what we gave him. He paid very close attention to all the details of that dress and we did just what he wanted.

Raul du Bois came from the stage and he was used to doing what he wanted. Raul didn't like having to sit down and discuss things with Mitch. In any movie, but particularly one of Mitch's, it has to be a collaboration. Once Raul realized this, things went more smoothly.

When I first knew Mitchell, he was a perfectionist and very sure of what he wanted, but he was nice about it. In the later years he became increasingly bitter and sarcastic. I would go show him a pile of sketches we had worked on for days and he would just glance on them and hand them back and say, "Dig deeper, Edith." What he really wanted was to do them himself, which was fine with me. He also became very foul-mouthed and would tell dirty jokes that offended people.

RAY MILLAND: Everybody thought *Lady In The Dark* was so wonderful at the time, but I always disliked it. Moss Hart was looked upon as a god or something; all these sweet young things were always fluttering after him and saying, "Oh Moss, you're so divine."

Can you imagine anything more inappropriate than Ginger Rogers playing a Moss Hart script? She was physically competent and she had been wonderful for *The Major And The Minor,* but this was way beyond her. And disappearing in the middle of shooting to get married was the last straw.

All the time we were filming, I tried to be very philosophical. I kept saying to myself, "Make the best of it. This too shall pass." I did my own singing of the Circus dream, and of course I couldn't sing, although I'd been a good singer when I was a child. I kept thinking "This too shall pass" and I plunged in and did it.

The costume Mitch designed for me for that number was out of this world. I had a tailcoat of paillettes of magenta and blue, white twill cavalry britches and boots up to the knee. Madame Karinska was one of the few who could take one of Mitch's drawings and figure out how to make it. She corrected him too, when he was off on something. For one thing, his military uniforms were always straight out of *The Student Prince.*

ELEANOR BRODER: Ginger Rogers was always very nice and never lost her temper. She and her mother, however, had a very annoying habit of talking to each other in baby talk in front of others so that they could not understand them.

PHYLLIS SEATON: That picture was complete chaos from start to finish. At best, it would have been an impossible project, and everything that could have gone wrong technically, went wrong. There were literally thousands of people on the stage at all times, the heat of the lights for the Technicolor was oppressive and the fumes from all that dry ice made everybody ill.

I was pregnant and I pleaded with the studio to let me quit the picture because I was sick everyday. They told me that if I stayed with it they would let me direct a picture on my own after the baby was born. So I stayed with it and I had a miscarriage. When I came back I asked them about my picture and they said, "We didn't really mean that, we just told you that so you wouldn't quit," and I never got to direct a film.

Ginger Rogers is a very lovely person, but she was a star with a capitol S. By that time she had already reached her zenith, and there was not too much I could do to help her. I was more of a stage manager on that picture than a dialogue coach.

FRENCHMAN'S CREEK - 1944

Lady In The Dark had finished shooting March 20, 1943, and less than three months later, Leisen was shooting another mammoth Technicolor epic, *Frenchman's Creek*. The insufficient interval between films allowed Leisen no time to regain his physical strength after the ordeal of *The Lady In The Dark*. In the eleven week period between films, Leisen had to cut, score, loop and balance the color on *Lady In The Dark* as well as begin pre-production on *Frenchman's Creek* which also involved extensive sets and costumes.

The task of preparing the costumes was so enormous that Leisen was forced to spend most of his pre-production time working in the wardrobe instead of working on the script. The picture started shooting with many of the costumes still unfinished, a script that needed revision and a badly miscast leading man. Like *Lady In The Dark*, *Frenchman's Creek* was a troubled project from start to finish, and ended up breaking all records as the most expensive film to date.

Also like *Lady In The Dark*, *Frenchman's Creek* was a feast for the senses but little else. Leisen's control and manipulation of the color was even more outstanding than in *Lady In The Dark*, so extraordinary that *Frenchman's Creek* ranks with *Black Narcissus* as the most beautiful color film of the decade. The camera movement, the blocking of the actors and all other technical functions are performed with magnificent expertise, and Victor Young's lush score is one of the best of his career.

Absent, however, is much evidence of Leisen's dramatic sense. The special ability of Leisen's that had made good films out of barely passable scripts and even injected a tender moment into the blaring *Big Broadcast Of 1938* should have done a lot more to pep up *Frenchman's Creek*. The Daphne du Maurier novel had to be laundered considerably to meet the requirements of the Production Code and what eventually emerged was a series of stunning tableaux strung together on an enjoyable but insufficient story.

The film opens on a parchment scroll which a hand slowly unrolls to reveal the credits. A very rich orchestration of "Clair de Lune" (the film's main theme) is heard on the track. In the first scenes, a proper 17th Century Lady, Dona St. Colomb (Joan Fontaine), tells her ineffectual husband (Ralph Forbes) that she is tired of repulsing the advances of his lecherous best friend, Lord Rockingham (Basil Rathbone) and informs him that she and their children are moving to Navron, their country estate. Her idyll there is broken by the news of French pirates terrorizing the countryside. Wandering about her grounds, she sees the pirate ship anchored in her creek. A pirate notices her too, kidnaps her and takes her to the captain. She is so charmed by the French pirate (Arturo De Cordova) that she invites him to supper and then tells her servant, in proper Hays Office terms, that she intends to "behave outrageously."

She accepts the pirate's invitation to come aboard his ship and spends several blissful days with him. Although they are shown to be engaging only in merry adventures innocent enough to pass the Hays Office, Leisen manages to insert a few oblique sexual references. Returning to her estate at dawn, Dona learns that her husband and Lord Rockingham have come down from London to help their neighbors to capture the pirates. That night at dinner, Dona uses her feminine wiles (including an impersonation of Nell Gwynn) to distract the men into inaction. The pirates capture their house instead.

The country squires locked up, the pirate pleads with Dona to sail away with him again, but she puts him off. Lord Rockingham, having escaped, views the scene and failing to seduce Dona by blackmail, tries to rape her. She struggles with him all over the banquet table, runs up the stairs and throws a suit of armor at him which kills him.

This fantastically staged piece of physical action is the film's dramatic climax and the romance with the pirate could and should have been

Joan Fontaine and Arturo de Cordova in *Frenchman's Creek.*

wrapped up right there with one additional scene. In an uncharacteristic misjudgment, Leisen continues the picture twenty minutes more, through an anticlimactic and unnecessary episode in which the pirate is captured and Dona cleverly arranges his escape. As he prepares to sail away in the rosette dawn, he again entreats her to go with him, but Dona says that she cannot, due to her responsibilities to her children.

Joan Fontaine was the perfect choice for Dona, and although the strained relations with Fontaine during filming were a disadvantage to Leisen, her patrician presence leant much credibility to the film. Hedda Hopper remarked at the time that Leisen was the first of Fontaine's directors to make her beautiful in a film, and throughout Fontaine was a glorious vision whose clothing Leisen made indicative of the film's mood. In the first scene, she denounces her husband and Lord Rockingham attired in somber black, but with a haughtily plumed hat. The serenity of her life on the estate is indicated next by a dull pink and grey striped frock. The color saturation of her clothing slowly but steadily increases as her passion for the pirate mounts. Rummaging through her trunk as she dresses for their first supper together, she pauses over a gown of scarlet silk interwoven with gold threads but chooses instead a darker gown trimmed in jet beads. Covering her escape to the pirate's ship, she first attends a reception in bright powder blue satin; the motif then warms into green as she awakens from sea sickness wrapped in a blazing emerald green sari the pirate had taken in plunder.

Returning home and plotting to distract the company, she dons the flaming scarlet and gold gown, and Leisen extends the power of the gown by packing the scene with reds and golds. There are men about, but we see only the dress, the masses of golden hair, her ruby and gold jewelry, goblets of burgundy on the table with an all-gold service and a bowl of oranges. In that setting she seduces the men away from their plan, flirts with the pirate in the presence of her husband and finally kills Rockingham.

This *tour de force* was Leisen's most triumphant moment in his constant quest for the subjective use of color. Screaming forth with extremes of color saturation only the original three strip Technicolor process could provide, the image is tempered nonetheless by Leisen's invincible good taste as manifested in the elegant shapes of all the brilliantly colored forms. With this scene alone, Leisen has won immortality.

The casting of Arturo de Cordova as the pirate reflected the wartime shortage of leading men, for his was the least effective performance in any Leisen film up to that time. Cordova simply did not have the variety, the charm or the strength to play the part interestingly or convincingly, and there was nothing Leisen could do to help him. He was attractive, but in a rugged, realistic way, which was inappropriate for the dreamlike romantic quality of the film as a whole, and mismatched to the fairy-tale-princess aura of Fontaine.

The details of the film were all fine. The casting in all the other roles was effective, with Basil Rathbone a most feisty villain as Rockingham. *Frenchman's Creek* gave Leisen his only chance to portray his great love for the sea, a passion he had inherited from DeMille, which added fervor to the film.

Whatever its faults, in retrospect, *Frenchman's Creek* repeated the great success of *Lady In The Dark*, proving that at the box office at least, Leisen could do no wrong. Despite this success, there came a certain wariness on the part of the studio heads in choosing Leisen's assignments, and though he remained at Paramount for seven more years, he was not given any more Technicolor pictures. Although nobody knew it at the time, the dye was cast and Leisen's decline had begun.

Leisen helps
Fontaine with
her dagger,
photo taken
10/1/43.

JOAN FONTAINE: I hated it! And I especially resented Phyllis Seaton's position as director *pro tem."*

I feel that in Frenchman's Creek *you were so involved with the visual aspects of the color, the costumes and the sets that you lost sight of the story values.*

MITCHELL LEISEN: You tell me what the story values were in *Frenchman's Creek* and I'll answer that. She falls in love with a pirate, leaves her husband and comes back in time to not get caught. That's all. It's as dull as dishwater and it was a lousy picture. It was one of those things, either I did it or I got suspended and my agent didn't want me to take a suspension. I should have but I didn't.

Joan Fontaine was furious that David Selznick had sold her to

Paramount for $2500 a week and he was only paying her $1200. She dug her heels in and said, "I'm going to give you $1200 worth of work and that's all." We had a dusty pink and grey dress for her and she couldn't understand the idea that she cold wear a pink dress with her red wig. She didn't want to wear the red and gold dress with that wig either. She ran screaming to Selznick who immediately sent us a twenty page memo, but when Fontaine finally saw the tests of those dresses, she had to admit they were perfectly beautiful.

Selznick kept sending us twenty page memos every day. He wanted to see all the dailies and OK them. Buddy DeSylva finally blew his stack and called Selznick to say, "You can have Miss Fontaine back. If you don't keep out of this we'll recast." I was in Buddy's office when he made the call, and for a fast ten minutes I thought we were going to start over with Ray Milland and Claudette Colbert in the parts, which would have been sensational. But Selznick apologized and agreed not to write any more memos and I was stuck with Fontaine and Arturo De Cordova.

He [De Cordova] was a Mexican from the Bronx. He could never pronounce the *g* in any word ending with *ing*. He'd say *huntin'* and *fishin'* and you could retake for days to get one good take out of him, but it just wasn't in him to say it. Somehow we finally got one take of him saying "going" and Alma Macrorie had countless copies made of that bit of sound track and she cut the *g* in everywhere he was supposed to say it.

Fontaine and Cordova were fighting all the time. The first scene we did at the studio when we returned from location (where things had been pretty lively) was a love scene. She jerked away from him, made a very insulting remark and he yelled, "I'll kill her." We had to use doubles for days just to get it done. We put her wig on her double and shot over the girl's back into his face. Then for the reverse shot, we sent him off, brought his double in and called for Fontaine. Then suddenly, Fontaine and Cordova walked in one morning arm in arm!

She pranced in one day when we were shooting the Nell Gwynn business and said she was sorry for being so difficult, but after all, the whole picture rested on her shoulders and it was a heavy responsibility. The whole company of distinguished British actors was so insulted they refused to work with her and we lost a lot of time patching that one up.

When we were up on location, the studio was only able to supply us with one outhouse because the war was on. Anybody who didn't want to use the woods had to stand in a long line. Miss Fontaine wasn't about to do that so she complained and complained until they finally found another one somewhere and sent it up to us. I was about to say that nobody could use it except her but she insisted that she wanted to be democratic and let others use it. Wouldn't you know that someone jiggled the handle when she was in there and she was livid. So I called the whole company together and said, on my microphone, "It took a lot of time and money to get this thing up here so please don't jiggle the handle when Miss Fontaine is taking a shit!"

It took us 104 days to get it in the can, but most of the overage was due to the fact that we got marooned in the fog on location and most of the time we could only shoot half the day. I finally got the idea of using the fog by making the last scene of the picture take place at dawn. Technicolor's slate said, "Shot under protest" because the consultant was certain there wasn't enough light, but there was. When we did the close-up in the tank back at the studio, we covered the ceiling of the stage with canvas, threw pink lights on it which reflected pink into the water.

ELEANOR BRODER: Natalie Kalmas was the Technicolor consultant and when she was divorced from Dr. Kalmas she had it in the agreement that she would continue in the job. She had her face lifted several times and after one job that did not turn out well, she always wore dark glasses. How she could judge the colors wearing those glasses I don't know, but we just had to play along with it. She also had a yen for Mr. Leisen and would bring up ridiculous objections just so she could talk to him. He was always trying to avoid her.

MITCHELL LEISEN: It was very difficult working with Technicolor because you didn't get color rushes and you never knew what the colors would be. They sent three frames of each take in color and that was projected along the side while the film ran in black and white. We cut it in black and white and then Technicolor made the first color answer print. The color would be way off and then you'd start fighting them, sending the scene back over and over until they finally balanced it in the printing.

The picture ends before the book does. In the book, she goes back to him and has three children by him, but we had to clean that up. Still I

Joan Fontaine and villain Basil Rathbone.

think we managed to get it across that they were living together in the scene after she's been seasick. It's quite obvious that she's naked in the bed when she throws the shawl around her shoulders before he comes in. She says, "We might fish in the cool of the evening," and he says, "We might."

ERNST FEGTÉ: We had only six weeks to get ready to shoot, due to the fact that Joan Fontaine had to do another picture right afterwards and it was the only time we could get her. That wasn't nearly enough time to prepare, and one of the reasons Paramount spent so much money on it was inadequate preparation and a lot of things that hadn't been thought through enough.

Raul Pene du Bois and Madame Karinska got screen credit for the costumes, but it was really Mitch who made most of them. Mitch was the only person who knew how many of the clothes of that era were actually put together, and in making them up from du Bois' sketches, he changed them a great deal from du Bois' original concept. Some of them were his designs from start to finish. He really had to rush and he was up in wardrobe the whole time. Whenever I needed to consult with him about a set, I had to go to wardrobe to find him.

Just prior to *Frenchman's Creek*, I had done *The Uninvited* with Lewis Allen. I had extensively explored the coastline from Jenner by the Sea to Fort Bragg. In the neighborhood of Albion, the coast exactly matched the coast of Cornwall in England. I used it for *The Uninvited* and I went back up there ahead of the company to make some continuity sketches showing the terrain and the sort of action which might be staged in it. The sketches were only for Mitch's reference, but he staged several scenes just the way I had pictured them.

The whole picture was completely mismanaged. The production department didn't send anybody to the location to watch expenses. Nobody was strong enough to tell Mitch he couldn't do what he wanted, so he just ran away with the picture, going way over schedule and spending more money. David Lewis was the most wishy-washy producer. All he ever did was play cards on the set with the actors. If Arthur Hornblow had been there, he could have kept the situation in hand.

The ship was gorgeous, all white and gold. It had been built in Hollywood on a pontoon. Then the pontoon was drawn all the way to Albion, which was quite a feat in itself. There was a little inlet from the sea which formed a gorgeous lake, but it was so shallow we could only sail at high tide.

The weather turned bad and we waited around for days before we could shoot the scene where Joan Fontaine comes out onto the deck of the ship with the pirate and sees the gulls flying around. The production department had engaged a sea gull trainer and we had to keep him up there on the payroll four weeks before we shot that scene. Finally the weather cleared one Sunday morning.

We set the camera up on the shore, Mitch said, "Let's have the sea gulls!" and the fellow opened up his crates and let them loose. The gulls hit the water and drowned! He had packed them so tightly they hadn't been able to oil their feathers.

So what could we do now? There was a kitchen in the camp and we sent some guys up there to get the garbage. We took it out to the mouth of the inlet at sea, and slowly lured the gulls up the inlet to the ship. Just before the take, we put some more garbage on the ship and they circled around it beautifully.

Mitch and I were both very good at cheating. We loved to use tricks so that it would look like we had fantastic production values without spending nearly as much money as the real thing would cost. We made much use of the hanging miniature technique. We built the first floor of the manor on location in the correct scale so that people could come out of the door on the first floor. But every time there was a long shot showing the whole building, the upper floors were a hanging miniature. It was built an inch to the foot and we hung it so that from a certain angle, the miniature and the real construction fused together. The sunlight hit them both the same way and when you saw it on the screen, you were sure it was a real two or three story building. Then we realigned it and came in for a closer shot. When we came back to Hollywood, I took the same miniature and added it on top of a building in the courtyard where they stopped to water their horses. We used another hanging miniature in the first scene in the gaming house. The balconies across the room were hanging miniatures, I did all of this as sort of a second unit while Mitch was off directing the actors, but he understood these things and encouraged me to the utmost.

An art director can suggest little dramatic things sometimes. In my research I learned that genteel ladies of the 17th century used to invite all their neighbors in to watch them give birth to a baby. In our scene, where Joan Fontaine visits Moyna McGill and Nigel Bruce as they await the birth of their baby, originally it was just the three of them. I suggested putting chairs all around the bed and filling the room with extras. Mitch loved the idea and that's what he did.

Frenchman's Creek ended my career at Paramount. After we were back from location, the head of the production department called me on the carpet and said I was prostituting my talent in an attempt to win an Oscar. I told him it was his fault for not having someone on the set to watch expenses; that was not my job. I said, "Mitch is not only directing, he's having to act as his own producer as well," and I walked out in a huff. I went right to Hans Dreier and he said, "Remember when we were in the Prussian Army, we always waited 24 hours before airing a complaint?" I came back the next day, still determined to quit, and I became a free-lancer. Ironically, I did win the Oscar for *Frenchman's Creek,* nearly two years later.

PRACTICALLY YOURS - 1944

Practically Yours gave Leisen another script by Norman Krasna, who had written *Four Hours To Kill* and *Hands Across The Table.* The results this

Fred said, "Claudette, there's only one thing wrong with this picture, we're both too damned old for it."

time were hardly as auspicious, though the picture somehow became one of the year's top grossers at the box office.

Ostensibly a comedy, *Practically Yours* had few bright lines and the contrived plot could not compensate for a situation so depressing that it prevented any possibility of humor. Bosley Crowther remarked in the *New York Times*, ". . . *Practically Yours* plants its kidding in a situation drenched in studied grief—the grief of a nation for a hero presumably lost in the war. It makes a solemn show of the pathos of the supposed fiance of this man and presents her as the shining symbol of other women who are bearing similar grief. And then it jumps blithely into cut-ups by bringing the hero back from the dead and having it turn out that the lady isn't his fiance after all."

James Agee commented favorably on a scene in which MacMurray belittles a newsreel account of his own heroics, and is told off by members of the audience who don't recognize who the detractor is. Colbert is modest, even mousy as a stenographer. It would seem a relief from the most persistent cliché of the Claude Binyon scripts that we are not asked to believe the heroine is an executive or a riveter, but with the Colbert character down to the MacMurray character's level of simplicity, there is no conflict between them to propel the story along.

Practically Yours ended Colbert's long tenure at Paramount and was thus her last picture with Leisen as well (although she subsequently was offered and apparently turned down *To Each His Own*). It was an inappropriate end for the team which had made *Tonight Is Ours, Midnight* and *Arise My Love* so memorable.

MITCHELL LEISEN: It was a pretty dreary job watching that yesterday. I was ashamed of it; it's supposed to be a brilliant comedy and it was about as funny as a crutch to me. It's a one-joke story, that's the problem with it. He says goodbye to his dog Piggy and they think he's talking to Peggy. That's it, and once you've spilled that kettle, you have nothing left. No matter how many people you put into it to make it live, it just doesn't.

Claudette's playing an ingenué, a sweet young thing, which was completely foreign to her. One day Fred said, "Claudette, the trouble with this picture is we're both too damned old for it." I don't remember what her reaction was. She told me at the time that she would love to play some mother roles if they would only offer her something that was well written, but they didn't and so she got stuck with this thing.

CLAUDETTE COLBERT: There was a sad lack of mature stories in the films of that period in the United States. It was the "Boy Meets Girl" era.

MITCHELL LEISEN: There was one scene in that picture I liked very much, where Fred goes to comfort Rosemary DeCamp when she gets the telegram saying her husband has been killed in action. He knew all along that the destroyer had been blown up and everybody lost on it, but he didn't tell her until he knew the telegram was going to come. Then Claudette went to see her and when she learned that Fred had already been there it was a complete revelation to her, the kindness and the gentleness. I always put dramatic moments in a comedy, and I thought it came off very well because it developed a side of Fred's character that you didn't know about.

CHARLES LANG: Claudette Colbert was a very big star on the Paramount lot, and she eventually had it put into her contract that she

MacMurray and Colbert with Rosemary DeCamp in *Practically Yours,* the last and least of Leisen's pictures with Colbert.

could choose her cinematographer. There were a lot of great cinematographers on the lot, but I guess I was associated with glamour and she liked my work, so from then on, I did most of her pictures.

It was always a pleasure to work with her. Every actor or actress has one side of his face that he thinks is better than the other, but with Claudette it was really true. The right side of her face had several problems, including a fairly deep scar on the right side of her mouth, so we kept it on the left side as much as possible. Full face could be all right if the light came from the left side, but we didn't do it very often.

Claudette wanted to play older characters, but the studio seemed to want to keep her in young roles and by the time of *Practically Yours,* it was a bit difficult to make her look the part in all the scenes. Make-up and lighting can take off fifteen years at most and not always that much. For Claudette I always used a key light above her head at a fairly sharp angle. Generally the sharper the angle, the more flattering the light, but we had to be careful that the shadow from the nose didn't run into the mouth. Since Claudette has a flat nose, I could place her key light at a sharp angle without worrying about the shadow on the upper lip. Then I filled it in with a broad, but a much weaker light, so there was still that beautiful modeling on her cheeks.

Practically Yours was her last picture at Paramount, and I did not work with her again. She did some independent productions and Joe Valentine used a completely different method of lighting her which was very attractive, having the light come from both sides. It was a flattering light and it worked well for the rest of the time she was making pictures.

KITTY - 1945

Leisen followed *Practically Yours* with *Kitty,* a far more satisfactory work. With its opportunity for exact historical reproduction, it was precisely the kind of picture Leisen could do better than anybody else, and its mixture of mannered comedy and gutsy drama suited him perfectly too. Many critics consider *Kitty* Leisen's best picture.

Kitty was a considerably cleaned-up adaptation of a novel by Rosamund Marshall which, in turn, was quite similar to the then-sensational *Forever Amber* and George Bernard Shaw's *Pygmalion.* Kitty (Paulette Goddard), a filthy cockney street waif of Restoration Era England, is discovered by a degenerate nobleman, Sir Hugh Marcy (Ray Milland), who cleans her up, teaches her speech and manners and has her pose for Thomas Gainsborough (Cecil Kellaway), all so that he can engineer a profitable marriage. Kitty first marries a tradesman, who conveniently dies, allowing her to marry the aged Duke of Malmunster (Reginald Owen). Learning that she is pregnant (and not knowing it is the child of her first husband), the Duke hysterically runs through the salons of his palace, announcing the good news. In a sublimely engineered tracking shot similar to the one he had used in *Tonight Is Ours,* Leisen pulls the camera back, through doorway after doorway, until the Duke finally collapses and dies. As the story ends, Kitty is a Duchess and is now free to marry Marcy.

Leisen's sense of historical accuracy was put to such good use in *Kitty* that he won citations from British historical groups who felt that *Kitty* was the most accurate film ever made about the Britain of an earlier day. His understanding of the period went beyond a mere reproduction of the fashions and architecture of the era, into an extensive examination of the mores of the period and indeed the very quality of its life.

Two views of Paulette Goddard as Kitty: Kitty, the beggar on the streets, was taken by Paramount's portrait photographer Whitey Shafer on a little set put together by Leisen; Kitty, the grand lady, was taken on September 9, 1944.

The sets and costumes were exquisite, but they did not become the stars of the film as they had in *Lady In The Dark* and *Frenchman's Creek* because Paramount prudently insisted the film be shot in black and white, which offered Leisen a much more limited range of possibilities for visual effects, and one that he had often explored before. The visual element of his work remained important, but it was expressed in terms of visually interesting dramatic scenes (i.e. the Duke's flight through the series of doors) as often as it was in extravagant tableaux, such as the exhibition of Gainsborough's paintings and the magnificent ball.

Moreover, Leisen had finally found in *Kitty* a story that seriously interested him, and actors with whom he worked effectively and happily. Committed to the story and the actors, he was careful not to let them be overpowered by the physical elements of the production. Paulette Goddard gave the best performance of her post-Chaplin career; Ray Milland was fine in the less important role of Sir Hugh Marcy; and the supporting cast which included Constance Collier, Patric Knowles and Sara Allgood as well as Reginald Owen and Cecil Kellaway was perfectly directed all the way down the line.

Because of the continuing problems with the backlog of unreleased pictures, *Kitty,* completed late in 1944, was not released until early 1946, when it became Paramount's top grossing film of the first quarter of the year.

MITCHELL LEISEN: I spent two years researching Gainsborough and the way he painted. We determined that the picture took place in 1659, and there's nothing in the picture that was painted by him after that year. The one that came up the following year, a portrait of George IV is in the studio being sketched by him at the time.

He painted by candlelight. Don't know why; he had his canvases laced on frames with leather thongs and he used a six foot brush to paint. When it came to paint the faces, he relaced the canvas so that the face was right at the edge, and then he painted with very small brushes and very fine detail. These things are very interesting to me, so we used them in the picture.

Getting copies of all his paintings for the exhibit was an enormous chore. I had hoped to be able to borrow the real Pinky and Blue Boy from the Huntington Library in Pasadena, but it was during the war and their security was very strict. So we had to settle for copies, but I made sure they were good copies, not just photo blow-ups or varnished prints. We had each painting individually painted by a staff of artists.

Goddard works on the tutelage of Constance Collier. Photo taken 8/2/44.

We just couldn't get the Blue Boy right; we made at least thirteen copies that I rejected. Finally one of the make-up men did one that was satisfactory.

When the picture was over, I wanted to send all the paintings on tour all around the country, to small towns that would never get a chance to see art like that. When I went to find them, however, they were all gone, all the executives at Paramount had taken them home.

Remember, we shot this during the war, so we had to be very careful how we made up our sets. I bought one authentic, paneled room from the Hearst Collection, and rented it to the studio. It was a very rare thing in that it had never been painted. Shortly after our picture took place, they discovered a practical method of painting wood, and everybody had their woodwork painted white. Somehow this room had escaped this, and when it was over, I gave the room to the Huntington Library for a tax write-off.

We learned in our research that the gentlemen of that era had two pairs of britches for every outfit. If they were going to a dance they never sat down, because their britches were so tight they couldn't. But if they were going to a dinner and had to sit, they wore the other pair which was much looser. The fashion for white wigs had already passed

Goddard with Cecil Kellaway as Thomas Gainsborough. The recreation of Gainsborough's studio was one of Leisen's proudest achievements.

in England by that time, so only the old people who were behind the times wear them in the picture; the younger ones just put white powder on their own hair, and the hair, whether it was red or black or whatever, showed right through. For the ones who did wear wigs, such as the Duke, who was Reginald Owen, we made them with hard edges at the hairline, instead of using the modern lace fronts. There was a lot of opposition to this, since it meant making many new things instead of using any old thing that was in stock at Paramount, but I put my foot down. I was king at Paramount and I got what I wanted.

The research people turned up a pamphlet showing the different ways of holding a fan to express yourself, so we wrote in a scene with Ray Milland giving Paulette a lesson in how to hold her fan. Ray had a blinding migraine headache that afternoon and I told him to go home and we would shoot around him, but he said, "You'll just waste time all afternoon," and he insisted on staying. Whenever we had some time to spare on *Kitty,* I shot extra stills. Usually you just shoot a lot of things in the gallery against a white background, but this was a special picture, so we made little sets from odds and ends of furniture we had lying around, and shot hundreds of poses.

This was a very challenging role for Paulette Goddard, and she worked with Phyllis Loughton for several weeks before we started shooting. We needed a special coach to teach her the cockney, and we had a hell of a time finding one. There were a lot of English actors around, but none of them would admit to being cockney or knowing anything about it. Finally we thought of Ida Lupino's mother, Connie Emerald, and she was perfect. We moved Connie into Paulette's apartment and they spoke nothing but cockney day and night. I spoke cockney with Paulette on the set; Ray did too. Whenever Paulette talked to anybody it was in cockney.

When it was time for Paulette to speak as the duchess, we moved Connie Emerald out and Constance Collier in. The first time we hear Paulette speak as the duchess, her voice is a full octave lower in pitch, as well as cultured, and we kept that lower pitch through to the end of the picture.

RAY MILLAND: I always liked working with Paulette. She was not a brilliant actress, she had no sense of timing and everything about her playing was mechanical and contrived. But nobody knew it better than she did, and she was completely honest about it; she is the most honest actress I ever knew. She worked her ass off trying to give it all she had, and in the end, her performances were quite all right.

Phyllis Seaton drilled Paulette on every little nuance to the point that she pretty well knew how she was going to do something by the time she came out onto the set. That was fine with me because Paulette always knew her lines perfectly. After every scene, Paulette, Phyllis and

Constance Collier would dash off to her dressing room to work on the next one, and they didn't come out until it was time to shoot. Constance said to me once, "I really don't know . . . it's as if she just doesn't hear what I'm saying."

PHYLLIS SEATON: Paulette Goddard is one of the most intelligent women I've ever worked with, but she has never projected her intelligence on the screen the way it projects when she is sitting talking in a living room. Her problem was to shift over from the pantomime techniques Chaplin taught her to the kind of dialogue comedy we did at Paramount.

I think I helped her a great deal to feel secure in her talent. We always had to prepare everything very carefully, and Constance Collier was a great help on *Kitty*. As a human being, Paulette is very spontaneous, but it was always very hard to get her to be spontaneous on the screen. She held everything in because of the strict discipline she learned from Chaplin. I worked on her voice quite a bit too.

MITCHELL LEISEN: At the beginning of shooting, Constance Collier said to me, "You are a very young man, but you are my director and I must act as you tell me. If what I do isn't what you want, you must tell me, until I do it the way you want it."

The first scene we shot with Constance, I said, "You're supposed to be completely gin-sodden. You mumble your lines, and at the end, grab wildly for the curtain to pull yourself up. It will come off the wall and cover you with dust." She said, "Fine" and she did it just like that. On the first preview, the audiences howled at that. Constance was a grande dame, but she didn't let that interfere with building up a good characterization. These are the great people, those who appreciate an idea and go ahead and do it.

MASQUERADE IN MEXICO - 1945

Leisen's next comedy, *Masquerade In Mexico,* was even less amusing than *Practically Yours,* although it had a few intriguing moments which offset the banality of the film as a whole.

The script by Karl Tunberg, loosely based on *Midnight,* had none of the wit or polish of the original and its execution in most departments was sluggish. Dorothy Lamour got one nice ballad to sing, and was

Leisen paints the mural for the ballet in *Masquerade In Mexico.* Photo taken February 28, 1945.

heard to sing a comic rendition of the Sextet from *Lucia di Lammermoor* with Mikhail Rasumny, demonstrating that her voice has a fine upper register which was never heard in any of her other films. Within the limits of the script she is fine and Patric Knowles did what he could in the Barrymore role, which was watered down to the point of being a very ordinary second lead. Ann Dvorak had the film's only credible moments as Knowles' unfaithful wife, and Natalie Schaefer was briefly diverting in the Rex O'Malley role as the wife's confidante. In the male lead, Arturo De Cordova was pathetically inept and he made no more films at Paramount.

In the midst of all the trivia, Leisen staged a very arty ballet which depicted several eras of Mexican history. Critics thought it inconsistent in tone with the rest of the film, which indeed it was, but it supplied one moment of pure Leisen elegance to a film which was otherwise sadly lacking in style. The mural in this sequence is similar in style to one that he painted on the walls of his dance studio on La Cienega Boulevard.

MITCHELL LEISEN: I only did it to get out of doing a picture with Betty Hutton. They told me they wanted me to do one with her and I said, "Anything but that." They thought about it and said that they needed to find a picture for Dottie Lamour and Arturo De Cordova and they had this big Mexican hacienda set standing from a picture that had been called off. So I said, "Why don't we remake *Midnight?*"

The basic story line was the same, but the characters were completely different, and after the ballet the story's different too. You'll notice we avoided doing the divorce scene from *Midnight*. It's just left high and dry. Patric Knowles goes up to Dottie's room and Arturo De Cordova makes a pass at Roberta Jonay. I wasn't about to have Dotty end up with Arturo at the end of the picture. There was nothing I could do to make him a serious love interest, so I just had to play him for laughs. He still couldn't pronounce the *ing* sound, so Alma Macrorie went to the vault and got out all the tracks of him saying *ing* that she'd made two years earlier on *Frenchman's Creek* and cut them in.

I couldn't have Dorothy play the part the same way Colbert had. Dottie's one of the smartest gals I've ever known, but she gives off a fairly dumb quality on the screen that you have to cash in on. You can't give her the clever machinations to do that Claudette can get away with.

That bit from Lucia revealed that she has high notes in her voice that we never heard before.

MITCHELL LEISEN: She has plenty of them. She studied singing quite hard, later on, and her voice is still excellent. We made a direct recording of that right on the set.

Dottie was very slim in that picture and designing her clothes was very enjoyable because I could do whatever I wanted. Edith Head helped me and did some of the street clothes, but I did the gowns. We kept her in black most of the time. The dress she wore when she danced with Billy Daniels was yards and yards of folded jersey and all around the bottom were black ostrich feathers. She handled it beautifully, it just floated through the air. There was nothing to keep the bodice up. That piece that went around her neck was no help at all. The whole thing was boned inside and we used rubber cement, tape and everything else we could think of to keep it up.

Dorothy
Lamour
dances with
Billy
Daniels.
Photo taken
2/16/45.

DOROTHY LAMOUR: I had never done much dancing up to that point. I had done a few steps in the production numbers, but none of this Veloz and Yolanda sort of ballroom dancing; I'd never had the time to learn. Mitch got Billy Daniels to teach me and we spent a long while until we really worked the number up well.

Sometime afterwards I suddenly discovered I was pregnant. I was overjoyed because the doctors had told me I would never be able to have a baby. Mitch always said he deserved some credit because having me do that dance must have tightened the muscles or something. The doctors disagreed, but I was too happy to care.

When Ridgely, our first son, was born, Bill and I asked Mitch to be one of his godfathers. He agreed, but then he had Eleanor do some research to find out what he was getting himself into. He made Ridge a beautiful christening gown from an heirloom he had in his family and trimmed it with ermine tails.

We had to get a bigger house to have room for the kids, and Mitch decorated the whole thing for us. He designed and made the furniture to be just in proportion to our height. The only trouble was that the upholstery was white and you can imagine how long that lasted with two little boys running around the house. We had it done over eventually, but we've used it ever since.

From then on, I had Mitch do all my evening gowns and everything I wore in my nightclub acts. He's always been ahead of the times and some of the innovations he had twenty years ago are just becoming the style now. He did a basic black dress for me about ten years ago that's perfectly timeless and I still wear it all the time.

When I started playing nightclubs, the first thing I did was to get Mitch to stage the act. He did all the lighting, helped me choose the material and even worked on the arrangements. He was with me that horrible night in Havana when the microphone started picking up police calls, and whenever I had any problems on the road, I went straight to the telephone and called up Mitch. He knows that business as thoroughly as he knows pictures and there was nothing he couldn't take care of.

MITCHELL LEISEN: I always did my research, even on something like *Masquerade In Mexico*. I went down and spent four weeks in Mexico City and took a photographer to make the process plates at Xochimilco. That was the filthiest water I've ever seen in my life. I stayed at the Rafona, the only so-called "European hotel" in Mexico City at that time. You'd go down to the coffee shop and there were flies all over the place and no two pieces of linen or silverware matched. I wanted to show it the way it really was, but the Mexican government raised hell and said, "No, it must be the most elegant hotel in the world."

Then they started to squawk about the ballet on the history of Mexico. We never shot the part of the ballet with the conquistadores. We were going to show the building of the Spanish cathedrals with the Indians forced to bring in the gold and pile it up, and carry the blocks of stone up the scaffold. At the climax of the thing, one of the Indians falls, is caught up and hangs: the crucified Christ. They wouldn't let us do it. Then Maxmillian and Carlotta were supposed to dance on a platform supported by the oppressed Mexican people. Juarez comes out from under the scaffold, shoots Maxmillian and Carlotta goes insane.

Leisen and Lamour prepare for the Xochimilco sequence. In the film it looked quite different, with the process plates Leisen shot in Mexico projected onto the background. Photo taken 2/8/45.

She finishes the ballet completely *non compis mentis*. Ann Dvorak would have been brilliant in that, one of the reasons we chose her was that she could dance, but the Mexican government wouldn't allow it. And then they wanted me to come down to Mexico City and stage the whole ballet! I said, "To hell with you!"

That was a fantastic set, and I wanted to use it again for a remake of *Death Takes A Holiday*. I thought it was just what the public needed as the war was ending, and Ray Milland would have given his right leg to play Death, but the studio said, "What do you want to do that for?" and tore the whole set down. Maybe it's just as well, because I wouldn't have had Sir Guy Standing for the remake.

TO EACH HIS OWN - 1946

Mitchell Leisen is often classified as "a woman's director," and while there is much justification in such a classification, Leisen's films were seldom "women's pictures" in the strictest sense. It is true that many of his films appealed more to feminine audiences and that Leisen often favored the female characters in his stories. However, there were always male characters who at least shared equally in the footage with the female leads, and were equally indispensable to the plot. Even considering Leisen's frequent use of role reversal in his comedies, his plots were always propelled by a male-female conflict in which the man was just as important as the woman.

To Each His Own is Leisen's only real "woman's picture." It is the only one of his films in which one female character remains the only focal point throughout the narrative, with the conflicts of this female character pitted against fate and the rules of society rather than a male character. There was certainly nothing original about the story; similar vehicles had already been constructed for most of the popular actresses of the '30s. Ruth Chatterton had had *Madame X* and *Sarah And Son,* Irene Dunne did *The Secret Of Madame Blanche,* Barbara Stanwyck was *Stella Dallas* and Bette Davis was *The Old Maid;* all of these parts were congruent somewhere with Olivia de Havilland's role in *To Each His Own.* Melodramas of unrequited mother love had gone out of style in the '40s. However, *To Each His Own* proved to be the last and the best. It was that magical thing that happens so very rarely, when a director like Mitchell Leisen is assigned a script from a writer like Charles Brackett and an actress of the calibre of Olivia de Havilland, and all three see in the project an opportunity for all the things they do best within their creative functions. *To Each His Own* was so well handled in every aspect of its execution that it surmounted the plot's limited credibility and the painful memories of earlier productions with similar storylines.

The story opens in wartime London on New Year's Eve, where we find a prim, middle-aged Miss Josephine Norris (Olivia de Havilland) and Lord Desham (Roland Culver) assigned to watch the city for bombing raids from a dark church tower. They form an instant dislike for each other, but an accident to Desham serves to break the ice and afterwards he takes Miss Norris for coffee, remarking that they are both, lonely people who fill in on holidays so that others may celebrate. Miss Norris warms slightly, but is distracted when an American GI tells her that another GI named Gregory Pierson is soon due to arrive in London by train. A woman in the train station complains about how long she's had to wait. We hear Miss Norris' thoughts as she reflects on how long she's had to wait for Gregory Pierson, and a flashback begins.

We see a lovely girl on a stepladder in a drugstore, a much younger Miss Norris, affectionately called Jody. She wears her hair tightly mar-

Ronald Culver, Olivia de Havilland and Leisen discuss the opening segment of the film. Paramount released few pictures of de Havilland as the middle aged Miss Norris and even had her pose in her usual make-up and 1945 clothes with John Lund for ad art stills in fear that seeing her this way would hurt the film at the box office.

celled and we learn that World War I has just begun. A frail, nervous girl named Corinne (Mary Anderson) jokes about her father's failing pianola factory and is joined at the soda fountain by a buxom house-wife named Belle Ingham (played by film editor Alma Macrorie). They leave and Alex Pierson (Philip Terry) enters, asks after Jody's ailing father and repeats his marriage proposal. When she again desists, he says, "You expect love to be all sky blue pink and trumpets blowing. It isn't like that." "If it isn't, I don't want it," says Jody.

An army flyer, Captain Cosgrove (John Lund) is brought into the drugstore to be treated for a minor injury. Hours later, dressed in white ruffles and on her way to a bond raising ball, Jody finds him still asleep in the back room. They talk and she is intrigued by the dashing hero. At the ball, Alex and Corinne inform Jody of their engagement. After-wards, Captain Cosgrove takes Jody for an airplane ride, intending to seduce her. Disarmed by her innocence, he admits his purpose and tries

Leisen shows John Lund how to dance with Olivia de Havilland in *To Each His Own*. Eleanor Broder behind de Havilland; Daniel Fapp behind the camera. (Courtesy AMPAS)

to turn back. Jody replies that the few hours until morning is the only time she will have with him, and Leisen ends the first sequence abruptly.

All of this plot passes within the first twenty minutes of the film. In this tale of almost epic sweep, every second counts. Every line of Charles Brackett's dialogue provides plot exposition, delineates the characters and establishes the milieu.

Leisen's greatest asset in making a good script come to life was his extraordinary knowledge of how to build tension and then relieve it at just the right moment, to exactly the right degree. Nowhere in his career is this instinct so well demonstrated as in *To Each His Own*, where such careful manipulation of mood is integral to the film's success.

In the second segment of *To Each His Own*, we are told that Jody is pregnant in a very subtle way. When Corinne Pierson and Belle Ingham come into the drugstore and ask for some milk, they say that they need to drink more milk because they are pregnant. After they leave, Jody calmly serves herself some milk, and Leisen cuts immediately. Had the scene been played more broadly, Jody's acknowledgement of her pregnancy would have created a false climax too early in the film. Underplayed as it is, the scene starts a feeling of tension which builds with each succeeding segment.

The tension escalates as Jody is told by a doctor that she must have an abortion or risk losing her life. The escalation continues as she overhears in a conversation that Captain Cosgrove has been killed in action and resolves to bear the child despite the risk involved. The next sequence (in which the child is born and is brought into town in an elaborate scheme to avoid detection of its origins) is again underplayed with no resolution of tension. Leisen even inserts a little joke by having the perennially pregnant Belle Ingham contemplate the foundling on her doorstep and comment, "Well, them that has, gets."

The tension continues to mount in scene after scene, as Corinne Pierson, who has miscarried, manages to adopt Jody's child. Jody, becoming desperate, tells her father the whole story and says she will stop at nothing, even a revelation of the child's illegitimacy, to get him back. As Jody finally breaks down, de Havilland becomes hysterical and weaves about the set in operatic mad scene style. The tension that has bound all of these short scenes together into a cohesive narrative is finally broken by this bravura moment, and the second sequence ends.

The next sequence begins quite pleasantly. Jody, plumper and with a different hairstyle, rings the Piersons' doorbell and we hear Olivia de Havilland's voice, again warm and mellow, offering a bit of narration to set the scene. Tension soon mounts as a conflict erupts between Corinne and Jody and Jody admits the child is hers in a vain attempt to get him back. The tension remains unresolved through a brief comical interlude in which Jody looks up an old beau in New York City. Finding that his cosmetics business is really a front for a bootlegging operation, she persuades him to legitimately go into the cosmetics business when the police start to close in.

A close-up of Jody on the telephone begins the next sequence. From her luxurious gown and opulent surroundings, we know that time has passed. It is the mid-'20s, and she has become rich. Her severely dressed hair and terse, nervous speech indicate that her personality has changed but her problem has not been solved. Powerful and ruthless, she blackmails Corinne Pierson into giving up the little boy, and showers the child with presents in a vain attempt to win his affection. When she realizes she cannot compete with the only mother he has ever known,

Griff Barnett and Olivia de Havilland in the "mad scene" from *To Each His Own*.

she quietly sends him back and moves to London to try to forget. As the flashback ends, the tension has not been broken, but continues to add impact to the scene in the train station in which Miss Norris confronts her grown-up son for the first time. His name is Gregory Pierson.

She invites him to stay in her flat and tries to not be disappointed by his breezy indifference to her. The invincible Lord Desham puts in an appearance and remarks, "The way you carry on one would think he is your own son." Leisen makes Miss Norris' reply another bravura moment that only Olivia De Havilland could have brought off with such forceful compassion. Her protective veneer of propriety finally scratched and in a state of barely controlled hysteria tinged with longing, Miss Norris exclaims, "He *is* my son. Oh, he doesn't know it and he never will. I thought for one week I was going to have him around. Just around. . . . I'd like to give him the sun and the moon and the stars. All his life I've wanted to. I hoped this week I could feel like a real mother— showering things on him, spoiling him. All he wants is his girl. I can't help him there."

Olivia De Havilland's rendering of this scene is superb. In the few sentences, she expresses all the conflicting emotions that had been suppressed in all the years during which the fey Jody became the severe Miss Norris. It is true that Brackett's dialogue here is perfection and that Leisen's instinct told him that this was the place to put the punch in, so he carefully guided de Havilland, urging her to a broader display of emotion until she soared. It remained to de Havilland, however, to portray the scene with such an extraordinary degree of conviction that she transcends all of the intrinsic banalities and gives the story a neat little shot of adrenalin just at the point where all other such tales become unbearably wearisome.

Leisen wraps the story up quickly, and knowing that the suspense was becoming painful, he throws much humor into the final minutes of the film. The boy and his English fiance are prevented from marrying by legal technicalities, but try to console themselves by going to a nightclub, followed at some distance by Miss Norris and Lord Desham. As they enter, the silliest of American nonsense songs, " Three Little Fishies" ("and they thwam and thwam all over the dam,") is being sung by a fellow with a heavy London accent. The boy keeps exclaiming, "Holy canarsie" as the waiter conducts the bewildered couple, Miss Norris and Lord Desham into a backroom where a wedding has been prepared. The boy and girl find out that Lord Desham has pulled strings and they are free to marry. As he signs for the license, Gregory Pierson says he's not sure of his correct birthdate, since he was adopted. Miss Norris shivers as Charles Brackett brings in this neat reminder that Pierson is still unaware of his real parentage. Leisen, knowing that the wedding is too highly charged emotionally and could cause a false climax, suddenly cuts to a barely related but very funny scene in the nightclub's kitchen where we find two cockney cooks busily assembling a bogus wartime wedding cake from various plastic parts.

The wedding party files back onto the dance floor and Lord Desham urges Miss Norris to tell Gregory her secret. She refuses, so Desham leaves her side, goes over to the boy and asks him why he thinks Miss Norris is taking such a deep interest in him, saying, "It's odd, isn't it? You're both American, but that isn't enough. You're both from the same little town. Not enough. Well, if you ever figure it out, let me know."

As the boy dances with his bride, he says, "You'd think she was my real mother." Suddenly he leaves the girl, strides over to where Lord Desham is dancing with Miss Norris, cuts in and says, "I think this is our dance, Mother." The scene quickly fades to the end title, as Brackett wryly notes in his scenario, "By one of those coincidences which will be jumped on by the critics but which the rest of us will enjoy, the orchestra at the moment is playing, "If you could care for me as I could care for you."

To Each His Own represents Leisen in absolutely top form. Transforming the basically incredible tale into compelling and memorable cinema requires great skill in all facets of filmmaking, and Leisen's talent proved equal to all aspects of the problem. He even demonstrated how his fine pictorial sense could enhance a film that seemed to offer few opportunities for visual beauty, since all the shots were interiors that had to be lit realistically, in keeping with the rest of the film. When Olivia de Havilland stands against the inky blackness of the drugstore, dressed in white ruffles and bathed in light, she is not only a vision of beauty but serves also to evoke the visual mood of James Montgomery Flagg and other popular illustrators of the World War I era.

Leisen's meticulous recreation of the period does not compete with the story but rather helps it by amplifying the feeling of realism. Hollywood films have never accurately portrayed the modes of eras in the recent past, and are particularly inaccurate in the matter of hairstyles. Even *Wilson,* which tried to be a historical document, showed the World War I era ladies wearing coiffures which were only slight modifications of the '40s look, big pompadours with the hair at the temples tightly drawn up. The real styles of World War I were exactly the opposite; the lines of the coiffures always had a downward direction, hiding the ears and obscuring the forehead. It was this style that Olivia de Havilland wore in the first sequences of *To Each His Own,* despite the fact nobody seemed to care and the '40s look was particularly good for de Havilland; it accentuated her high cheekbones and balanced her enormous eyes.

The Second World War had been over for ten months when *To Each His Own* was finally released in May of 1946. It was highly successful at Radio City Music Hall and racked up sensational grosses even though the public clearly wanted realism and message pictures and no more sentimental romances or "women's pictures." By the end of the year, *Variety* reported that *To Each His Own* had already returned $3,500,000 to Paramount on an investment of $1,600,000. It went on to double that figure with the European release, and Charles Brackett's title, *To Each His Own* eventually became a new American idiom, due in part to the very popular song which was composed by Jay Livingston several months after the picture's release.

JAY LIVINGSTON: That line was from an obscure poem by John Donne that Charles Brackett insisted on using. The studio didn't care but Victor Young said, "I can't write a song for that because I don't understand it" so that's why I got the job. The song was never heard in the film though to this day people insist to me that it was.

For Olivia de Havilland, *To Each His Own* was an all-out triumph. It reignited her career after her long legal battle with Warner Brothers and an indifferent, though popular comeback picture called *The Well Groomed Bride*. Portraying a beautiful, wide-eyed ingenue for the last time, de Havilland took the character farther than she had ever gone before, encompassing an incredible gamut of emotions yet never once losing her grasp of the complex and tragic figure's psyche. In doing so, she finally made the transition into meatier, less conventional roles in literary films like *The Snake Pit* and *The Heiress*, becoming the foremost American screen actress of the post-war period. *To Each His Own* brought de Havilland her third Academy Award nomination, and this time she won.

OLIVIA DE HAVILLAND: I am very proud of *Hold Back The Dawn* and *To Each His Own*, especially *To Each His Own*. I'm so pleased to see it still works today. What other *Madame X* story still holds up like that?

When Paramount sent me the script of *To Each His Own*, I knew immediately it was a part I had to do. It was a very long part and it offered a lot of opportunities for an actress; it was fascinating to see how the character changed. Yet I knew it would be very difficult to make a sentimental story such as this believable. The front office proposed a man named Lewis Allen for the director. He had made some good films, but I watched them very carefully and in the end I flatly refused. He didn't have that special something to make this kind of property work. I said, "There's only one man on the Paramount lot, perhaps in all of Hollywood who can direct this and that's Mitch Leisen."

Despite his great sophistication and urbanity, Mitch had a marvelous empathy and understanding of rural America, and I knew this because he had been so good for *Hold Back The Dawn*. Jody in *To Each His Own*, was the same sort of character as Emmy of *Hold Back The Dawn*, but in a much wider context and over a much greater span of time. Charles Brackett, who wrote and produced it, was also a very sophisticated man, and yet he knew these people. He could make them come to life.

Mitch was in New York, so they sent him the script and he absolutely detested it. Nonetheless, I continued to insist on him; they spent a long time reworking it and eventually he was persuaded. He supervised all the pre-production work and he brought out the best in everybody. He inspired Edith Head to design some beautiful clothes that were perfectly in period.

The first days on the set, he was a real pro. Even if his heart wasn't in it, he was determined to do a good job and he couldn't have been more helpful and charming.

Then the most marvelous thing happened. Towards the end of the second week of shooting, I could see him beginning to get enthusiastic about the picture. The third week started and when he came on the set in the morning, he was whistling and smiling. By the end of that week, his enthusiasm was boundless. He had realized that this was not just another job to get through, but indeed would be one of the best pictures of his career. What a relief his change of attitude was to me! I had insisted on Mitch and if it hadn't worked out, it would have been my fault.

Did you know that the story was very similar to something that had just happened in his own private life?

OLIVIA DE HAVILLAND: No. How extraordinary! He never told us.

Just before we started shooting, I had toured the South Pacific entertaining the troops and I caught a rare disease. My doctor managed to cure me when I got back, but by weight shrank to 97 pounds which was 17 pounds under normal. Shooting in continuity, we could turn this to an advantage. Being very thin at the beginning of the story helped me to build the characterization. It gave the girl a frail, sensitive quality. Mitch lit me very carefully; in every scene I had a key light and a broad to fill in so I wouldn't appear too hollow cheeked.

You are very beautiful throughout the first sequence, but you are most beautiful in the scene in the airplane.

OLIVIA DE HAVILLAND: Mitch diffused me! It was the only time he did that. It was his trump card and he was saving it up until it really counted.

Mitch had me eat a big lunch every day, so that when we got to the next segment where the girl is pregnant, I was slightly heavier. It was almost imperceptible, but the cheeks were fuller and there was the feeling that time had passed. Unfortunately at that point, we had to go back and retake some of the scene in the drugstore because it was John Lund's first film and he had moved around too much. I had only gained about five pounds, and you only saw my back since they cut in the close-ups of me that had been done earlier, but I was always very conscious of the weight difference. It could have been a hundred pounds to me.

By the time we were filming the final segment where I'm middle aged, I had gone several pounds over my usual weight. Edith Head got me a "frankly forty foundation garment" which was really a corset several sizes too large. We filled it in with cotton.

The aging of my face was accomplished with the most brutal lighting of my face Mitch could devise and very careful make-up. I had seen a series of photographs in *Life* magazine which traced the changes in Winston Churchill's face from youth to middle age. As a young man, he had had a very full mouth, with a full upper lip like mine. As he got older, his upper lip shrank and got thinner and thinner until it disappeared. We did the same thing for Miss Norris, and Bill Wood, who was the make-up man, carefully painted fine little lines around my eyes and broke up the jaw-line to give me a slight double chin.

When we went on the stage to make a test, I was also decked out in a very brilliant white wig. When I stepped on the set in that wig and the gold lamé evening dress, all the electricians wolf whistled at me! I didn't look like a middle aged lady, I was a glamorous platinum blonde. Mitch and I thought about Ray Milland's wife Mal. Her hair had gone white when she was 27, and she became even more beautiful. We decided that white hair was far too exotic for Miss Norris who had become something of a drab little wren. Mitch had them dress my hair the way he thought Miss Norris would do it, fashionable but severe. The hairdresser wanted to put a few gray streaks in but Mitch wouldn't hear of it. He said, "Women with grown sons don't have to have gray hair these days, especially Miss Norris who's in the cosmetic business. Just don't put any brilliantine on it."

JOHN LUND: Olivia had what they called a "Garbo face" in the business. Gene Tierney did too. That meant they could be photographed from any angle with any lighting. The only problem photographing Olivia was that she had pronounced bags under her eyes but they would disappear with the right lighting. After we looked at the rushes of the scene where I was dancing with her in the beginning of the movie, Mitch said, "We've got to do it over, I can see the bags under her eyes." There were a lot of extras in the scene so it was expensive to reshooot it, but that's the kind of perfectionist Mitch was. When she was supposed to look older, the bags under her eyes were very useful.

OLIVIA DE HAVILLAND: This fantastic attention to details is one of the things that made Mitch Leisen a great director. You watch *Hold Back The Dawn* and *To Each His Own,* and no matter how fine the detail is, it is correct for the locale and the time. Most importantly, it adds something to the picture dramatically.

MITCHELL LEISEN: George Marshall used to drive me crazy. His *Incendiary Blonde* had so many anachronisms. It's supposed to be 1908, and Betty Hutton lights a cigarette with a modern Ronson lighter. Then they're riding in an absolutely modern pullman car, instead of one of those horrible horsehair things they used to have. He used to just laugh it off. "Nobody will ever notice that, Mitch." I said, "They may not put their finger right on it, but they'll sense it isn't right somehow, and then you've lost them."

The beginning of *To Each His Own* takes place in a drugstore, and by some miracle, Sam Comer of the prop department found a complete drugstore of that era in storage. We duplicated the room exactly and everything you see on the shelves is in its correct place: the patent medicines of the time and beargrease for the hair. We hired the druggist who had kept it all those years as a technical consultant. He told us how he wrapped the face powder in tissue paper and how he made cold cream and we used all that.

When the Government said we couldn't spend more than $5,000 on new materials during the war, we often bought authentic rooms of the period to get around it. It didn't matter how much they cost since they were used materials, and I liked them because they were the real thing. When Olivia becomes the successful cosmetician, her office is an original mahogany paneled room that somebody had installed in the early '20s. The important thing to me always was to create the right atmosphere. If you remind your audience in a hundred little ways that this is 1918, then the plot and the characterizations become more real and compelling.

OLIVIA DE HAVILLAND: Mitch was a marvelous director from the actor's point of view. Phyllis Seaton was with us again on *To Each His*

Two scenes cut from *To Each His Own* after extensive previewing: Josephine calls on her friend Mac Tilton—who she believes is in the cosmetics business—and is greeted by his Brooklynese speaking secretary; and a moment of heavy drama, the now wealthy Josephine returns to New York after giving up the child.

Own, and she helped a lot. John Lund and I would run through our lines with her in my dressing room while Mitch was on the set lining up the shot. We would talk over the emotions of the scene, the characters and what they were thinking. But it was always Mitch who knew how to take all of the raw material and make the film.

The scene in which she tells her father that she's going to get the child back no matter what, and he says she can't, and she gets hysterical, was extremely hard to do. Mitch said, "I see it this way. She hasn't given up hope all this time, but now she loses control. She says this line and she falls across the counter. She straightens up a little and stumbles across the room and falls again on the other side." He demonstrated the motions to me slowly and it began to take form in my mind. It was right and I did it that way.

It was always Mitch. Whenever I needed help, he knew what to tell me. Then I could see it, then I could do it. *To Each His Own* could not have been made without Mitch, without his ability to see how every little bit of the film related to the film as a whole.

He always knew exactly how much rehearsal to give us. He blocked it out, gave us our movements and our props. He asked us how we thought it should be done, and he did it that way whenever he could. Then he rehearsed it several times, until we were comfortable with our props and knew where our marks were on the floor. At precisely the right moment, he said, "Let's take it." You could go ahead and give it everything you had on the first take because you knew exactly what you were doing. So many times we printed the first take and did one more for protection. Then we went right on with the next scene, still fresh.

I've worked with so many other directors, who are very good in other ways, but they don't give the company enough time to rehearse. Then there are still others who are unable to see in the first takes the values they are looking for. On the first take you don't dare give it 100% because you know there will be so many more takes. You must pace yourself, so you give maybe 40% or 50% on the first take and gradually work up to 85% or 90% with the tenth take. All the other actors in the scene are getting worn out and you may struggle through 35 or 40 takes before you finally get it right. By that time you're all used up.

With Mitch you knew you could give 95% on the last rehearsal, then 100% on the first take and 100% on the second, and that was it. You went on to the next thing, full of energy and enthusiasm, and got that done right away too.

Every one of the characters in *To Each His Own,* down to the smallest bit part, is fully realized, even the little old lady who tries to con a bottle of whiskey out of the druggist during Prohibition. None of them is on the screen very long, but you remember them. They each have their moment. Using Alma Macrorie as Belle Ingham was inspired casting. She was so perfect and natural and so was Victoria Horne as the nurse, Daisy. She's married to Jack Oakie.

Mitch was a master at building up a characterization. He knew how to use business, just the right business. The tea gown Edith made for the '20s segment was marvelous, smoke blue chiffon trimmed with chinchilla. I remember it was August and blazing hot and Mitch kept saying, "Don't you dare perspire!" Not only was it high style, but it gave me so many little things I could do, managing the train as I went around a corner and managing the chinchilla sleeves when I used my hands. That long cigarette holder—Jody has not only started smoking, she knows how to use one of those things. These are the things that enrich a characterization. They support the performance of the dialogue.

MITCHELL LEISEN: I turned *To Each His Own* down when Charlie Brackett sent it to me in New York. It was about a girl who has an illegitimate child, loses him and suffers and suffers. It was *The Sin Of Madelon Claudet* rewarmed, and as such it wasn't too interesting; it had been done to death. But Brackett kept insisting I do it. We talked it over many times and finally I got the idea of making her a real bitch in the middle of the story when she takes the child away from Mary Anderson. We made her a real Simon Legree and then it began to work.

It was the first time an illegitimate child had been used in a film since the Code came in in the '30s. We sent our script to the Hays Office and they sent it back with a flat refusal. They told us we couldn't make it at all. We never paid very much attention to the Code. The point was, if you did something in good taste, it didn't become offensive. We went ahead and shot the picture anyway, and when it was cut, we showed it to the censors. They came out crying, "This is the most beautiful picture we've ever seen." So they made an exception and allowed an illegitimate child. It was only when you did something in bad taste or showed a lack of discretion that you got into trouble.

When we saw that favorable reaction, Charlie and I both jumped on them and said, "There's one scene missing that we've just got to have. That's where they tell her she's got to have an abortion." There was no

Josephine is told she must have an abortion. The censors insisted that another doctor had to be seen at the beginning of the scene so the set was rebuilt and de Havilland (now twenty pounds heavier than she had been when the rest of the first episode was filmed) returned.

such scene in the original version. They let us make it; we put it in the picture and it made all the difference in the world.

ELEANOR BRODER: You're forgetting the Catholic Church. First we previewed it without the scene at all. Then we shot the scene and put it in. The third time, we cut the scene out again and the favorable reaction went down by about 20%. So then we talked to the Catholic Church and they said one doctor wouldn't do, we needed two or three doctors in a conference. Then we did a whole retake, just to show another doctor leaving when Olivia came in.

MITCHELL LEISEN: There was another scene added after the preview in which we see Olivia taking the little boy back to Mary Anderson and afterwards Olivia sobs and sobs. Charlie insisted we shoot it. I said, "If the audience sees Olivia cry, then they won't cry." But Charlie said "I want that extra bucket of tears," so we went back. It was at least two weeks after we went back. It was at least two weeks after we had finished shooting. The set had been struck and it had to be rebuilt. We had to pay all the actors for all the time that had lapsed as well as for whatever time we took to shoot it. I think one of the actors was already on another picture.

Altogether it cost $70,000 for those extra scenes. We kept the one in the doctors office, but when they cut in the other one of Olivia crying, all the tensions went right out of the whole thing. I was in New York the next time it was previewed and I got a wire from Charlie saying, "You were right, they didn't cry." And he threw the scene out the next day.

We must have had twenty previews of that thing, until we got it just right. It was blood, sweat and tears all the way. One night we ran it down in Long Beach, and Charlie and I got into such a fight afterwards out in front of the theatre that he refused to ride back into town with me. I still don't know how he got back.

Then there were problems with the scene where she tells her father she's going to get the child back, and he said, "And have him be the town bastard?" The censors weren't about to let anybody say "bastard" but I said, "I'm not using it as a curse word, I'm using in its legitimate sense, an illegitimate child. If you don't like it, you take it out of the Oxford Dictionary."

In the end, however, we had to change it because of Olivia. The father read the line to her and she went absolutely white and blew up sky high. It just threw her completely. It was such a shock to her that we had to go back to the alternate line, "The little boy in the blue suit who has no father" whatever the line was.

Olivia was so wonderful in that part. Nobody else could have played it as well as she did, to be so beautiful and innocent in the beginning, then grow to be a bitch and finally the lonely Miss Norris. Olivia is a very flexible actress. She listens to what you have to say, and she will do her best to do it as you want it. However, I never imposed a performance on any actor; I didn't want 20 Mitch Leisens running around the stage. Olivia and I worked it all out together. I have always said that if the actor understands what his character is thinking in a scene, he will not blow the lines. He may not say them exactly as they are written, but he'll get the point across all the same. Olivia always came up to me before each scene and said, "Now tell me what I'm thinking." I gave it to her and she said, "Now give me my pitch." She used her normal voice at the beginning and as she grew older, her voice dropped in pitch, lower and lower, until it became the voice of a mature woman.

Aging her naturally wasn't too hard. She didn't worry about her image or any of that routine. She was an actress playing a part, and she wanted to do everything possible to make it believable. Danny Fapp is a very clever cameraman. He took away her broad and angled the key light as unflatteringly as possible. All the while we had to keep some fill light on John Lund, since he was playing her son and had to look young. Her harsh lighting would have made him look old too.

I was convinced that Olivia was going to get the Award for *To Each His Own*. At the party at the end of shooting, I gave her a charm bracelet with a little miniature Oscar. Then we opened the curtains and there was a muscle man, painted gold and naked except for a big gold sword. Olivia was so stunned, all she could say was "His eyes are blue, an Oscar with blue eyes."

John Lund was a very brilliant young man, considering this was his first picture. He had starred in *The Hasty Heart* in New York and was brought out here from that to be put under contract to Paramount. I got him, and I had quite a time trying to get him to stop projecting as if he were in a theatre. You always have this problem with stage actors, getting them to use a normal tone of voice. John also had a rolling gait; he wove in and out of the camera range when he walked. So I said, "You come back here and look through this little eyepiece. I'm going to do exactly what you're doing. Where am I now?" He said "You're cut in half." I said, "that's exactly what you're doing. I can't keep panning back and fourth to keep you in the picture; you must walk a straight line. Just imagine there's a cord in the back of your neck and pull it."

I also had to teach him to move and shift his weight so the shadows wouldn't fall on whomever he was talking to. It's quite obvious in that one spot of the drugstore scene; his shadow is on Olivia's face and suddenly you see him move to one side. He suddenly woke up to the fact that he was casting a shadow. It wasn't obvious to anybody who didn't know what was going on, so I used the take anyway. Once we got these problems squared away, John was just fine.

My big fight with the studio was to have him play his own son. They couldn't see that at all. That was the punch to me, that the second he stepped off the train, not only does she recognize him, but you recognize him as well. I said, "It's of vital importance. If it's another actor, the point is lost completely. It's got to be the same guy." So I finally convinced them.

For the first part of the picture, we used John's own blond hair. For the second part, I rinsed his hair a light brown because I figured her genes would have some influence on the color of his hair. I thought John was much better looking with light brown hair, but he absolutely refused to do it again.

I love Roland Culver as Lord Desham; I think he's just sensational, really sensational. When he's giving her instructions, "Hang onto the guide rope" and then he falls off himself. Then that touching scene in the Officer's Club where he tells about his life passing in front of him. That was a long scene and he did it all in one take. And wasn't Alma Macrorie great in that? She was just incredible. She said, "God knows, I've cut enough pictures to know what's wrong. When they don't play it right, I have to correct it, so I know." She cut *To Each His Own* too and I had to fight her sometimes. She'd want to cut something of her own part and I'd say, "No, leave it alone." She was really giving a performance, not just playing herself.

ELEANOR BRODER: When Alma read the script, she wanted to play the part of Belle Ingham, the expectant mother with a messy house and a pack of kids. Alma was a superb cutter, but she had never acted before and the first day on the set she was very nervous. Mr. Leisen rehearsed it with her and said, "When the camera moves, you walk over to that mark." The first couple of takes she went way over her mark on the floor. Mr. Leisen went over and over it with her and finally he lost his temper, which was very rare for him, and he said, "For Christ's sake, Alma! You're going to have to cut this thing and you know if you don't stay within that mark I won't be able to hold you in the two shot." From then on, Alma stayed on her marks.

MITCHELL LEISEN: I never had another part Alma could have done, but later on she got a part in a Bing Crosby picture as a ballerina. Bing got delayed up north on location for six or seven weeks, and Alma practiced her dancing every day. By the time the company got back, Alma had lost 50 pounds and they had to pad her up again!

I thought that your device of telling Jody is pregnant by having her drink a glass of milk was very clever.

MITCHELL LEISEN: I thought so too. It wasn't in the script; we just did it. I was getting awfully tired of that routine of showing her knit little things. You may have noticed also that when they're up in the plane, there's no sound on the track at all except a very faint train whistle. I always kept track of my pictures through the cutting and when they were doing the sound recording, I told them to put that sound in.

ELEANOR BRODER: It came time to shoot the scene where John Lund and the British girl get married. It was on a set we hadn't used yet, so the day before, we finished shooting where we were, and Mr. Leisen and I went over to the new set with Mr. Brackett to choose the camera angles. Mr. Leisen walked back and forth, reciting the dialogue and looking through the viewfinder, trying to picture how the scene would be filmed. The way the script was written at that point, Olivia was supposed to tell John she was his mother and go into a long speech explaining the whole story. Then there was the wedding ceremony and that was the end. This scene had been read many times by all concerned and nobody had objected to it being played that way, but when it came right down to actually doing it, Mr. Leisen knew instinctively that it wouldn't work. Yet he couldn't put his finger on the trouble. He just said, "It's no damn good, Charlie, I won't shoot it." Mr. Brackett couldn't understand this at all and he got very angry and said, "You'll have to shoot it." Mr. Leisen said, "You'll have to get somebody else, I won't do it" and he ran out in a rage.

He got as far as the studio gate when he decided that this was no way to behave. Besides, he was beginning to see what the matter was. He went up to Mr. Brackett's office and he said, "The problem is too much exposition. This picture is full of plot and by the end of the picture the audience will be very keyed up emotionally and they just won't stand for any more. Besides, when the boy finally understands the picture is over. It would be very anticlimactical to go on and show him get married to some girl we don't know at all."

Mr. Brackett got the point and the two of them sat up late that night working out a new ending. When we arrived on the set the next morning, the whole thing had been rewritten. The wedding now took place first and the boy finally recognized his mother in the very last seconds of the film. It was Mr. Brackett who gave John Lund that perfect closing line, "I think this is our dance, Mother," but it was Mr. Leisen who made him do it.

MITCHELL LEISEN: The big thing about this picture for me is the punch line at the very end when he realizes that she's not just some nice

"I think this is our dance Mother."

lady as he had always considered her to be. He says, "I think this is our dance, Mother." You can't improve on something like that; it is absolutely perfect. It could not have been done any other way; I just knew it and I finally made Charlie see it. You see him dancing with her for just fifteen seconds, and then I cut right away. The theatre owners kept writing to us, "Please add a little bit on the end to let people dry their tears. We turn on our lights and the customers are crying so hard they can't see their way out of the theater."

Author's note: To Each His Own was recently preserved by the UCLA Film Archive using money from the David Packard Foundation and the National Endowment to the Humanities. The original nitrate camera negative was gone as well as the nitrate fine-grain made in the '40s for foreign dupe negatives. All that remained was a poor safety fine-grain made in the '50s and Paramount's original 35mm vault print which had been run a great deal and certain parts were very scratchy and/or full of splices. By examining each scene carefully, preservation officer Robert Gitt was able to see which print was better for each section. For the scene in which Josephine and Corinne fear that Griggsy has swallowed the safety pin, neither print was usable so a third, very low-contrast copy found in Italy had to be used. The sound track was re-recorded.

LUX RADIO THEATER

MITCHELL LEISEN: DeMille never actually directed any of those things. They always had somebody else to do that, and DeMille just read the introductions and filled in between the scenes. Then he had a fight with the union over a dollar so they let him go, and he recommended that I take the job. I earned $3000 a week for a couple hour's work, but I tried to copy him and they didn't like it. I didn't like it either because it was on Sunday night and I couldn't go down to my boat. I only did about seven of them.

Bill Russell was to take over from me, and he got such stage fright he couldn't even talk. They finally put him at a chair and table at one side of the stage, but he just could not do it. He collapsed and they sent for me at the last minute. I had to do it completely cold; I got there just in time to start and I'd never seen it before. Ordinarily, I had time to take a red pencil and underline the important words.

This happened to be the anniversary show for Lever Brothers, and I made a booboo by calling it "Lever" to rhyme with clever rather than "Leever". I remember distinctly Eleanor sitting in the front row with the Oxford Dictionary. At the end of the performance, the director came down and said, "How do you pronounce b-o-q-u-e-t?" I said, "Bookay." He said, "I'm sorry, but you said "bucket." I said, "I did not," and Eleanor said, "Yes, yes you did!"

ELEANOR BRODER: They had various people from Paramount in the lower echelons do the commercials. They asked me if I would perform

DeHavilland and Leisen at the *To Each His Own* wrap party.

and talk about Lux, to say how nice it made my skin, etc. I got $100 for doing it; I had to pay $54 to get into the union; it put me in the next income tax bracket, and I was petrified besides.

SUDDENLY IT'S SPRING - 1947

Continuing the pattern of an annual "big picture" alternated with a modestly budgeted comedy, Leisen was next assigned a clever Claude Binyon script titled *Suddenly It's Spring.* The title came from one of the songs in *Lady In The Dark* and had no particular significance in the story, which was yet another variation on the theme of role reversal by Binyon who was nominally the producer.

Fred MacMurray had moved to 20th Century-Fox when his contract with Paramount expired in 1944, but he returned for this one film. Claudette Colbert was first announced for the female lead, but Paulette Goddard eventually did the part, and although Goddard was much less

Arleen Whelan, Fred MacMurray, Paulette Goddard, Leisen and film editor Alma Macrorie in a typical publicity picture.

skillful than Colbert, she worked hard and her performance is enjoyable. Macdonald Carey in a supporting role is quite all right too; sporting a bowler hat that flatters the planes of his face, and timing his delivery well, he is much more effective and attractive here than he was later to be in *Dream Girl* and *Song Of Surrender*.

Suddenly It's Spring is probably the best of the three Claude Binyon scripts Leisen directed. The characters MacMurray and Goddard play are more realistic and are not unbelievably young (they've been married awhile but were separated by the war and now MacMurray wants a divorce). Binyon's dialogue is amusing; his situations are not as far fetched; and the turns of the plot are less predictable than those of *Take A Letter, Darling* and *No Time For Love*. Released early in 1947, *Suddenly It's Spring* went on to be one of Paramount's top grossing films of the year, returning $2,450,000 to Paramount on an investment of $1,372,000.

ELEANOR BRODER: Claude Binyon was Fred MacMurray's favorite writer and Fred always tried to get him on any picture he did. Binyon's brand of humor was to have a scene start in the most ordinary, natural way possible, and then suddenly throw a twist in at the end. The way Fred played it was to read the line with the twist in the same matter of fact way as all the other lines, so that you didn't catch on to the twist right away.

Mr. Binyon was also the producer, supposedly, but Mr. Leisen had to take care of most of the things himself. Binyon was very shy and every morning, when he came on the set, he looked around nervously and asked, "Where is she?" because as soon as Paulette laid eyes on him, she rushed over in her peppy way, saying "Oh, come on, Claude, give me

Goddard and MacMurray in *Suddenly It's Spring.*

some better lines" and that got on his nerves. Whenever Mr. Leisen asked him to rewrite a scene, Mr. Binyon would go stand in a corner with his face to the wall until it came to him.

Paulette was married to Burgess Meredith and she was very much in awe of his talent. She used to say, "You tell Burgess to act like an Indian, and wham he's an Indian. He looks like one, talks like one, he can do everything right on the spot." Paulette had to work out every little thing before she ever stepped on the set. Doing a comedy with her could be excruciating because she had no sense of timing at all. Alma Macrorie's cutting got her through a lot of scenes, but there were some scenes she just had to do right in the shooting.

There was one scene in *Suddenly It's Spring* where she and Fred were on a train in the pullman car. The wife is trying to get her husband back, but she's being very subtle about it and he doesn't catch on. Every take we did, Paulette either played it so fast that it was blatantly obvious she wanted him back, or she did it so slowly it wasn't seductive at all. After I don't know how many takes, fifteen or twenty, I went over to Mr. Leisen and said, "The production department is getting nervous. When do you think she'll get it right?" he said, "Heaven knows. If and when she does get it, it will be totally by accident. She won't know that she did it any differently than all of the other takes she's done already." Finally we got a take we could print, and it was strictly by accident. She couldn't time the next scene either, and there we went again.

GOLDEN EARRINGS - 1947

Bringing Marlene Dietrich back to the United States for her first post-war American film, Leisen created *Golden Earrings,* one of his most bizarre and relentlessly romantic works. The fairy tale plot with highly erotic overtones cast Ray Milland as a stuffy British soldier who is imprisoned for spying in Germany in the final days before World War II. He manages to escape, and crawling through the woods, comes across a solitary gypsy woman (Dietrich) cooking her evening meal over an open fire.

Dietrich announces spookily that the water spirits had forecast Milland's arrival when her last husband had been executed for a petty crime. To elude his Nazi predators, she transforms him into a gypsy by dying his skin and piercing his ears for the golden earrings which are fre-

Dietrich plays the piano for Billy Daniels on the set of *Golden Earrings*.

quently mentioned in the dialogue and which at one point, become the subject of a lusty song by Murvyn Vye. They experience various amusing and mildly exciting adventures until Milland is delivered into safety and must leave her as duty calls, but they are reunited in the end.

Among the Paramount directors, only Leisen was enough of a romanticist to take this silly plot seriously, and he plays it straight for the most part, though Dietrich's reading of some of the lines is so broadly played as to get into Mae West territory and inevitable send-up. The pictorial quality broke much new ground for both Leisen and cinematographer Daniel Fapp. It owed something to Sternberg via Dietrich, who controlled all of her own lighting and kept the face Sternberg had created for her; it showed the influence of post-war Italian neo-realism and at the same time was reminiscent of the fairylands created by Hal Mohr for *A Midsummer Night's Dream* and Lee Garmes in *Zoo In Budapest*. A strange fusion of Leisen's meticulous accuracy and his fertile imagination added intrigue to the Dietrich legend and boosted the popularity of this highly profitable film.

MITCHELL LEISEN: Marlene came back from the war very much changed. She's never gotten over the horrors she saw there. She slept for months in jeeps, on floors, even bare dirt, and I tried to tell her she should write a humorous book about her experiences, but it was no laughing matter. She told me that she was walking through a little French village one afternoon after VE day. All around her was rubble and she couldn't understand why because all the buildings along the street were still standing, with curtains blowing in their windows. Then she looked through one of the windows and she saw that there was nothing behind. The fronts of the buildings were still standing but everything behind them had been destroyed and there was not a single person there.

I went out to the airport to meet her, and the first thing she did when she got of the plane was say, "I must call the General in Paris." I said, "But you've just come from Paris!" She said, "I know, but he made me

Ray Milland tries his earring on.

The reunion at the end of the film.

promise I would call; he was worried about me." She told me she had been participating in a ceremony, in Paris, and as she walked off the stage, a GI came up to her and said, "The General expects you at his apartment." Marlene said, "But I don't know the General." "He expects you," said the GI. "So," said Marlene, "I went over there and stayed two weeks. He wants me to marry him, but I can't be an Army wife. What would I say to the other army wives?"

The studio didn't want Marlene at first, but I insisted. The whole point of the story was that this gypsy woman was so seductive underneath all her filthy clothes and greasy hair that the stuffy English man couldn't help falling in love with her. I said, "There's only one woman who can be glamorous under all that and it's Marlene." After she accepted the role, Marlene decided to do some research. She visited all the gypsy camps around Paris and even stayed in one of them for several days. She learned all about the way they lived and how they dressed. Before she arrived here, we went on location in the mountains and did some long shots with Ray Milland and a double wearing Marlene's costumes. When Marlene got here, she took one look at those costumes and refused to wear them because she knew they weren't authentic. We had a terrible time making clothes Marlene would wear that resembled the ones on our long shots enough.

Ray Milland didn't want to make the picture. He didn't like Marlene; he thought he was too young to do it, so he was a real bastard at first. He calmed down a little by the end, but he and Marlene fought the whole time. When we were shooting the scene where he first meets her as she's eating the stew, over and over, Marlene would stick a fish head into her mouth, suck the eye out, and then pull out the rest of the head. Then, after I yelled cut, she would stick her finger down her throat to make herself throw it up. This whole performance made Ray violently ill.

There was a little fire under the pot, but the water wasn't hot; we put dry ice in the pot to give off the vapors. When we broke for lunch, the prop man stupidly forgot to put the fire out. We came back, and when Marlene saw the water bubbling merrily along, she assumed it was just the dry ice. She stuck her hand in and let out a blood curdling scream. She had a second degree burn. I suggested we call it quits for the day, but she wouldn't hear of it. She wouldn't even allow us to restage the scene and use her other hand. We cooled the water off and she kept sticking her burned hand in the pot with the dry ice all afternoon.

JAY LIVINGSTON: Paramount was a very democratic studio. Everybody ate lunch in the same dining room, including the head of the studio. Ray Evans and I had a table right in front by the door and when Marlene Dietrich came in the first day, all in her gypsy make-up, we asked her to eat with us. She ate with us through the whole shooting. One day she came in and she was very annoyed with Ray Milland. They had finished shooting one scene and there was some time before lunch so Mitch said they would rehearse the next scene and then shoot it after lunch. It was a love scene and when Ray found out he had to embrace Marlene, he sort of snarled and said, "Aw, I'll kiss her after lunch!" Marlene said, "Those Englishmen are so cold!" Ray was known all over the studio as being quite a ladies' man, but he didn't like it when the woman took the initiative.

RAY MILLAND: "I thought she was very overrated and she was always on the make."

ELEANOR BRODER: On the first day, when Marlene realized she wasn't going to get anywhere with Ray, her eye fell on Murvyn Vye, who

Dietrich and
Mervyn Vye.

was playing the second lead. The two of them were very anxious for the shooting to wrap up so they could get over to her dressing room.

MITCHELL LEISEN: Marlene made herself up, of course, and she decided to wear a very dark base make-up. On top of that, she kept getting soot off the bottom of the pot and rubbing it into her face until she was photographing darker than the inside of a hole. She also kept poking holes through her dress with her nails until finally I slapped the back of her hand and told her to cut it out.

Marlene's daughter Maria Seiber was with us on *Golden Earrings* working as her mother's dialogue coach. Maria was a brilliant actress and she did a lot of radio, but she was so heavy that acting in pictures was out of the question. Then she married Bill Riva and had her first child, and the same thing happened to her that had happened to Katherine DeMille; her metabolism changed and she became so slender she could even wear Marlene's tiny clothes, which pleased Marlene no end because she was very proud of Maria.

ELEANOR BRODER: There was a jurisdictional strike during the shooting of *Golden Earrings* and the studio decided it didn't want us crossing the picket lines. We shot late every day until the pickets went home, then we were allowed to go home, eat dinner and take a bath, but everybody had to report back to the studio at 9:00 p.m. and stay overnight. The stars both had beds in their dressing rooms, and Mr. Leisen had had one ever since his first heart attack, but for the rest of the crew and the featured players, it was murder. There as no place for us anywhere. I finally found an empty office across the hall which barely had room for three cots. I stayed there with Lupe, our script girl, and Phyllis Seaton's sister Frances, who was our overall dialogue director. It went on for weeks, and it was murder.

JAY LIVINGSTON: I wrote the music for the song, "Golden Earrings" with Victor Young and Ray Evans and I wrote the lyrics. I don't know why Marlene didn't sing it except that in the script it said the Mervyn Vye character would sing it even before the parts were cast. He did it beautifully — he had sung on the stage.

Dietrich, Milland and Leisen.

LEISEN'S DECLINE

Golden Earrings, released late in 1947, proved a bonanza at the box office. By the end of the year, *Variety* reported that it had already returned almost $3 million to Paramount (on a $2 million investment) and it went on to clean up in the newly reopening European market. It was to be the last big commercial hit of Leisen's career. His next four pictures were outright flops.

Critically, Leisen's descent was neither precipitous nor immediate. It had already started when *Lady In The Dark* and *Frenchman's Creek* had failed to reach fullest dramatic potentials (although nobody noticed it at the time since both films grossed highly). Leisen had again hit his stride with *Kitty* and *To Each His Own,* both fine in content and sublime in form, and both very profitable. While *Suddenly It's Spring* and *Golden Earrings* were not as outstanding in terms of aesthetics, they continued Leisen's pattern of steady box office success.

Leisen struck out commercially for the first time in his career with *Dream Girl, Bride Of Vengeance* and *Captain Carey, U.S.A.,* all of which were also soundly panned by the critics. His subsequent films at Paramount, including *No Man Of Her Own* and *The Mating Season* garnered more positive reviews and performed respectably at the box office, but by the beginning of the '50s, Leisen's average was clearly way below what he had enjoyed a decade earlier.

The quality of American films in general declined during and after the Second World War. In the halcyon days of the war and immediate post-war period, virtually every film released made money regardless of its quality and the box office was no longer an effective guide for future production, with the result that many of the great talents of the '30s momentarily declined. Some recovered and continued, others didn't.

Mitchell Leisen was not immune to these trends within the industry, and in addition, his work in this period reflects a general decline in the studio operation at Paramount which up to that time had supported him well, for Leisen remained at Paramount while much of the key talent he needed for his films was departing.

A whole generation of capable and popular players had been groomed into stardom at Paramount in the '30, but by the end of the war, most of them were gone. M-G-M, 20th Century-Fox and Warner Brothers kept their important stars under long term exclusive contracts, but Paramount relied more on non-exclusive multiple picture deals. Thus, Paramount stars were often free to make pictures at other studios or drift into independent production.

Of those with who Leisen had worked most successfully, Carole Lombard had signed a lucrative contract in 1938 but never worked at Paramount again; Fred MacMurray and Claudette Colbert had left, and were eventually followed by Ray Milland and Paulette Goddard. When casting pictures, it became necessary to use Macdonald Carey, who was not the new Ray Milland the studio hoped for, and John Lund, whose talent was in the realm of character parts, not with the juvenile leads the studio gave him because of his good looks.

Moreover, many of the talented people who had supported Leisen were no longer available. Preston Sturges, Billy Wilder and even Claude Binyon turned to directing. Dorothy Parker retired from screenwriting, Virginia Van Upp moved to Columbia, Norman Krasna, Oscar Hammerstein II and Howard Lindsay and Russell Crouse all went back to Broadway. Among the producers, Arthur Hornblow Jr. had moved to M-G-M, B. G. DeSylva returned to songwriting and Charles Brackett was almost always teamed with Billy Wilder.

Leisen was most often assigned to Richard Maibaum and the association was an unhappy one. Unhappy also in his personal life, and discouraged with one disappointing project after another, Leisen grew disheartened and the creative fires within him wavered. He had acquired the reputation of producing expensive pictures, and although none of his films were seriously over budget, the budgets he demanded and got were sometimes considerably higher than the studio felt the project warranted. With the declining box office, a loss of confidence on the part of the front office was evident to Leisen in all his day to day dealings, and in turn, it showed up in his films. Frank Capra related in his autobiography, *The Name Above The Title* how the management at Paramount was now insisting that no Paramount picture, (other than DeMille's) could cost more than $500,000.

Leisen's increasing dependance on Phyllis Seaton to work with the actors was also noticed. Nobody complained when it was a Paulette Goddard Picture; it was well known that Goddard needed Seaton's constant help on every film, even when the assignment wasn't as demanding as with *Kitty*. When Leisen began requesting Seaton on virtually every film, tongues began to wag. Early in his career Leisen had been anxious to delegate the art direction and costume design and to prove he could work effectively with actors. He did prove it. Now, however, he seemed to be losing interest in that aspect of the job. The fact that he involved himself with the *Bride Of Vengeance* costumes so much that he actually took screen credit for them coincided with the fact, as Macdonald Carey says, "That was the picture where Phyllis Seaton really took over." Some observers thought that Seaton was just stepping in to help make good pictures, others thought she was trying to further her own career at his expense (ironically just the same as Leisen had once taken over on *Tonight Is Ours* at the expense of Stuart Walker).

Despite all these problems, however, Leisen eventually regained his equilibrium. His last three pictures at Paramount, without Seaton and with moderate budgets, showed a return to the high quality with which his name had always been associated.

DREAM GIRL - 1948

The first outright failure of Leisen's career, *Dream Girl,* is also the saddest of his several disappointing films of the late '40s because the ingredients of the film, for the most part, were fairly sound. For this reason Leisen is blamed much more than he would be for his subsequent flops.

Paramount paid a record price for the screen rights to Elmer Rice's popular play *Dream Girl* and sent out reams of publicity to the effect that a "new" Betty Hutton would emerge as a dramatic actress in the

The "new" Betty Hutton in *Dream Girl.*

film. Although Leisen was denied the use of Technicolor, no other expense was spared, for the maintenance of Betty Hutton's popularity was a matter of great importance to the studio.

Whether or not Hutton really could act remained undetermined with the release of *Dream Girl.* Gone for the most part was her old screeching hyperactivity, and in some scenes she showed evidences of sensitivity and reflection completely unknown heretofore. Nonetheless, her performance was monotonous, pitched in an unvarying, not-quite-awake key throughout. Perhaps Leisen pushed Hutton to the absolute limits of her dramatic capacity, but this seems unlikely since the rest of the film was equally unconvincing. He made a crucial error in changing the Hutton character from an average working girl (like those Carole Lombard and Jean Arthur had played so well for him) into a bored rich girl just so he could have more lavish sets and costumes.

Despite the money spent, *Dream Girl* has the air of a very cut-rate *Lady In The Dark.* The dream sequences are unimaginative and shed little light on the character Hutton plays. Ever grinning, Macdonald Carey doesn't exhibit enough strength to convince anybody he could bring Hutton out of her daze. Only the dependable Walter Abel escapes *Dream Girl* with any dignity.

MITCHELL LEISEN: Nobody liked that one. All of Betty Hutton's fans were disappointed when she didn't go around screaming "Murder he says" and the rest of the public who couldn't stand her didn't go either.

The day she came in to do the make-up and hair tests, her hair was curled within an inch of her life and her face was absolutely caked with make-up. Her hair was naturally almost white and I had them put a dark blonde rinse on her and style it very simply, in a great big knot. Then I gave her a street make-up. She argued all the way through it, but when she saw the tests, she came out of the projection room yelling, "I'm beautiful, I'm beautiful!"

She sincerely believed that she would win the Oscar for *Dream Girl* and nobody had the heart to tell her otherwise. The day the nominations were announced and she wasn't one of them, she was devastated. I always ducked when I saw her coming on the lot after that.

I think Macdonald Carey is a very nice guy, a fine father and lately he's been very good on his soap opera. But he was so wishy-washy in those days, and the studio wanted me to use him in everything. I couldn't get any life into him.

MACDONALD CAREY: When he wrote the play, Elmer Rice stole the whole damn thing from *Lady In The Dark*. Actually the part I played was more fully written than Charley Johnson in *Lady In The Dark* but the big thing was to change Betty Hutton's image and the whole studio was aware of it. That put the rest of us into secondary roles, which we realized as we went along. Betty was a very pushy babe and that got her into problem after problem. She had a claque that included her hairdresser and make-up artist and she made great friends of Phyllis Seaton and Alma Macrorie.

The first week, at the end of each day, we would go to see the rushes and this clacque would sit up in front and laugh uproariously at everything Betty did. When the close-ups of me, Walter Abel and Peggy Wood came on, there was utter silence. Peggy and Walter stopped coming after a couple of days but I stuck it out until the end of the week. Apparently Alma really believed it because when she assembled the rough cut, it was one endless close-up of Betty. They had the first preview and it was a disaster. For the next preview, Alma replaced some of my two-shots and over the shoulder shots and it went better. For the third preview, she even used some of the master shots. It got a little better but it was never wonderful because while the heroine had been a poor working girl in the play (and needed some escape from her humdrum life) Mitch made her life so opulent that there was no need for her to escape into her fantasies.

ELEANOR BRODER: Mr. Leisen was very unhappy in his personal life during that period, and *Dream Girl* and *Bride Of Vengeance* were his lowest ebbs. And the production of *Dream Girl* was often very exasperating. One of the days we were shooting the wedding, we had hundreds of extras on the set and every delay was costing a fortune. Nothing went right. As the camera pulled back and went up the crane, there was too much friction and it squeaked. We had a man assigned to wet it down, that's all he had to do, but he left the set for some reason and nobody else on the camera crew would touch it. It wasn't their jurisdiction. Finally, Mr. Leisen went over and put the water on himself, and everybody on the set froze because he didn't have any right to do that. "You

Macdonald Carey, Betty Hutton (as Portia, sort of) and Patrick Knowles in a scene cut from *Dream Girl* after the disastrous preview. Photo taken June 3, 1947.

Leisen confers with Macdonald Carey and Betty Hutton on *Dream Girl.*

damn unions," he said, "next thing you'll be having toilet paper tearers."

SONG OF SURRENDER - 1949

Song Of Surrender was the last of Leisen's films to take place in a rural America populated by distinctive provincial characters. It was a project Leisen was never fond of (he was often at odds with Richard Maibaum, the writer-producer) and yet his work here is as precise and well judged as in any of the films he enjoyed making. *Song Of Surrender* suffers from major casting error, but the script is sound and Leisen's visual concept is one of his most interesting.

As usual, Leisen mastered every detail of the era (the turn of the century) and the locale (New England). The basic conflict of the story is the confrontation between the sternly disciplined Puritan life of the local inhabitants, and the much freer society of a band of New Yorkers who come into the region to spend the summer.

Leisen's exposition of the extremes of behavior represented by the two groups is the film's greatest strength. As the story opens, a sophisticate from New York (Macdonald Carey) calls upon Elisha Hunt, (Claude Rains), the curator of a dark little museum to ascertain the value of a musket he has found on the grounds of his estate. A severely dressed young woman named Abigail (Wanda Hendrix) enters and Hunt orders her to make some tea, cautioning her to bring only two cups. Hunt explains that Abigail is not his daughter but is his wife. She

Macdonald Carey and Wanda Hendrix in *Song Of Surrender*.

returns with the tea, and he chides her for having put on her good dress. A neighbor who has gone bankrupt is to auction his household goods the next day, and Abigail begs to be allowed to attend. Hunt at first refuses, but sensing her disappointment, relents and gives her a dollar, saying that if she bid on something, her presence at the auction would seem more proper.

Having meticulously presented the constraints of Abigail's existence, Leisen's camera quickly sweeps across the valley to the estate of the New Yorkers who are spending the evening in polite debauchery. In a very brief sequence we learn that Bruce Eldridge (Carey) is unenthusiastic about his engagement to a wealthy heiress, and is indifferent to the pleasures of her friends.

In Leisen's long establishing shot of the auction, we see the city folks as a small cluster of white figures amid the locals who are dressed in black. Each group openly resents the other, as the New Yorkers consistently outbid the locals. Abigail impulsively outbids the amused Eldridge for a gramophone, despite the obvious disapproval of her neighbors. She apparently has never heard music before and is enchanted by the Caruso recordings; they relieve the harshness of her life. When her husband insists that she get rid of the phonograph, she contrives to keep it. Eldridge hears her playing it while Hunt is away and persuades her to go dancing with him, but fails in his efforts to seduce her. Learning of all this, Hunt wrathfully denounces his wife from the pulpit of the church and she flees to New York in terror. Abigail returns to her husband, but he has suffered a nervous breakdown and conveniently dies, allowing Abigail to marry Eldridge, whom she has inspired to an altruistic career in politics.

Aside from the tacked-on happy ending, Richard Maibaum's script is compelling and highly realistic. His dialogue for Clause Rains is well conceived, particularly in the difficult denunciation scene wherein Hunt justifies his revelation of his wife's indiscretion on the basis that other members of the congregation will profit thereby.

Rains' absorbing performance dominates the film; there is a streak of madness in his austerity and a frightening conviction when he uses the case of the family that had to auction its possessions as proof of divine retribution. Wanda Hendrix was a most promising newcomer, and carefully prepared by Phyllis Loughton and directed by Leisen, her portrait of Abigail is compassionate and sincere. Macdonald Carey, however, is very weak as the third side of the triangle, and much of the picture tumbles because of his inability to make Eldridge come to life.

It is impossible to believe that Abigail could ever be led astray by such a bland and uninteresting seducteur.

Predictably, Leisen and his cinematographer Daniel Fapp created a striking visual style for *Song Of Surrender* which was unlike any other Leisen film. Fapp, who had earlier created a romantic lighting scheme for *To Each His Own,* reflected the influence of the post-war Italian neorealism in *Song Of Surrender.* All of the interiors of Rains' house are harshly lit from one source. During the day, small windows cast a faint, low angle beam of light through the kitchen; at night a single kerosene lamp burns.

During production, the film was first known as *Abigail, Dear Heart* and then became *The Sin Of Abby Hunt.* Reflecting on the great popularity of the song "To Each His Own," Paramount retitled the film *Song Of Surrender* and had a title song written. It was sung, somewhat ludicrously, under the titles by Buddy Clark, and the same recording, complete with lush orchestration, was heard to eminate from Abigail's gramophone in the final scene as she embraces Macdonald Carey. "Song of Surrender," however, did not lead the hit parade, nor did the film duplicate *To Each His Own*'s commercial bonanza. 1949 was a bad year in general at the box office; the reviews were mixed and the picture had no boxoffice names. Although Wanda Hendrix's performance is faultless, a better-known actress might have drawn to *Song Of Surrender* the audience is deserved. Unknown as it is today, it remains one of the most satisfactory of Leisen's lesser works.

MITCHELL LEISEN: I wanted to remake *Death Takes A Holiday,* but the studio wouldn't have it and instead I was assigned to Richard Maibaum to make this fool thing about Connecticut. You might say Maibaum and I were friendly enemies. We didn't dislike each other personally, it was just that we didn't see eye to eye about anything. Having worked so closely with Hornblow, Brackett and DeSylva, the situation with Maibaum was very hard on me. The pictures I made with him were pretty disastrous for my money. Some of them weren't all that bad, but they weren't my favorites either. Technically I didn't have script approval in my contract and my agents didn't want me to turn down any pictures because I was getting quite a big salary and the studio was hoping they could break the contract.

Whenever I got stuck with a script I didn't like, I had a tendency to distract myself with the technical details and the costumes. On *Song Of Surrender,* everything was correct for the time and place. An old woman had died and Frank Richardson, who was the head of the wardrobe, bought up all of her old clothes, which were originals from the great French coutouriers of the period. We didn't change a thing, we just altered them to fit the actresses. Eva Gabor had a black net dress studded with real turquoise.

At one point, Macdonald Carey and Wanda Hendrix sit on a hill and he plays Caruso's recording of the "Shubert Serenade" for her and translates it as he goes along. We couldn't actually play the record as he talked, because it would have picked up and we couldn't have balanced the two things on the track. Yet Macdonald had to hear it somehow so he could keep in sync. I finally rigged up a little broadcasting system; she had a receiver hidden in her hair and there was a wire hidden in her clothes that was connected to an earphone he wore. That way he kept in sync.

We sent back to have the Caruso recordings pressed from the original masters, but the one of "Shubert's Serenade" was so tinny it hurt the ears and would have distracted from the mood of the scene. So we took a modern one and tricked it up to sound old, but not that old.

I thought Wanda Hendrix had a great potential. I wanted to do *Romeo And Juliet* with her, but the studio wouldn't have it. I guess it wouldn't have been as good as Zeffirelli's anyway. He really made it come alive. After I saw his version, I went home and reread the text, and I found he'd cut out pages and pages because he didn't need them. That picture really moved.

BRIDE OF VENGEANCE - 1949

Although it was panned by the critics and was a complete failure at the boxoffice, (Leisen's third in a row), *Bride Of Vengeance* has certain rare and unique qualities which make it a fascinating film to see today. The performances are all bad in this tale of how Cesare Borgia inveigles his innocent sister Lucretia into marrying and poisoning the Duke of Ferrara. Even so, the constant splendor of Leisen's images gives *Bride Of Vengeance* a persistent fascination that overcomes at least some of the dreadful acting and scripting.

Leisen's recreation of Renaissance Italy is a marvel of historical conception that had seldom, if ever, been equalled. It surpasses even Leisen's own *Frenchman's Creek*. The Italy of the Borgias is dark and sinister. Even in the daylight, a treacherous mood darkens the exteriors,

Make-up test of
Lund for the role
of Cesare
Borgia. Photo
taken 7/28/48.

while the interiors of the palace are always drenched in shadow. Frequent trips into dungeons and catacombs are blacker still; torches illuminate only patches of the walls, the rest is pitch black save for sporadic highlights of water trickling over stones.

Despite the opportunity for period work, Leisen felt that the original script by Cyril Hume and Michael Hogan could not be filmed, and was determined to take a suspension rather that film it, though he was dissuaded from this course by his agent and business manager. The noted novelist and playwright, Clemence Dane was brought in for a rewrite which seemed an improvement, although much of Dane's dialogue was in a stilted psuedo-Shakespearian blank verse which Paulette Goddard was vocally incapable of delivering. John Lund also rewrote certain scenes, but received no screen credit.

Paulette Goddard in two costume tests. One taken 8/6/48, shows how Leisen recycled the mink skirt from *Lady In The Dark* into a cape.

Lund tried hard to be the Duke of Ferrara, and his performance is the best of the three principals. Macdonald Carey was better than usual as the evil Cesare Borgia, but Paulette Goddard was hopeless in the role of Lucretia. Phyllis Seaton's most intensive efforts for once could not carry Goddard through, and Leisen seemed content to ignore Goddard's performance completely and concentrate on trying to make her look younger. He designed complex headdresses which hid the double chin and pared down the massive forehead, and had cinematographer Daniel Fapp light Goddard with painstaking care. He staged many of Goddard's most important scenes completely in longshots, when using close-ups could have covered some trims that would have picked up the sluggish tempo a bit. The distance, the flat lighting and heavy diffusion all combined to make Goddard's face completely devoid of expression and thus weakened the characterization further. The success of *Kitty* and *Suddenly It's Spring* had prolonged Goddard's tenure at Paramount, but *Bride Of Vengeance* was such a catastrophe Goddard never worked on the Paramount lot again.

MITCHELL LEISEN: That was a lousy story about a big cannon that went boom. They kept casting these cannons from iron and every time they fired one, it would explode along with the charge. Finally they hit upon the idea of cooling it in water which tempered the iron. They filled it with shrapnel, fired it and that was it. I said, "Maibaum, you're an ass to think anybody would care about this after the atomic bomb," but we had to make it anyway.

In order to do the explosion scene, we first shot a field, supposedly the field outside the gates, and then we shot the same field after the explosion. We rigged up the gates of the castle on a soundstage with an enormous process screen on the other side showing the field. After the explosion, the image changed and showed the devastation. Very simple. On the first take, a spark went out and hit the screen and it went up in flames. A $2500 screen! Farciot Edouart was ready to kill himself.

We had about a hundred extras as soldiers, but we made it look like a lot more. They ran through the set, out the door of the soundstage, down the alley between the stages and came in through the other side. Then they picked up some different shields and banners and ran through the same take again.

Originally Ray Milland was supposed to play the Duke of Ferrara with John Lund as Cesare Borgia, but Ray refused to do it. We had already worked out all the make-up and costuming for John to wear as

Cesare, but we decided to recast with Lund as the Duke and have Macdonald Carey portray Borgia. Paulette did Lucretia, and the picture shows Lucretia as she actually was. In reality, she was very charitable and by all intents and purposes was a good woman. She even opened a home for wayward girls. She was not the poisoner you read about. The best way to get at the truth of these matters is to examine contemporary writings of the period, but it did not help the picture to show a Lucretia the public would not believe in.

You share credit for the costumes with Mary Grant.

MITCHELL LEISEN: She is Vincent Price's wife and a very talented woman. That was the only time I ever took a credit on one of my pictures for anything other than directing, although I did some of the clothes for almost every picture I directed. At least I had some fun working with the Renaissance period. I wanted the actors to wear codpieces, because that was the period. We made them up and tested that way, but the studio was not about to allow that and in the end, they just wore tights. We took the skirt of Ginger Rogers' mink dress apart and used it to make sleeves for Paulette to wear in *Bride*.

JOHN LUND: Mitch's insistence on authenticity for the costumes took us forever to get dressed in the morning. There were no modern conveniences like zippers or hooks and eyes. Mitch produced everything exactly as it was done in the early Renaissance. The sleeves were always separate from the body of the garment, they were all tied on with a complex series of lacings. If there was ever a change of schedule that required us to change costumes, there would be a real panic just over the time it took to get us laced up into the other costumes.

Surely Phyllis Loughton should be considered the co-director of *Bride Of Vengeance;* she worked harder on that than anything else she ever did at Paramount. Phyllis went into a script so deeply that she often read greater significance into scenes than the writers had really put there. If I was supposed to say a line like, "Give me that calendar," Phyllis would say, "Remember that's the same calendar that was on his desk in the first scene," which was something that probably had never occurred to the writers, but it made sense nevertheless. We began to see cross references all over the place and whole new relationships developed between the characters.

I think a lot of this was due to the fact that Phyllis was and is married to George Seaton, who was and is a better writer than 99% of the people who were writing at that time. George wrote this complex kind of relationship into his scripts, so Phyllis just assumed that the writers she worked with had gone into their situations just as deeply. She proceeded accordingly, and it helped the films.

PHYLLIS LOUGHTON SEATON: We worked like demons on that, trying to make something out of it, but it was hopeless; there just wasn't anything in the script you could work up. What were we trying to say with this picture? What did it prove? Nothing! That dialogue just could not be performed by the people we had. Garson Kanin once said to me, "Good direction can make a good script better, but there's nothing in the world the director can do to make a bad script good."

Mitch eventually gave up trying to make any sense out of that story and concentrated all his energy on the camera work. He carefully composed every frame of the film for maximum effect. I remember one occasion when he went in for a closer shot of John Lund. There was a candlestick right behind John's head and Mitch moved that candlestick just half an inch so the composition he saw through his viewfinder would be perfectly balanced. Mitch's ability to reproduce exactly the look and feeling of a particular period is unerring and as far as that was concerned, *Bride Of Vengeance* was perfect. Today, a Visconti can make a *Death In Venice* and will get praised to the skies for this period work, but there was a different audience when we made *Bride Of Vengeance,* and nobody cared.

Part of the problem on *Bride,* of course, was the lack of a rapport between Mitch and Richard Maibaum. Personally, I think Dick is a great guy, and there's no doubt of his talent, but somehow, he and Mitch didn't work well together. A good pairing of producer and director is as hard to set up as a good marriage; if we could figure out what makes some relationships work while others don't, we'd have more good marriages and more good pictures. It had a lot to do with respect. Mitch grew to respect Arthur Hornblow's judgments and when Hornblow told Mitch he couldn't do something he wanted to do, Mitch could appreciate the reasons Hornblow gave and would eventually agree that Hornblow was right. It was the same way with Charlie Brackett. But when a conflict arose between Mitch and a producer he did not respect so much, Mitch would go away still certain that he was right.

RAY MILLAND: *Bride Of Vengeance* was the only time I took a suspension to avoid doing a picture in all the years I was at Paramount. I had

Paulette Goddard and John Lund in *Bride Of Vengeance.*

just been to see the Fox picture, *Prince Of Foxes* when I received the script. It had a horrible title, *A Mask For Lucretia* and it was a horrible script, and it was the same story as *Prince Of Foxes,* about the Duke of Ferrara and the Borgia Family. Henry Ginsberg, who was the head of the studio, didn't know anything about *Prince Of Foxes,* and the producer, Richard Maibaum, insisted there would be a rewrite. They asked me to go downtown to the Singer Sewing Machine Company and be measured for a form for the costumes. I agreed, but I begged them not to spend any money on my costumes until I had approved of the revised script. They said they would wait.

Then they went and made up the costumes anyway, and a few weeks later I got a call to come to the gallery to make the costume tests and do the publicity shots with Paulette, which we usually did at the end of shooting or during a break, not before shooting even started. They insisted that they had written another script, and I refused to go to the gallery until I saw it. Finally they brought me a script and it was the same old thing. I absolutely refused and I was suspended for the eight weeks it took to shoot it.

They made it without me, and it was an unmitigated bomb. There was nothing Mitch could do to save it. Paulette couldn't play Lucretia, it was beyond her range—she's too earthy. It opened in New York and closed the same week. The critics really roasted it and Richard Maibaum stormed all over the lot. He was certain that I was in league with the New York critics who panned it because they wrote the same criticisms of it that I had made before they ever started shooting.

RICHARD MAIBAUM: The studio was very worried about Mitch and they assigned us to work together thinking that I could get him going again. I admit I didn't succeed, but I don't think it was wholly my fault because the pictures I produced with other directors turned out quite well. Mitch just wasn't the same man who had directed *Hands Across The Table* and all those pictures. He spent all his time lighting the set and draping Paulette Goddard's skirts, and ignored the acting. Phyllis Loughton had to gradually do more and more until she was directing the whole picture by default. When Mitch finished a take, he'd glance at Phyllis and if she nodded, he'd yell, "Print it."

MACDONALD CAREY: Phyllis Seaton always did an awful lot of midwifery beyond what was needed, but on this one she really took over. Once I asked Mitch about something in the character and he said, "Oh, you go work with Phyllis on that." She had him in some kind of thrall. I think a lot of people who had not gone to college or done theatre were impressed with her, but I had a college degree in Theatre and had done virtually every Shakespeare play. I was always friendly with her and she was always very subtle about how she gave me her advice. She'd start talking about something in a conversational way and gradually get around to what she really wanted to say. However, I do remember once she told me rather directly that I should open my eyes wider to express anger!

Johnny Lund and I had a conversation while we were shooting that and we both agreed we wanted to play 'character parts' and didn't like it when the studio put us in romantic leads. This was a very artsy-fartsy thing to say since in retrospect obviously it was the guys doing the romantic leads who would get the big build up.

Did you ever see Leisen arguing with Richard Maibaum?

MACDONALD CAREY: No, they were always very civil around us. Richard and I had gone to college together and I thought he was a good producer. He produced *The Great Gatsby* which I was in and I thought it came out very well.

CAPTAIN CAREY, U.S.A. - 1950

Leisen hit an even lower ebb with his next picture, *Captain Carey, U.S.A.* Indeed, it was the worst film of his whole career. Of his several difficult collaborations with Richard Maibaum, *Captain Carey, U.S.A.* was the only really hopeless script, coupling cardboard characters with a plot so labyrinthine that even a laborious explanation at the end left viewers in doubt of what it was all about. *Song Of Surrender* and *Bride Of Vengeance* had at least given Leisen interesting locales and eras to work with, but the post-war Italy of *Captain Carey* did not inspire him at all. Sadly, it was his only encounter with Alan Ladd, an actor he much admired. The only distinction of *Captain Carey, U.S.A.* is the song "Mona Lisa" which was introduced in the film. It subsequently became a standard and won the Academy Award for Best Song.

JAY LIVINGSTON: When I got the script it was titled something else and I went to see Mitch and see what kind of song he wanted. He didn't care as long as it had an Italian feeling because the accordion player had to play it as a signal. So Ray Evans and I wrote "Mona Lisa" and Mitch liked it. Then the studio changed the title to *After Midnight* and they told us to write a new song with that title. So we wrote another lyric. We had the singer come in with a 45 piece orchestra and he recorded the "After Midnight Lyric" but there was a short time left over so I asked him to record it again with the "Mona Lisa" lyric. The the studio changed the title again to *Captain Carey, U.S.A.* and I went to the front office and asked them if we could go back to the "Mona Lisa" lyric. They played them both and said, "All right, if you want to." We sent the music to every Italian singer, Vic Damone, Frankie Laine, and they all turned it down. Finally they decided to ask Nat King Cole. Nat was such a good pianist that he didn't want anybody playing anything for him, he just wanted to get the music and try it out by himself. However, Paramount insisted that I be allowed to play and sing it for him and he finally agreed. While I was playing it for him, his little daughter kept running around and making a lot of noise which worried me, but Nat agreed to record it. And of course his daughter was Natalie who now sings it beautifully.

Alan Ladd and Leisen on the set of *Captain Carey, U.S.A.* Photo taken 6-13-1950

ELEANOR BRODER: Although Mr. Leisen was very fond of Mr. Maibaum as a person, somehow they just could not work well together. There would be long paragraphs in Mr. Maibaum's scripts explaining who the characters were, what their background was, and what the situation was, and Mr. Leisen would say, "Where are any of these points made in the dialogue? You say she's this, that and the other, but how do we get it on the screen?"

The first page of the *Captain Carey* script gave long descriptions of what was going on in Italy during the war, but the dialogue only carried plot points, and when we went to preview, the audience was immediately restless because they didn't know what the situation was. The general reaction was poor, and the next day I wrote a criticism explaining the problem as I saw it. Mr. Maibaum wrote four new scenes which were added onto the beginning. That solved the problem, but it would have been a lot easier if he and Mr. Leisen could have determined the problem before we started shooting.

MITCHELL LEISEN: Alan Ladd was a very quiet, serious man, a very conscientious actor. Every time his wife came onto the set, he'd get nervous and they'd get into a fight. Finally he barred her from visiting the set, which suited me fine.

NO MAN OF HER OWN - 1950

Fortunately, *Captain Carey, U.S.A.* ended the spiral of ever worsening films, and in his last three productions at Paramount, Leisen's career enjoyed a brief renaissance. There were marked changes in Leisen's style, but he demonstrated that he could still make a good picture if the material was moderately interesting. His last three pictures for Paramount were quickly and cheaply made, in keeping with the studio's new economy wave, but they all turned out well. With Phyllis Seaton no longer around, there was no question that he was directing the performances, which everyone agreed came out well.

No Man Of Her Own was the first and best of the three final pictures. Leisen remained as skillful with a thriller as he had been in the days of *Four Hours To Kill* and the plot, taken from *I Married A Dead Man* by Cornell Woolrich (under the pseudonym of William Irish) is the most ingenious Leisen ever tackled.

Barbara Stanwyck, pregnant and unmarried, is on a cross country train where she is befriended by another pregnant woman who is going with her husband to meet his wealthy parents, who have never met her or even seen a photograph. The two women are in the ladies' room when the train crashes, and when Stanwyck regains consciousness, she discovers herself in a hospital, having given birth and been wrongly identified as the wealthy woman. The woman and her husband are both dead, and Stanwyck decides to continue the ruse. Assuming the other woman's identity and passing her son off as the grandchild of the wealthy parents she moves into their mansion.

No Man Of Her Own was Leisen's only venture into the realm of film noir. The movement towards darker images which Leisen and Daniel Fapp had started with *Golden Earrings* and continued with *Song Of Surrender* reached its climax with *No Man Of Her Own*. The brief moments on the train and in the hospital are the only high key scenes in

Jane Cowl and Barbara Stanwyck in *No Man Of Her Own.*

the film; all of the others are black, enveloped in dense shadows. When Stanwyck arrives at her in-laws' enormous Victorian mansion, it is twilight. The interiors are all dark, lit harshly by a single bulb in the ceiling. The chase which comprises the last half hour of the film is even blacker, illuminated only by occasional street lamps.

The narrative structure is also very much that of Film Noir. By using the flashback device, Leisen emphasized the fatalism of the story, opening the film with John Lund and Barbara Stanwyck sitting in their living room, awaiting the arrival of the police. It is the afternoon of Easter Sunday, but the room is dark. She wears a white lace coat over a black dress. Putting her child to bed, Stanwyck muses over what has happened, and the flashback begins.

Leisen had freely interpolated humor into the thrillers he made in the '30s, but in *No Man Of Her Own,* the terror and despair are unrelenting. Leisen opens the flashback with the most brutal scene he ever shot. The pregnant and no longer young Stanwyck is in the hall of a shabby rooming house, hysterically pounding at the door of Lyle Bettger, who is the father of her child. After an interminable pause, Bettger shoves an envelope at her under the door. She rips it open and finds a transcontinental train ticket, and in her panic, does not notice a large stack of bills fluttering to the floor.

Leisen was never farther from his theme of role reversal than here. Gone is the plucky, assertive heroine that Goddard, Colbert and Stanwyck had portrayed in earlier films. She has no control over her destiny, she can react only passively to the situations which confront her. Stanwyck plays the woman with every nuance her vast experience had taught her. She is the vital force of the film, that which transforms the clever but incredible plot into compelling drama.

MITCHELL LEISEN: I read the book and I knew I wanted to do it but the studio wasn't interested. I gave the book to Barbara, and she told the front office that if they didn't give her that picture, she wouldn't do anything for them.

Sally Benson did a screenplay which I rejected completely and I adapted it myself. Catherine Turney came in and wrote some additional scenes (which we discarded) and the whole beginning which we used. I could not take any credit because I was not a member of the Screen Writers' Guild but it didn't matter to me one way or the other.

Barbara Stanwyck is a fantastic actress. When she makes a gesture as she speaks a line, she has a way of suspending that motion for a split second in mid-air on a certain word which gives an imperceptible emphasis to just that word.

She did all her own stunts in the picture. To stage the train wreck, we built the set of the ladies' room inside of an enormous wheel, about twenty feet in diameter. We rotated the wheel to make the train crash and roll over, and Barbara and Phyllis Thaxter were right in there, falling from side to side.

ELEANOR BRODER: When stage actors are rehearsing a play, they have weeks to get used to handling their props, so that often, when they make a picture, they have trouble with props. There was a scene where Barbara and Jane Cowl are taking down a Christmas tree. Jane had a very hard time handling the props and she got so upset she blew her lines on take after take. Finally Mr. Leisen just gave her some tinsel to wrap around a piece of cardboard and she still blew the lines. After each take, Barbara put the ornaments back exactly where they had been before. There were so many takes the production office started getting on our backs and the tension was so thick you could cut it with a knife.

So Barbara started kidding around. Between takes when she needed the make-up man, she called out, "Hey, wrecking crew!" When she got up on the ladder for another take, Buzz Boggs reached up to check with his light meter and she pretended she was kissing him. The whole crew howled and it certainly improved the atmosphere on the set.

THE MATING SEASON - 1951

Reunited with Charles Brackett for the last time on *The Mating Season,* Leisen produced his best comedy in years, a social satire full of funny lines but with the same generous interpolation of tender moments that had made *Remember The Night* so effective.

Brackett's script was rich in irony. John Lund is a poor but ambitious company employee who marries wealthy Gene Tierney and lives way beyond his means. When his hard-working mother (Thelma Ritter) comes to visit at the same time as her own bitchy high society mother (Miriam Hopkins) comes to live with them, Tierney mistakes her for the new maid. The complications ensuing are predictable but enjoyably developed and there is a new mellowness in Leisen's work which indicates that his style was in transition. Ostensibly Ritter's role is supporting but he allows her to dominate the film because her character is the most interesting. Gene Tierney is among Leisen's loveliest heroines even if her role is rather one-dimensional and there is a certain candor in the delineation of Lund's aggressive personage which helps to lift the film out of the classification of simple situation comedy.

MITCHELL LEISEN: That was a good script and it was very good to be working with Charlie Brackett again. Gene Tierney was a doll, it's always easy to work with Johnny Lund and I adored Thelma Ritter. She and Phyllis Seaton were lifelong friends, you know. They were all wonderful, Charlie Lang was the cinematographer and everything went along fine until we started shooting the scenes Miriam Hopkins was in.

ELEANOR BRODER: Miriam Hopkins drove Mr. Leisen crazy. She just couldn't get it into her head that she was playing a supporting role and was not the star of the picture. Every night she figured out all the things she could do with her lines and she'd come to the set full of enthusiasm and proceed to tell us how the whole thing should be done.

Leisen, Charles Brackett, Gene Tierney and John Lund on the set of *The Mating Season*. Photo taken June 27, 1950.

Her ideas were very good but they detracted from Gene Tierney and John Lund who were the real stars of the story.

Mr. Leisen was always polite to her and never attempted to discourage her. He filmed whatever she wanted but he had no intention of using those scenes in the picture. In the scenes between Johnny and Gene, where Miriam was in the background reacting all over the place, Mr. Leisen simply changed the lens on the camera so she was out of focus or out of the frame. He shot extra close-ups of Johnny and Gene so he could cut to them in the middle of the scene instead of using the medium shot with Miriam all the way through.

Miriam always offered so much unsolicited advice we could never get any work done. One day when she was not on the set, we had to move to another stage to shoot with a transparency and Mr. Leisen had everybody take the long way around so they wouldn't walk past her dressing room and tip her off that the company had moved. Another time we had it all set and Miriam looked at the final run-through and took Gene by the shoulders and said, "I think it would be better if you stood like this." She wasn't even in that scene!

DARLING, HOW COULD YOU? - 1951

Late in 1950, Leisen began shooting *Rendezvous,* an adaptation of James M. Barrie's *Alice-Sit-By-The-Fire,* which would prove to be his last film at Paramount. Perhaps one of Barrie's lesser works, *Alice* had remained a very popular play in summer stock and had just been revived with great success as a vehicle for Helen Hayes and her daughter, Mary MacArthur. Paramount had announced in 1948 that Charles Brackett would adapt and produce a version of *Alice* which would mark Mary Martin's return to the screen but it was never made. It was also proposed to Gloria Swanson as a follow-up to *Sunset Boulevard,* but she refused to make a test on the grounds that *Sunset Boulevard* had proven her capabilities. By the time it was assigned to Leisen, with Harry Tugend producing, it had become a less ambitious project, starring Paramount contractees Joan Fontaine and John Lund and was shot in a quick 33 days, making good use of the still standing Washington Square set from *The Heiress.*

The story is very simple. Lund and Fontaine return to the United States after some years abroad, during which time they have had very little contact with their two children. They have difficulty overcoming the indifference of the children, who have been raised by a grand-mother, and have to straighten out their adolescent daughter Amy who wrongly suspects the mother of having an affair with a medical student.

While the plot of the play is hardly suspenseful, Barrie's dialogue is enjoyable when well played and Leisen directed it with a certain quiet humor, again indicative that his style was changing. (Had he done it in the '30s, I think some of the scenes would have been busier.) Joan Fontaine brought the right fey and whimsical quality to the part of Alice without being overly stylized, while John Lund seemed a bit too pragmatic and down to earth in the part of the father. By contrast, a brilliant though little known actor named Peter Hanson, cast as the medical student, had just the right stylized overplaying complete with exaggerated facial expressions to suit the text. The pivotal role is that of Amy, the daughter, and Mona Freeman brought it off very well. Although she was in her early twenties at the time, Freeman was quite convincing as a 12 year old child, even in the sequence in which the girl decides to impersonate a *femme fatale* gets dressed up in her mother's clothes and goes off to seduce the medical student. Producing a child's voice imitating a woman's voice is a tricky thing to attempt, but Freeman brought it off well.

Leisen reassures Joan Fontaine on the set of *Darling, How Could You?* Photo taken November 21, 1950.

JOAN FONTAINE: I only did it because Miss (Ethel) Barrymore suggested it.

MITCHELL LEISEN: I dreaded working with Joan Fontaine again, but the first day, during a break, she came up to me and said she was just doing it for the money, she wasn't out to prove anything anymore and she would act it whatever way I told her. And that's just what she did, she couldn't have been more delightful and fun to work with. It's the most complete reformation I've ever seen. We had a ball doing it.

CHICO DAY: When the war ended and I came home, I went to Mitch's house to see him. He had injured his leg and was laid up in bed. During the time I was gone, he had gotten used to working with Johnny Coonan as his Assistant Director (he was William Wellman's brother-in-law) and he was very cold toward me and made it clear he didn't want me to come back. That was all right with me, the Production Office at Paramount assigned me to other directors. I worked with Mitch again briefly on a short subject that Billy Daniels was supposed to be directing but Mitch really did it himself. Other than that I didn't see him.

When the Production Office was getting ready for *Darling How Could You?* they told Mitch that they couldn't assign Johnny because he was already working on another film. Mitch got very angry but the other director wouldn't release Johnny so I was assigned. Mitch absolutely refused to talk to me during the whole production. When we finished one set-up, I automatically knew what came next from the call-sheet and I would summon the actors we needed. If I needed to tell him anything, I would type it in capital letters on a memo and give it to Eleanor Broder at the end of the day. That way I stood next to him through the whole film and we never talked to each other.

Since you hadn't had any quarrel, didn't this behavior bother you?

John Lund, Mona Freeman, Joan Fontaine and Peter Hanson in *Darling, How Could You?*

CHICO DAY: No, that was just the way he was. I don't think most people realized how much pain he was in from his heart and his bad foot. He always hid it very well but sometimes his heart would bother him and he'd have to sit down. He was afraid to tell anybody for fear the studio would think he wasn't strong enough to direct.

At this point, Leisen renegotiated his contract with Paramount, so that he was obligated for only one film per year, rather than two. Why had he chosen to remain so long at the same studio, especially when changes in the front office had made his position insecure? Part of it was that Paramount was his home and he liked working there. He had long standing relationships with craftsmen in the art, wardrobe, hair and make-up departments and he knew they would know how he wanted things done. Also he was well aware that at Paramount, producer-director teams enjoyed more autonomy than at the other studios, and even so, he had often stretched the studio's tolerance to the limits.

Had Charles Feldman placed Leisen at other major studios or with independent producers in the mid-'40s, Leisen could have commanded more important assignments than he got when he branched out in the early '50s. He would also have had the opportunity to work with stars, producers and writers who never crossed his path at Paramount. In the '50s, major directors like Robert Wise and Howard Hawkes were forming their own production units, and shopping projects from studio to studio, but this was not Leisen's style. *No Man Of Her Own* was one of the few times he found a property he liked and stayed with it from inception to completion; usually he waited until something was offered to him. The fact that he was known throughout the industry as being "difficult" was no help and possibly Feldman had been trying to line up outside jobs ever since *The Lady Is Willing* with no success. Possibly Feldman was also finding he could not get Leisen his Paramount salary at the other studios either.

In the halcyon days of the early '40s, Feldman had negotiated a fantastic contract with Paramount, which provided, among other things, that henceforth all of Leisen's pictures would be billed "A Mitchell Leisen Production" in type 75% of what was used for the stars' names. Leisen was to be paid $4000 a week. If the second of the films overlapped into the next contractual year, Leisen was to be paid a bonus of almost $3000 per week and that had happened on both *Frenchman's Creek* and *Golden Earrings*.

Leisen and Feldman were soon aware that the studio was trying to break the contract and this they resisted by every means possible, including accepting scripts like *Bride Of Vengeance* and *Captain Carey, U.S.A.* which he could have rejected earlier. However, the scripts he was offered after *Darling, How Could You?* were so bad he finally had to agree to a compromise of his original contract. It was decided that his unexpired time equaled five pictures, with *Darling, How Could You?* counted as the first, he now owed Paramount four films, at the rate of roughly one per year. He and Eleanor Broder moved their offices from the Paramount lot into the dance studio on La Cienega Boulevard. He could accept other offers provided he gave Paramount a 72 hour notice during which time Paramount could give him their own assignment.

YOUNG MAN IN A HURRY - 1952

Feldman's problem was to convince the other studios that Leisen could still work quickly and cheaply. Eventually he came up with *Young Man With Ideas* at M-G-M which was to be produced on about the same scale as the last three Paramount pictures. The Arthur Shekman script was all plot with little character development and it gets a bit tedious at times although Glenn Ford is sympathetic as an idealistic young lawyer.

It was Leisen's first film intended for release as a second feature, following M-G-M's early '50s policy of double-billing what would have been a minor A release a few years earlier, hoping to strengthen box office draw. *Young Man In A Hurry* received favorable notice from the press, but it quickly came and went, leaving Leisen's career at a standstill.

How did you feel about going over to M-G-M after all the years at Paramount?

ELEANOR BRODER: I felt we were going to Alcatraz. Everybody over there was so unfriendly and it's such a large place. It's fifty miles from one office to another but our office was smaller than the one we had had at Paramount. We had to share a little suite with Vincente Minnelli. There was a tiny outer office for Minnelli's secretary and me. It was so small the only way we could put the desks was back to back so we sat there facing each other all day long. Mr. Leisen and Mr. Minnelli both kept their doors open and when they needed something, they'd call out.

Leisen confers with Glenn Ford and Nina Foch on *Young Man In A Hurry.* The special light attached to his chair indicates his cataracts were already impairing his sight.

How did you feel about the M-G-M style?

MITCHELL LEISEN: The distinct Metro style was set up by Cedric Gibbons who was head of the Art Department. Whether it fit the story or not, he was going to have his sets paramount. In *Young Man,* we were supposed to have a dinner party in a golf club in Billings, Montana. I picked out a set that was standing and we had the people all ready to go in business suits, but oh no, that was not M-G-M. Gibbons did the most elaborate country club you've ever seen all bright white and everybody dressed to the teeth in white ties and tails.

Then one scene took place in a bookie joint. We used some tacky real estate office on Washington Boulevard for the exterior, but when Gibbons did the interior, it looked like something out of *House And Garden.* He had copper lamps with plants growing out of them. In a bookie joint! He wanted it a certain way. That was the M-G-M style and that's what you got.

I only did it because I needed a job. They had already signed Russell Nype because of his great success on Broadway in *Call Me Madam*. Russell is a great singer but he has never built himself up as an actor, I had seen him in *Call Me Madam* and I said to Bill Wright, the producer, "I think we had better go to New York and get a look at this guy." We sat in the audience and Nype looked about eighteen years old. Bill said, "You mean that's the guy we've signed up?" I said, "That's it." He said, "Christ, have we got problems." We went backstage to see Ethel Merman and she said, "I'm doing everything but fanning my armpits to keep things alive."

Russell came out to L.A. and I did a test of him in the courtroom scene. Then Dore Schary had everybody come to a conference room and read the script aloud. When it was all finished, he put his arm around my shoulder and said, "I certainly feel sorry for you, Dad." The head of the studio! That's the kind of bastard he was.

Ruth Roman had the female lead and she was something else again. She did every trick in the book to steal the picture. She and Russell went to lunch together every day and she had him around her little finger. In their scenes, Roman just chewed Russell up and spit him out in little hunks.

After about a week, Russell got dumped and he went back to *Call Me Madam*. Glenn Ford was put into the part and then the battle started. Glenn wasn't about to take anything from Miss Roman. Once, her dialogue cued his following speech. It had to be very nasty from her in order for him to jump on her with his line. So she read the line as sweetly as could be. Glenn said, "I can't answer with my line." "Well" she said, "I'm talking about my children and I can't read it any other way."

Glenn went to his dressing room and wouldn't come out. I called the producer and, "You'd better come down here and settle this one. It's not my fight." He read Roman the riot act and she read the line the right way finally. It was that kind of bitchy little trick all the way through it. She did everything she could to upset his performance. Glenn was a pretty smart hombre and he didn't let her get away with very much.

TONIGHT WE SING - 1953

Leisen then went to 20th Century-Fox for the first time in his career to direct what was ostensibly a biography of impresario Sol Hurok. At first, Darryl Zanuck had assigned his contractee Jean Negulesco to the project and intended to have Oscar Karlweis portray Hurok. The real Sol Hurok did not approve of this casting (he wanted somebody handsomer and more famous so the part went to David Wayne and Karlweis was cast in a supporting role instead). Negulesco went to M-G-M for *Scandal At Scourie.* After he bowed out, Feldman secured the job for Leisen. The pastiche of popular classical music had been inspired by the success of *The Great Caruso;* Ezio Pinza, Roberta Peters, Tamara Toumanova and Issac Stern lent their talents and the numbers were tastefully staged by Leisen.

This was Leisen's first color film since *Frenchman's Creek* and although strict budgetary limitations cramped his style a little bit, he made much use of glass shots and managed to create his customary opulence in staging two operatic excerpts. Giving the rest of the picture an A picture look took all of Leisen's ingenuity, a flashback to similar conditions on *Tonight Is Ours* and a prelude to the extensive television work he would later do. Alfred Newman's score thriftily recycled a theme he had originally composed for *A Royal Scandal* (1945).

The staging of Roberta Peters' two arias in the middle of the picture is a good example of how Leisen got a lavish feeling while carefully watching the expenses. We see her at a formal dinner party with many guests when it is announced that she is going to sing. Tracking in as she begins, Leisen shows us many extras and a very large orchestra; the establishing shot and the dolly shot were as much as he could crowd into one day's shooting. Planting his camera in front of the crowd, Leisen keeps Peters in such close shots as she sings "Sempre Libera" from *La Traviata* that few extras are needed to fill in the background and the sides. To get a feeling of motion without pulling back and having to fill the room with people again, Leisen cuts to the door where Byron Palmer enters and starts singing the offstage voice of the aria. Peters goes over to the door as she finished the aria, passing a few people. The two sing the duet from *Madame Butterfly* by the door, again in a close shot, but with enough people around to continue the illusion of the large crowd we saw at the beginning of the scene.

Economics also prevented Leisen from ever showing an audience at

David Wayne, Isaac Stern and Byron Palmer in *Tonight We Sing*.

the performances (except for a brief shot of a small crowd in the gallery) but he makes up for this with the splendid pageantry of the two operatic excerpts. The kermesse and prison trio scenes from Gunoud's *Faust* are both strikingly executed; while the eye for visual detail and flair for color are apparent, they are never allowed to become prominent enough to detract from the music. It is the processional scene from *Boris Gudanov* however that is the film's artistic climax, even though it is the first number in the picture. The stage is choked with massive crowds decked out in ritualistic clothes of all colors (but reds and golds predominating as in the banquet scene in *Frenchman's Creek*) all obscured by the burning of smoky incense.

Sadly, Leisen was not allowed to match the magnificence of the operatic numbers with the ballet numbers. Originally two big production numbers were planned for Tamara Tounamova but one was dropped before shooting and the other, a lavish depiction of the song "Autumn Leaves" was cut at the order of Darryl Zanuck. In the cheaper dances which replaced the above, Toumanova got her requisite two appearances, but her share of screen time became very small. In the first, we see her alone onstage, dressed in red against an ultramarine curtain as she performs Anna Pavlova's famous forty *fouettes en pointe*. The second gave Toumanova a small corps de ballets for a spirited dance. The symmetry of the dance pattern, the floating quality of the dancers' long skirts and the billowing ultramarine drapes (which filled the space eliminating the need for a set) made it all very pretty indeed.

Issac Stern, portraying the celebrated violinist Eugene Yssaye, also played twice. In the first number, he rehearses briefly in his stateroom, in the second, he is onstage with a pianist, the camera angled to reveal none of the audience except a few people in a stage box.

The fictional biographical material about Hurok which links it all together is innocuous and never takes up much time between the numbers. David Wayne was miscast as Hurok and Anne Bancroft had little to do as the wife but Ezio Pinza as Chaliapin, Toumanova as Anna Pavlova and Issac Stern all carried off their brief dialogue scenes credibly. In *Tonight We Sing*, only the music mattered, but the rest was agreeable too.

CONSTANCE MOORE: Darryl Zanuck was looking for somebody to direct the biography of Sol Hurok and Charlie Feldman suggested Mitch. Zanuck said, "He'll cost too much. This isn't any $10,000,000 picture." To prove he could make a high quality picture on a relatively small budget, Mitch went through the script item by item and prepared a cost breakdown down to the last extra. Zanuck approved of it and Mitch got the job. Mitch stayed within the budget and when it was over, he was as proud as could be. Of course he would have loved to spend a lot of money on it but he was glad to get the chance to prove what he could do with less.

MITCHELL LEISEN: Actually I brought it in $100,000 under budget and Zanuck was ecstatic. We were supposed to have Hurok first see Anna Pavlova from the wings in an elaborate ballet. Zanuck and I couldn't agree how it should be done so we just cut the number out and saved a lot of money.

George Jessel was supposed to be the producer of this but he was hardly ever around and I had to take care of everything myself. Every morning I'd get a call from him and he'd ask, "How are you doing?" and I'd say, "Fine. Where are you?" One day he was in Chicago, the next day Kansas City and so on. Jessel was very close to Hurok, however, and he persuaded Hurok to let us film his story. It was hard to get any

Ezio Pinza as Challiapin in the "Boris Gudanov" scene from *Tonight We Sing*.

reality into it because Hurok wouldn't let us tell very much about his life. We couldn't even mention his first wife. Most of the artists were under Hurok's management.

Working with Ezio Pinza was a fantastic experience. He was fascinated by Chaliapin and gave a true picture of what Chaliapin was really like. He studied every photograph of Chaliapin, talked to everybody who ever knew Chaliapin and listened to every recording Chaliapin ever made. When Pinza sang the arias, it was as Chaliapin had sung them, not the way Pinza did it himself when he sang the same roles at the Met.

Issac Stern is such a funny fellow. I was in stitches half the time with the stories he told about all the great conductors he'd worked with. Although he was not an actor, he wanted to give a true portrayal of Yssaye, not just go through the motions. He found out everything he could about Yssaye and I directed him very little. He did it on his own.

Roberta Peters was adorable. We pre-recorded her tracks and played them back on the stage while we shot silent takes of her singing. I told her to sing right along with the track and I was sure she was just mouthing it silently because I couldn't see the muscles in her throat moving at all. She insisted she'd been singing right along with the recording, and to prove it she sang "Sempre Libera" all the way through, *a capella*. It was the most glorious thing to hear and yet there wasn't any movement.

Byron Palmer, who played the juvenile lead, had a fine voice but it was not operatic. He couldn't keep up with Pinza and Peters so we hired Jan Peerce to make the tracks but Byron sang right along with the others when we shot the numbers, and that was something to hear!

One of the ways I saved money was not building new sets for the operatic scenes. My wife had sung with the San Francisco Opera company so I knew the stage designer up there and we rented their sets very reasonably. The set for *Boris Gudanov* was fantastic and must have cost them a fortune. We used their costumes for that too and with the money we saved, I was able to put more extras on the stage.

The prison set (for *Faust*) had a big black pillar painted down the middle of the backdrop. That was too tacky so I built a real pillar with a circular staircase winding down around it. Pinza made his entrance creeping down the stairs rather than sneaking out from behind a flat. The area to the left of the pillar was not used in the action the trio, so I built a torture chamber and very briefly, you see a guy being stretched on racks. There are a few lines sung by a chorus of nuns offstage. All these things enriched it and San Francisco incorporated them into their production. They later asked me to direct a new production of *Faust* up there but I declined.

Cutting the picture was an ordeal. Zanuck always did his cutting at night and if the director wanted to have any say about it at all, he just had to stay up until 2:00 a.m. when Zanuck ran it. He ordered one can of beer, for himself, and he dictated to his secretary what had to come out. The next morning, the Editorial Department got little notes typed in red ink and capitol letters saying "So and so must come out." You could argue with Zanuck but most of the time it didn't do any good. The main production number had been a ballet to the song, "Autumn Leaves." It had been popular in France for many years but wasn't known in the U.S. yet. I had always liked it so we staged it for Tamara Toumanova and brought a fellow out from New York for $500 a week to be her partner. It was really beautiful but Zanuck took one look at it and decided the boy's prick showed through his underwear too much and ordered it cut out, just like that. No amount of argument could persuade him, although a few seconds of it with Tamara alone was inserted before the titles as a prologue.

That very same year, the English lyrics to "Autumn Leaves" were written and it became the smash hit of the year. Everywhere you went you heard it and it just broke my heart to think we had filmed that beautiful number and then lost it.

MY COUSIN RACHEL and RED GARTERS

After *Tonight We Sing,* Leisen almost made two other films, either of which could have restored his status as a topnotch director, and both of which, one could argue, would have turned out better in his hands. His ever deteriorating relationship with Paramount, however, kept him from realizing either.

M-G-M had loaned George Cukor to Fox for *My Cousin Rachel.* Initially he and producer Nunnally Johnson believed they had persuaded Greta Garbo to return to films in the title role. Cukor worked at length on the script with Johnson, scouted locations in England and discovered Richard Burton. However, Garbo changed her mind and when Cukor was not able to persuade Vivian Leigh to take over, he lost interest and agreed to do the modest *The Model And The Marriage Broker* instead. Darryl Zanuck, highly pleased with *Tonight We Sing,* asked Leisen to take over *Rachel.* He was ecstatic; it was the best project he'd had in years: a top quality story from a best selling novel, a big budget, an interesting period and best of all, another chance to work with Olivia de Havilland.

Paramount, however, refused to let him go, telling him instead to begin preparing a musical biography of the Duncan Sisters, to star Betty Hutton and Ginger Rogers. When Hutton decided she wanted to play both roles and threatened to walk out unless her husband was assigned to direct, the studio seized the opportunity to terminate its contract with her and the picture was never made. Although Leisen was paid in full by Paramount, *My Cousin Rachel* was already shooting at Fox under the workmanlike direction of Fox regular Henry Koster.

It was during this period, Leisen directed the 1953 Academy Awards broadcast, his only experience with live TV. At Paramount the management changed again and Leisen was told, early in 1953, to report for work on an unusual musical western called *Red Garters.* The pre-production period was excruciating for him for, inexplicably, he was barred from most of the conferences. When Edith Head loyally came to discuss the costumes with him, she was forced to visit him secretly in his home one evening. Shooting began on May 11, 1953 and Leisen continued until May 19, when he was fired and replaced with George Marshall. At the same time, Pat Crowley replaced Anna Maria Albergeti and Gene Barry replaced Don Taylor. None of Leisen's footage remained in the final film and scrapping this week of shooting cost Paramount $250,000.

JAY LIVINGSTON: Ray Evans and I wrote the songs for that. The problem was that Mitch wanted to make the whole thing too arty and stylized. He was very stubborn and the last straw was a scene in a saloon. Mitch wanted to have everybody standing there like statues and they told him that a saloon has to be rowdy. He absolutely wouldn't budge, so they fired him.

YVONNE WOOD: I designed the mens' costumes for that and Edith Head did the women. The genesis of that picture was one number in the Bing Crosby picture *Just For You,* which Elliot Nugent had directed. There was a Mexican musical number that took place on a stage in a theatre. When I saw that the art director had made a sketch for the set that was just a suggestion, just an outline, I suggested to producer Pat Duggan that we do the costumes the same way, going for big, broad effects. He said, "Well, fine, if you can get Edith to design for the women that way." This was difficult because Edith had spent a lot of time in Mexico and she knew exactly what the native costumes looked liked. I said, "Edith, this is supposed to be a number on a stage, not real people in a town square. Eventually she got the idea and when it was well received, they decided to do a whole picture like that with a Western story.

I had heard for years how Mitch gave Edith a hard time and insisted on coming to all her fittings, so when I'd made my appointments with the actors, I called him up and told him when to come over. He said, "Oh no, honey, I'm very busy. You take care of that yourself." He took me to lunch every day, either to Lucy's or Oblath's. He talked alot about his ex-wife who had lived in Paris and he was so sexy and charming that I would have thought he was coming on to me if I hadn't known about Billy Daniels."

He was bisexual.

Oh really? Well it wouldn't have worked out, I was married at the time. Pat Duggan (the producer) was a charming man too and I never saw any friction between him and Mitch and I don't know why they fired Mitch.

He was making it too arty.

Well, he overplayed his hand and it's a pity too because George Marshall wasn't the right person for it. He was a very good director, I worked with him on *Tap Roots* and he was a very funny guy, but he didn't have the special imagination needed for something like this.

PAT CROWLEY: I only worked with George Marshall and I didn't even meet Mitch until we did a TV show later. However, everybody kept telling me what a creative genius Mitch was and Marshall used everything that Mitch had prepared so in that way I think he had an influence on the picture.

BEDEVILLED - 1955

Another plodding thriller, *Bedevilled* was a little more interesting than *Captain Carey, U.S.A.* because of some nice travelogue shots of Paris in Cinemascope and color. It was Leisen's first and only experience with the aspect ratio and although he disliked it, he used it with more taste and imagination than was usually evident in 1954.

In their early scope films, 20th Century-Fox told their directors to utilize the master shot all the way through since there was plenty of room to get all the actors into the same scene. Fox encouraged the other studios who rented the scope process to do the same thing since it obviously saved time over the conventional technique of breaking the scene down into two shots and close-ups. Also, the lens fattened faces when it got too close. The problem with this method was that it created static filmed plays, similar to the early talkies, and without cutting during a scene, a director lost the dramatic punch of a close-up as well as the ability to direct attention to a certain character at a specific moment.

Although logistics and the severe limitations of the lens gave Leisen fewer angles to work with, he still insisted on covering scenes from several sides, which bothered M-G-M since it felt this was unnecessary

Anne Baxter's face, already wide when photographed with a normal still camera lens here, became even broader when photographed in the close-up with the primitive Cinemascope lens. Nonetheless Leisen shot close-ups because he felt the film needed them and some were used in the final editing.

but the film did have a certain fluid quality which was often lacking at the time.

ANNE BAXTER: Mitch was terrified of the wide screen! Many directors I knew then didn't like it but they managed to adjust. Mitch just couldn't. It went against every instinct he had and it made him so insecure that he started acting like a desperate man. He was coming on to every handsome man who crossed his path including an actor in the picture that we all knew was not interested. The actor complained and Mitch was behind schedule so M-G-M took him off the picture.

Was it John Sturges who finished it.

No, I don't think so, but I can't remember now who it was. M-G-M sent somebody to "can" it and he really did. We finished everything Mitch hadn't done in a few days.

MITCHELL LEISEN: M-G-M had money tied up in France. You couldn't take the money out of France so we had to make a picture to use up the frozen funds.

All the street scenes were shot right in Paris. Over here, people are polite and stay out of your way, but there, they'd get into a violent argument with the police and say that they own the ground as much as the motion picture company does and they're not about to leave. We were shooting in the airplane ticket office on the Champs Elysees. It was a tiny place and we had to use arc lights to counteract the sunlight from outside. The arcs were throwing off a blue smoke so by the time we were ready to shoot, the room was so full of smoke we had to turn the arcs off. In the first shot of Steve Forrest, you see the street outside and it's normal and rather empty. You cut to the reverse of the travel agent and when you cut back to Steve, there are 2000 people looking on from across the street.

Later I was talking to George Davis, who went over there, and he said, "The police wouldn't do anything so we just rented a whole bunch of police uniforms from a costume company and dressed a whole bunch of extras as policemen. We had 50 extra police and we got the crowds to do what we wanted."

Then we were shooting in the yard of a little church in Montmartre. The priests wouldn't allow us to shoot inside the little church, they also wouldn't allow Victor Francen to go in so we had to fake him coming out the door. The priests kept walking back and forth through the scene. We couldn't stop them so finally we went to another church.

We had trouble with the script. They could never decide whether the character Anne Baxter was playing would turn out to be a good woman or a bad one so we had to shoot in the meantime and there was no way we could build up the character without knowing that. We had Leonard Spigelgass come up from the South of France to work on the script and we had daily conferences in my room, but Leonard was more interested in a romance at the time than in getting the script out.

Steve Forrest was something else. He came to the set one morning and he said, "I've been up all night and I'm sick to my stomach. I can't figure out the inner meaning of the word 'it' in that sentence." Steve was supposed to be a young priest. They outfitted him here, made a test and sent it over. His suit was the most violent shade of ultramarine blue you've ever seen in your life. M-G-M just said that it was bad and to get something else in Paris. Well, there are no places you can go in Paris to get suits his size. We finally took a grey flannel suit of mine and altered it for him. Then his trunk arrived and he decided he would wear a brown suit of his own instead. We had to get a duplicate because of the fight scene which was very early in the shooting and we didn't dare run the risk of the suit being wrecked. We tried everything, even painting it, but nothing matched.

Helen Rose had made a dress for Anne Baxter which they sent over with a note that there was too much cleavage and that we would have to do something about it. There was nothing to do but get a whole new dress. We went to Jean Dessus to get her wardrobe made which took time and how. Anne also insisted on living in Versailles which was completely at the other side of Paris from where we were shooting so she was usually late. We started shooting at noon, having eaten lunch, then had a sandwich break at 4:30 and continued until 7:30.

Anne and I were the only ones in the whole company who spoke both French and English and we had to translate for the whole company. The crew complimented me when I left. They said, "Your French is excellent but we can't place your accent. You don't have an American accent or a British accent." I said, "Well, we had a Russian art director, a German art director, a set dresser from Normandy and someone else from the South of France, all speaking French with different accents. My accent is a compendium of all that."

Nothing ever worked right. We were supposed to shoot at Versailles but the fountains were turned off and nobody could turn them on. Finally, the morning we were set to go out there, it was pouring rain. The roof of our stage leaked, so the rain came through the roof. The walls were so thin that twice a week, when they had a fair outside, you could hear the music coming in. The result was that we spent days making useless shots to keep going. Suddenly the producer came to me and said, "You're off the picture. John Sturges is coming." They just didn't like what they were seeing on the screen, so without a word, they sent Sturges to take over. He arrived the next day but they asked me to please finish the fashion show I was shooting.

All told, I did about four fifths of it. I didn't shoot the chase through Les Invalides although I had chosen the camera angles. When I got back, we tried to set up an interview with Dore Schary to see what the hell was the problem and to make suggestions about the cutting. Schary refused to let me speak to him. He was the bastard of all times. We stood up and cheered when he was fired from M-G-M. I tried to get my name taken off of it but there are certain rules and I had done most of it. Two disasters came at once, *Red Garters* and *Bedevilled* and that really was a crushing blow.

THE GIRL MOST LIKELY - 1957

Leisen spent many more months unemployed and was convinced his career was over when he was summoned to the briefly revived RKO to discuss a remake of Garson Kanin's *Tom, Dick And Harry*. After a long period of inactivity, General Tire and Rubber had purchased the studio to obtain its backlog of films and for a brief time, re-entered production of new films, albeit most of them remakes of past hits. Of the several that were done, only *The Girl Most Likely* impressed critics as being equal to the earlier version. It was the last film made on the RKO lot prior to its sale to Desilu and as it turned out, Leisen's last film as well.

The whimsical story had a pretty girl, (Jane Powell) getting herself engaged to three men at once and fantasizing what life would be like with each one. Budget limitations kept Leisen from dream sequences as elaborate as he had done in *Lady In The Dark*, but his ideas were fully as imaginative, and the score, written by Hugh Martin and Ralph Blane, was delightful. Gower Champion staged two very colorful production

Jane Powell in the "Crazy Horse" dream sequence from *The Girl Most Likely*.

Leisen and Jane Powell, night shooting at Balboa.

numbers, one at the beach in Balboa, California, the other in a Tijuana bazaar. Leisen's touch remained evident throughout and his love of business to underline a long dialogue scene was demonstrated as Jane Powell unrolled her hair and dreamily tried to decide which of her three beaux to marry.

Leisen found producer William Dozier congenial and might have had a place at RKO had the studio continued. However, Leisen was wearing out. Script Supervisor Pat Miller recalls, "I was telling some friends how much fun it was to work with Mitchell and they said, 'If only you could have known him twenty years ago when he really sparkled.'" Few saw *The Girl Most Likely* however, for though it was completed by mid-'56, it remained unreleased when RKO shut down its distribution facilities. Universal picked it up and released it in January 1958 as a second feature to Disney's *Old Yeller*.

MITCHELL LEISEN: William Dozier was trying to keep RKO going. He called me in and asked me what my fee for a picture would be. I said, "$50,000 for ten weeks' shooting and up to ten weeks preparation free." He said, "I'll give you a straight $3000 per week." Since I worked over twenty weeks, I ended up collecting a lot more money.

Carol Channing was supposed to play Jane Powell's girlfriend but she never showed up for any make-up or wardrobe tests and we got worried. Finally she waltzed into Dozier's office and demanded she be given the starring role. She had just been second banana to Ginger Rogers in a flop called *The First Traveling Saleslady* and she said she didn't mind being second banana to a "big" star, but Jane Powell wasn't big enough. She also had all kinds of stupid gags, like having two girls walk down the street and having one of them fall into an open man hole and disappear. Dozier fired her right on the spot and we were stuck with the picture about to start and no actress. Gower Champion was standing in the office when this happened and he suggested Kaye Ballard, who'd never done a picture before. She worked out fine.

When we start shooting, there were a couple of other companies shooting on the RKO lot, but they finished and we were the only company left. When the studio decided we no longer needed a certain department, it was shut down and if we needed something after that, we had to make do ourselves. It was really eerie.

Jane Powell was a good sport about everything. When we went down to Balboa to shoot the scene where she jumps out of the boat and into the bay, it was October and cold as hell, but she jumped right in like it was bath water. For the scenes of her dripping wet, we soaked the dress in baby oil, which kept her a little warmer.

LEISEN ON TELEVISION

After the debacles of *Red Garters* and *Bedevilled*, his agents urged him to consider television. He had already directed the 1953 Academy Awards broadcast and did not want to do live TV, but by the late '50s, the medium was moving its focus from New York to Hollywood and from live programming to filmed. Its impact on theatre attendance had been so profound that working in television was often the kiss of death as far as future film work was concerned. Yet there were a few programs, such as *G.E. Theater* (produced by the powerful talent agency, MCA) which

Snapshot of Fred MacMurray, Pat Crowley and Mitchell Leisen on the set of "The Bachelor's Bride," and episode of *G.E. Theater,* Leisen's first filmed television show.

were of sufficient quality to attract the regular participation of important film stars. Fred MacMurray had signed to make his filmed television debut on a G.E. episode called "Bachelor's Bride" and as a favor to him, Leisen agreed to direct it.

The program aired late in 1955 and received lukewarm reviews dampening Leisen's enthusiasm about the new medium. Although G.E.'s schedule of two days of rehearsal and three days of shooting was extremely generous by industry standards, getting 24 minutes of film in a week was still faster than Leisen was used to working. He found the standards of that script and the ones he was offered afterwards to be very low and he turned his back on television when he was offered *The Girl Most Likely.*

In 1958, however, he was lured by an offer to direct three episodes of *Shirley Temple's Storybook,* one of the most expensive and prestigious series on the air at that time. In addition to directing Temple's introductions to all of the episodes, he directed three episodes entirely: "Sleeping Beauty", "Hiawatha" and "Mother Goose". Shot on a soundstage, "Hiawatha" employed a harsh, contrasty lighting scheme producing a look different from anything he'd done earlier in feature films. It gave the adaptation of Longfellow's epic poem an almost surrealistic quality. "Mother Goose", shot in 'Columbia Color' contained charming performances by Elsa Lanchester, Carleton Carpenter and Shirley Temple.

MITCHELL LEISEN: Getting a halfway decent show on the air with the kind of schedules and budgets we had to work with took every trick I'd ever learned in all the years I'd been making pictures, but it was a challenge and I enjoyed it. I found Shirley Temple to be a very conscientious, hardworking woman with no great drive to recapture her former glory. She's very short and when we were filming the introductions to the various episodes, I went to Western Costume and got out all of Carmen Miranda's old platform wedgies. They were hideous things, gold plated alligator skin encrusted with glass jewels, but they literally made Shirley five or six inches taller. I took her to Don Loper's salon to have gowns made with long, full skirts that covered everything.

MARVIN WALD: Alvin Cooperman conceived the idea of the *Shirley Temple Storybook*. She was a housewife in Northern California and he sold her on the idea that she would just have to come to Los Angeles one day a week to film the introductions. After she got into it, she said, "I'd like to act in something with my children." They had been watching her in all her old movies on TV and thought that acting would be fun.

Cooperman used to play tennis with Henry Greenburg who I knew and he told Henry he was desperate for an idea for Shirley and her kids. I had this idea about "Mother Goose" and Henry offered to introduce me to Alvin but only if I shared the credit with him and gave him half the money. I had to agree since there was no other way I could meet Cooperman. Originally Mother Goose's role was bigger and Shirley's part of Polly was rather minor but after she read the script, she told Cooperman, "I love it and I want my part built up." So I added some things like the Commedia de larte sequence for her and that meant I had to cut some of Elsa Lanchester's scenes. She was a trooper and she didn't complain.

Did Leisen work with you on the script?

No, not at all. I'd write something and Cooperman would take it to Shirley and he'd come back and tell me what she thought. I went on the set to watch the dance numbers but I didn't do any rewriting while they were filming. Shirley hadn't danced in some years and she wasn't too limber at first but she got into it. She did her own singing. Her three kids were cranky and whining all day. They hated waiting around. She thought that was very funny and said, "You think being a child actor is fun. This is what I had to do for years." I don't think they ever brought it up again.

Mitchell was charming and enthusiastic throughout. I was a little surprised he was doing television but I didn't say anything. We worked on it about a month, counting the rehearsal time. When they had a screening for the company at NBC, Shirley had gone back home. Charles Laughton came and was shocked to see how much of his wife's part had been cut. He went over to Mitch and said, "You are a swine, sir. You cut out so much and "Mother Goose" is the title role. If I weren't a gentleman, I'd thrash you." Mitch didn't lose his cool, He just said, "I shot the script they gave me. And after all, Shirley Temple is the star of the series."

RODDY MCDOWELL: I was living in New York when they offered me the episode, "People Are The Same All Over", doing theater and live television. I hadn't been in front of a motion picture camera in about six years. I wasn't too interested until they told me who was going to direct it and then I said I'd do it on one condition: that Mitch would agree to show me his prints of *Death Takes A Holiday* and *Murder At The Vanities*. (I should have asked for *Cradle Song* too!)

Mitch agreed and he gave a dinner party for me and showed the films. Working with him was a delight. I felt I learned so much about comedy in that week, even though the story was a drama. And I felt he had a very definite air of the '30s about him.

Did you feel that he was longing for those days?

No. He was looking ahead, full of plans. He was going to Las Vegas to direct a night club show.

MITCHELL LEISEN: My favorite *Twilight Zone* was "The 16mm Shrine", which starred Ida Lupino as a faded movie queen. I'd known Ida at

Roddy McDowell and Susan Oliver in "People Are The Same All Over" episode of *The Twilight Zone.*

Paramount and in the meantime, she'd become a very important television director in her own right. On the first day, Ida came to me and said, "Listen, Mitch, let's get this straight. I'm the actress and you're the director. I'll do anything you tell me but I'm going to steal from you like crazy."

Harry Tugend, who had produced *Practically Yours, Golden Earrings* and *Darling, How Could You?* persuaded Leisen to return to *G.E. Theater* for a number of episodes filmed in 1958 and 1959. Ray Milland brought him into the *Markham* company for seventeen episodes and his agents got him assignments on *Pete And Gladys, Thriller, Wagon Train* and *Follow The Sun.*

Within the rigid cost restrictions of television, Leisen tried to maintain the same high standards for which he had been known in features and gave the illusion of much higher production values that the budgets had really allowed. His perfectionism undaunted, he once wrote a

Ida Lupino and John Clarke in the *Twilight Zone* episode, "The 16mm Shrine."

memo to the prop man for the three day shoot of *The Maureen O'Hara Show* pilot (which didn't sell).

> "Since the doors of the closets will be open, there must be clothes inside, but they must be the right clothes, not any old thing borrowed from studio wardrobe. Try to borrow items from the personal wardrobes of Maureen O'Hara and Tony Randall, if that is not possible, find out their sizes and make sure everything in the closet is the correct size. Get sporty outfits for her and cocktail dresses since she's a sophisticated woman."

Leisen pragmatically accepted the routine nature of these television assignments but a few turned out to be outstanding. One *G. E. Theatre* episode entitled "The Incredible Jewel Robbery" starred Harpo and Chico Marx and was filmed entirely in pantomime. Groucho turned up for the final scene and it was the last appearance of the three together in any medium. On another *G.E. Theatre*, Leisen directed Maurice Evans and Piper Laurie in an act of George Bernard Shaw's *Caesar And Cleopatra*.

George
Bernard
Shaw's
*Caesar And
Cleopatra*
with
Maurice
Evans and
Piper Laurie
on *G.E.
Theater*.

As always, there were interesting projects that were never realized. In 1960, Revue producer William Frye conceived an hour long situation comedy series entitled *Mother Climbed Trees* to star Joan Fontaine and be directed by Leisen. The pilot for the series was never made although Leisen later directed a half hour *G.E. Theatre* episode based on the same material starring Jan Clayton.

Probably most important of all of Leisen's television films is an hour long *Thriller* episode, "Worse Than Murder". John Baxter noted how this film carried Leisen's fascination with role reversal farther than any of his theatrically released films. Writing in the February 1966 issue of *Film Digest*, Baxter stated:

"Worse Than Murder" is, in many ways, a summation of all Leisen's films, a final statement of a bizarre attitude. Here finally his cynicism is allowed full play. Constance Ford is the quintessence of every tough, cynical, masculine woman in his earlier films, a Goddard without charm, a Colbert without humor, a Lombard without love...Arrogantly she sleeps with her landlord, in return for help and free board—and in the after-sex scene, it is she who lies replete and contented on the bed, while her lover sits nervously on the edge. No artist ever had a better summation of his work. "Worse Than Murder" is the essence of Leisen, his final, utterly paralyzing statement.

RAY MILLAND: I was co-producer of my second television series, *Markham,* which I loathed. We kept trying out new directors, all of whom went over schedule and over budget and the final results were so bad there was nothing to show for it. Finally I got to the end of my tether, so I went to Lew Wasserman and told him I wanted to bring Mitch in. He said, "But he's the most expensive director in the business!" I said, "Not anymore, he's been doing television."

We brought Mitch in on a trial basis for one show, and he did so well that we kept him for the rest of the season. He stayed on schedule and under budget and the shows he directed were by far the best of the lot. He could make the tackiest sets look lavish just by the way he lit them, and he did a lot to help out the worst of scripts. There was always something of the old grand manner about Mitch, even though he was just doing television. Every day when we finished shooting, Mitch's chauffeur would come in, dressed in uniform, and hand Mitch his portable bar. Mitch would mix himself a Bloody Mary and sit on the set all alone, thinking about the next day's work.

CONSTANCE MOORE: I guested on two episodes of *Markham* that Mitch directed and I can remember walking on the set the first day and having the feeling that I'd been there before. It was all so familiar and I couldn't understand why. Then I realized that the tea service was Mitch's, the ashtrays and the other accessories had all come out of Mitch's apartments. I started to rib Mitch about it and he said, "Sh, don't let anybody know, but I had to do it, nothing in the prop department was right."

Mitchell Leisen worked more consistently in television for three years than he ever had in feature films but his great burst of activity came

Jeanie Cooper and Barbara Hale in Leisen's "Night Club" an all female episode of *G.E. Theater.*

quickly to an end when he was hospitalized for bleeding ulcers and emphysema. *Markham* and *G.E. Theatre* both went off the air and after Leisen refused to go back and re-shoot part of the *Mother Climbs Trees* episode, he didn't get any more offers from Revue. He then attempted, without success to join the staff of *My Three Sons.*

FRED MACMURRAY: He sent me a telegram asking for the job. He was, well, you know, a homosexual and he had gotten into some trouble on a picture he was making in Europe. With the three young boys we had working on the show, I just didn't think it was right. So I never answered the telegram.

Forty years of incessant hard work and frequent illness had taken their toll, and by his early sixties, Leisen lacked the strength to go on. He suffered from chronic heart troubles (alleviated somewhat by a pacemaker) and emphysema, so that even a short walk taxed him. Circulatory problems numbed his limbs and impaired the sight of one eye, while a cataract clouded over the other.

He told his agents he considered himself retired from directing, but he did work several days on a project called *Here's Las Vegas* as a favor to old friends. One sequence of Constance Moore singing ended with her raising a wineglass in a toast, another was a striptease of Jayne Mansfield (who Leisen characterized as a "pig.") Some of his footage ended up in a luridly advertised compilation entitled *Spree* and Leisen was listed as one of the directors, much to his chagrin.

As a favor to another old friend, Albert McCleery (who had written *The Lady Is Willing*) Leisen created the costumes for an ambitious 1963 pilot, *Alexander The Great,* which was never sold. He helped Broder run Leisen Enterprises and kept a workroom going making gowns for Dorothy Lamour, Constance Moore, Mamie Van Doren and Marilyn Maxwell.

Then suddenly in 1966, an old colleague from *G.E. Theatre,* Doug Benton, invited Leisen to do three episodes of *The Girl From U.N.C.L.E.* at M-G-M. Although he was now so weak that he had to spend a week in bed after each show, Leisen plunged into his last assignments with characteristic vigor and the three programs he directed were considered excellent for their genre.

DOUGLAS BENTON: I was Harry Tugend's associate on a lot of *G.E. Theatre* shows that Mitch directed and I knew how good he was. When it came to producing *The Girl From U.N.C.L.E.,* I was really in a spot because I just couldn't get the kind of production values the studio expected with the budget we had. I knew there was only one person who could bail me out and that was Mitch. Mitch insisted that he had retired, but I knew he still wanted to work, and it wasn't hard to persuade him to come back.

God, he was good. I don't think he ever knew quite how good he was. He knew this was television and he adjusted to our limitations pretty well. He always wanted to cover everything with two cameras on the day he did the action stuff and it was really beautiful. He always managed to get so far ahead of schedule that he could take one sequence and shoot it right, just the way he would in a movie, with plenty of camera movement and really beautiful composition.

I really miss him. There are times when I want to go out to the Motion Picture Country Home, drag him out of bed and make him do another show for us. He was really tops.

When you were doing television, did you ever say, "You have to keep your hand in, even if your heart's not in it?"

MITCHELL LEISEN: I don't remember, maybe I did. Of course, it wasn't the same. Before was The Golden Era. Before we had the best writers, the greatest stars, the most expert crews and we had enough money to work with to really do something big when we wanted to. Those days are gone and they'll never come back, but I am satisfied to know that I was able to adjust to the new medium and do a good job on its terms.

What are your personal favorites among your own films?

MITCHELL LEISEN: *Cradle Song,* certainly, *Death Takes A Holiday, Swing High, Swing Low, Hold Back The Dawn, To Each His Own. The Eagle And The Hawk,* the way it was originally. *Remember The Night.* Those made me the happiest when I saw them again, but I'm quite proud of some of the others too.

THE RETIREMENT YEARS

The end of Mitchell Leisen's life was very unhappy. More alone than ever and increasingly unable to create and thus distract himself, he passed several empty years, superficially busy with Leisen Enterprises. Forgotten by the industry that had made him great, he maintained his friendships with Dorothy Lamour, Constance Moore and Phyllis Seaton. Enough people rented his rehearsal hall to keep it going and he made some dresses and altered others to fit his friends. Then I came along with the Oral History grant and he devoted many hours to working with me.

Bearded, long-haired and generally wearing tie-dyed hippy clothes, my appearance must have been painful to this still immaculately groomed man, but he was kind to me and never said anything about it, although for Christmas he gave me the kind of knit shirt he wore. On the few occasions when we went somewhere together in public, he went to great lengths to describe the Oral History we were doing to any acquaintance he ran into lest that person might mistakenly think I was the lover of the moment.

Marlene Dietrich came to see him one evening in the apartment with far from cheerful news. All she wanted to talk about was the circulatory problem in his left leg that went back to his childhood clubfoot operation. Dietrich pulled up her pants to reveal ace bandages on her legs and said morbidly that she thought they too would have to be amputated.

Early in 1970, Leisen was hospitalized for gangrene in his left leg. Suddenly Natalie Visart was back in the picture. She had always stayed in touch with Leisen and Eleanor Broder in her twenty five years of marriage to Dwight Taylor. After some years on the East Coast and an increasingly difficult marriage, Natalie longed to get out of the cold weather and when interior decorator Gladys Belzer (Loretta Young's mother) offered her a job, she decided on an extended visit to California. She and Eleanor Broder kept me up to date on Leisen's medical condition. Finally it was necessary to amputate his leg and he was moved to the Motion Picture Country Home. Eleanor struggled to keep Leisen Enterprises in business for some time, but when it became clear that he would never be strong enough to leave the Home, she sold the furniture and closed up shop.

At first I was not allowed to visit, but soon Natalie and I were driving out once or twice a week and I was able to complete my interviews. The two years he spent at the Home were fraught with incessant physical pain but there were a few bright moments; Ray Milland appeared one day with a cocktail shaker full of Bloody Marys; another time Natalie brought Katherine DeMille and Myrna Loy out. "Myrna always had legs like a piano," was Leisen's comment. Dorothy Lamour and Phyllis Seaton came too. These visits were not hard on Leisen's pride since these ladies had seen him in recent years and knew of his emaciated condition. Constance Moore got permission for Mitchell to spend several weekends at her home and also appeared when there was a screening of *Take A Letter Darling* in the Theatre at the Home. Connie Moore was always a most accommodating friend. I once asked her why her grand piano was emerald green. She replied that one day Mitchell had gotten the idea they should paint it and she said, "OK, we'll paint it" and she even helped him do the work.

I received a call one day from an office at Universal Studios. The secretary explained that Olivia de Havilland wanted me to drive her out to the Home to see Mitchell. I agreed and at first Mitchell did too. Then he had second thoughts and excitedly told his nurse that a lady was coming to see him and he didn't want to see her and she should telephone me and call the whole thing off. The nurse apparently thought the lady he was referring to was Natalie and after calming him down, did nothing about it.

I picked up Olivia at the Beverly Hills Hotel. When I had met her a few months earlier in Paris, her hair had been a pretty strawberry blonde, causing her to look very different. Now Universal had dyed it back to the familiar brown, a fur coat covered a few extra pounds, and when we arrived, she put on some red lipstick making her look startlingly like she had in *To Each His Own.* "Give me a minute, David." she said. She took several deep breaths, put on a radiant smile and flung open the door to Mitchell's room. "Mitch, darling" she cried, in a voice and manner that was her own but with a little feeling of the Lorraine Sheldon-Margo Channing glamorous star thrown in.

She acted as if she and Mitchell were still in the same positions in life they had been in in 1945. She talked of the roles she was being offered and asked his advice on what part she should do next. She talked of her home in Paris and asked him how to redecorate it. (Although she had no real plans to redecorate.) He talked about when he'd lived in Paris with Stella. She gave him a magnum of champagne and a pound of caviar, knowing full well that he could eat neither. He accepted them with glee. She knew instinctively the kindest way to deal with the 80 pound body and the missing leg was to make no mention of them. Two hours passed like a moment and when it was time for his lunch, she wheeled him into the dining room, placed him at the assigned spot and leaned from behind him to give him a kiss as every eye in the place looked on. The next day she was due to go back to Paris but she had the limousine take her back to see Mitchell one last time before going to the airport.

The effect of her visits on his morale was miraculous and his physical condition improved markedly. In May of 1972, Delta Kappa Alpha, the cinema fraternity of USC, had a special day to honor Leisen as part of a series entitled "Comedy in the Thirties." Leisen's doctors allowed him to attend, and after a most hearty welcome following *Easy Living,* he discussed his films with the student audience for over an hour. Leisen could still rise to his former brilliance on occasions like this.

His physical condition continued to weaken, however. In September he suffered a stroke which the doctors predicted would prove fatal, but somehow he rallied, and the cause of his death, several weeks later, was emphysema.

George and Phyllis Seaton made all the arrangements for the funeral, and the chapel at All Saints' Episcopal Church of Beverly Hills was jammed to capacity with many of the behind-the-scenes personnel that Leisen had worked with: technicians, hairdressers and researchers, but there was little star-power in evidence. Olivia de Havilland, John Lund and Constance Moore attended; Barbara Stanwyck sent flowers; Dorothy Lamour and Ray Milland, both tied to commitments in the East, sent Eleanor Broder their condolences.

Constance Moore gave a lovely luncheon afterwards and it was a very happy occasion with many old friends reunited for the first time in years. We all felt relief that his ordeal was finally over.

The relationships that came to me as a result of this project continued to enrich my life long after it was over. I got another Oral History Grant to interview George Seaton. Dwight Taylor closed up his Connecticut home and moved to California to be with Natalie. The Taylors had suffered severe financial reversals throughout their marriage but they lived in great style in an apartment owned by Natalie's old friend, photographer John Engstead. Natalie continued to work for Mrs. Belzer who loaned her beautiful furniture for the apartment. When she would suddenly decide she needed a table from the Taylor apartment for a home she was decorating, Mrs. Belzer would send a truck over to pick it up along with another nice table to take its place.

Often I would arrange screenings of films written by Dwight, designed by Natalie or starring Myrna Loy. Myrna didn't especially like watching her old movies but she enjoyed evenings with the Taylors when she was in California so she went along. After we watched *Parnell* together, we all thought it was very good and couldn't understand why it had been such a flop. Myrna even agreed to see *When Tomorrow Comes* despite her lifelong disagreement with Irene Dunne's politics. Afterwards, she kept ribbing Dwight, saying, "Why didn't you write scripts like that for me, Dwight?"

One day Natalie called me with the horrible news that her beloved son Peter had been killed in a San Francisco gay-bashing. She asked me to be one of the pall-bearers; another was Loretta Young's son Christopher. On the other side of the ledger was the birth of Laurel Taylor's beautiful daughter Chloe. Increasingly Natalie suffered, as Mitchell had, from emphysema and eventually she and Dwight moved to the Motion Picture Home where they died in the mid '80s.

POSTSCRIPT

The first edition of this book was only available for a short time yet it seems to have been widely read, judging by all the times it has been quoted. I have always been happy whenever it was quoted, for I could see that I succeeded to some extent in making Leisen's work known. Yet I still get the general feeling that Leisen is best remembered for his blatant homosexual behavior, and for having directed five films which, despite his participation, are usually attributed to their writers, Preston Sturges and Charles Brackett and Billy Wilder. Leisen was a Renaissance man in the 20th Century, so skillful in so many fields that he never quite settled down to become predominate in any one of them. Motion pictures, by their very nature more complex than any other medium, offered him the opportunity to express all his complex, bizarre and beautiful concepts. If they did not solve his personal unhappiness, they kept him busy, and made him rich and famous (at least for a time). These cinematic expressions of Leisen's talent, his taste and his troubled soul mark a lasting contribution in the history of American motion pictures.

FILMOGRAPHY

Only those films for which Leisen was credited and those which he clearly remembered making have been listed in this filmography. He certainly had a hand in at least several other Paramount and DeMille films, but no attempt has been made to guess what these films were, nor do we speculate about the number of films in which he appeared as an extra or bit player. The feature films are listed in order of release, the television shows in the order of production. All films were released by Paramount unless otherwise noted.

MALE AND FEMALE
Producer-Director: Cecil B. DeMille
Cinematographer: Alvin Wyckoff
Costumes: "When I was A King of Babylon and You Were A Christian Slave" *sequence:* Mitchell Leisen
Release date: November 30, 1919
Cast: Gloria Swanson, Thomas Meighan, Bebe Daniels, Lila Lee

CONRAD IN QUEST OF HIS YOUTH
Director: William DeMille
Written by: Olga Printzlau
Set Decorations: Mitchell Leisen
Release Date: November, 1920

MIDSUMMER MADNESS
Producer-Director: William DeMille
Written by: Olga Printzlau
Production Manager: Mitchell Leisen

Release date: December, 1920
Cast: Lila Lee, Conrad Nagel, Lois Wilson

FORBIDDEN FRUIT
Producer-Director: Cecil B. DeMille
Cinematographer: Alvin Wyckoff
Costumes for Cinderella Ball Sequence: Mitchell Leisen and Natasha Rambova
Release date: February 12, 1921
Cast: Agnes Ayres, Theodore Roberts, Kathlyn Williams

ROBIN HOOD (United Artists)
Director: Allan Dwan
Art Direction: Wilford Buckland
Costumes: Mitchell Leisen
Release date: November 5, 1922
Cast: Douglas Fairbanks, Enid Bennett

ROSITA (United Artists)
Director: Ernst Lubitsch
Producer: Mary Pickford
Cinematographer: Charles Rosher
Costumes: Mitchell Leisen
Art Director: William Cameron Menzies
Release Date: September 3, 1923

THE COURTSHIP OF MILES STANDISH (Associated Artists)
Director: Frederick Sullivan
Written by: Al Ray
Cinematographer: George Rizard
Costumes: Mitchell Leisen
Release date: December 30, 1923
Cast: Charles Ray, Enid Bennett, E. Alyn Warren

THE THIEF OF BAGDAD (United Artists)
Director: Raoul Walsh
Art Direction: William Cameron Menzies
Costumes: Mitchell Leisen
Release date: March 23, 1924
Cast: Douglas Fairbanks, Anna May Wong

FAUST
Director: Ernst Lubitsch
Cast: Mary Pickford
Leisen made a costume for Mary Pickford, who filmed a test scene as Marguerite under the direction of Lubitsch. He designed several other costumes and was about to start making them when Pickford decided not to make the films.

DOROTHY VERNON OF HADDON HALL (United Artists)

Director: Marshall Neilan
Producer: Mary Pickford
Costumes: Mitchell Leisen
Release date: May 25, 1924
Cast: Mary Pickford, Allan Forrest, Estelle Taylor

THE ROAD TO YESTERDAY (DeMille-Producers Distributing Corp.)

Producer-Director: Cecil B. DeMille
Written by: Jeanie Macpherson, Beulah Marie Dix
Cinematographer: Peverell Marley
Art Direction: Paul Iribe, Max Parker, Anton Grot
Set Decoration: Mitchell Leisen
Release date: November 15, 1925
Cast: Joseph Schildkraut, Jetta Goudal, Vera Reynolds, William Boyd

THE VOLGA BOATMAN (DeMille-Producers Distributing Corp.)

Director: Cecil B. DeMille
Written by: Lenore J. Coffee
Cinematographers: Arthur Miller, Peverell Marley
Art Direction: Max Parker, Mitchell Leisen, Anton Grot
Costumes: Adrian
Release date: April 4, 1926
Cast: William Boyd, Elinor Fair, Julia Faye

HIS DOG (DeMille-Pathe)

Director: Karl Brown
Written by: Olga Printzlau
Cinematographer: Fred Westerberg
Art Direction: Mitchell Leisen, Edward Jewell
Costumes: Adrian
Release date: July 25, 1927

THE FIGHTING EAGLE (DeMille-Pathe)

Director: Donald Crisp
Written by: Douglas Z. Doty
Cinematographer: Peverell Marley
Art Director: Mitchell Leisen
Costumes: Adrian
Release date: August 29, 1927

THE ANGEL OF BROADWAY (DeMille-Pathe)

Director: Lois Weber
Author: Lenore J. Coffee
Cinematographer: Arthur J. Miller
Art director: Mitchell Leisen
Costumes: Adrian
Release date: October 3, 1927

THE WISE WIFE (DeMille-Pathe)
Director: E. Mason Hopper
Written by: Zelda Sears, Tay Garnett
Cinematographer: rank Good
Art Direction: Mitchell Leisen
Costumes: Adrian
Release date: October 24, 1927

DRESS PARADE (DeMille - Pathe)
Director: Donald Crisp
Author: Douglas Z. Doty
Photographer: Peverell Marley
Art Director: Mitchell Leisen
Costumes: Adrian
Release date: October 27, 1927

THE FORBIDDEN WOMAN (DeMille - Pathe)
Director: Paul L. Stein
Author: Clara Berenger
Cinematographer: David Abel
Art Director: Mitchell Leisen, Wilfred Buckland
Costumes: Adrian
Release date: October 29, 1927

THE KING OF KINGS (DeMille - Producers Distributing Corp.)
Producer-Director: Cecil B. DeMille
Written by: Jeanie Macpherson
Cinematographer: Peverell Marley
Art Direction: Mitchell Leisen, Anton Grot (and Paul Iribe)
Costumes: Earl Luick, Gwen Wakeling
Release date: October, 1927

CHICAGO (DeMille - Pathe)
Director: Frank Urson
Author: Lenore J. Coffee
Art Direction: Mitchell Leisen
Costumes: Adrian
Release date: March 4, 1928

POWER (Pathe)
Director: Howard Higgin
Written by: Tay Garnett
Cinematographer: Peverell Marley
Art Direction: Mitchell Leisen
Release date: September 23, 1928

CELEBRITY (DeMille - Pathe)
Director-Screenplay: Tay Garnett
Cinematographer: Peverell Marley
Art Direction: Mitchell Leisen
Release date: October 7, 1928

SHOW FOLKS (Pathe)
Director: Paul L. Stein
Written by: Jack Jungmeyer, George Dromgold
Cinematographer: Peverell Marley, David Abel
Art Direction: Mitchell Leisen
Release date: October 21, 1928

LOVE OVER NIGHT (Pathe)
Director: Edward H. Griffith
Written by: George Dromgold
Cinematographer: John J. Mescall
Art Direction: Mitchell Leisen
Release date: November 25, 1928

THE GODLESS GIRL (DeMille - Pathe)
Director: Cecil B. DeMille
Written by: Jeanie Macpherson
Cinematographer: Peverell Marley
Art Direction: Mitchell Leisen
Costumes: Adrian
Release date: March 31, 1929

DYNAMITE (MGM)
Producer - Director: Cecil B. DeMille
Written by: Jeanie Macpherson
Cinematographer: Peverell Marley
Assistant Director: Mitchell Leisen
Art Direction: Cedric Gibbons, Mitchell Leisen
Gowns: Adrian
Release date: December 13, 1929

MADAM SATAN (MGM)
Producer-Director: Cecil B. DeMille
Assistant Director: Mitchell Leisen
Cinematographer: Harold Rosson
Written by: Jeanie Macpherson, Gladys Unger, Elsie Janis
Costumes: Adrian
Release date: September 20, 1930

THE SQUAW MAN (MGM)
Producer-Director: Cecil B. DeMille

Written by: Lucien Hubbard, Lenore J. Coffee, Elsie Janis
Cinematographer: Harold Rosson
Assistant Director and Art Director: Mitchell Leisen
Release date: September 19, 1931
Cast: Warner Baxter, Lupe Velez, Eleanor Boardman

THE SIGN OF THE CROSS
Producer-Director: Cecil B. DeMille
Written by: Waldemar Young, Sidney Buchman
Edited by: Anne Bauchens
Cinematographer: Karl Struss
Assistant Director, Art Direction and Costumes: Mitchell Leisen
Release date: December 1932
Running time: 115 mins.
Cast: Claudette Colbert, Fredric March, Elissa Landi

TONIGHT IS OURS
(working title: THE QUEEN WAS IN THE PARLOUR)
Director: Stuart Walker; *Associate Director:* Mitchell Leisen; *Adaptor and Dialoguer:* Edwin Justus Mayer; *Based on:* "The Queen Was In The Parlour" by Noel Coward; *Cinematographer:* Karl Struss; *Costume Design:* Travis Banton.
Shooting dates: November 23 - December 16, 1932
Release date: January 21, 1933
Running time: 75 mins.
Cast: SABIEN PASTAL: Fredric March; NADYA: Claudette Colbert; GRAND DUCHESS EMILIE: Alison Skipworth; PRINCE KERI: Paul Cavanaugh; GENERAL KRISH: Arthur Byron; ZANA: Ethel Griffies; SEMINOFF: Clay Clement; ALEX: Warburton Gamble; LEADER OF MOB: Edwin Maxwell.
Synopsis: Nadya meets Sabien Pastal at a masked ball and they fall in love. She tells him that she had been a duchess in her native ruritanian land, but had fled to Paris upon the death of her husband and never intends to return. She and Sabien plan to marry but she is forced to return home and assume the duties of queen. A year passes during which the country is torn by revolution and Nadya plans to marry Prince Keri, but Sabien comes back into her life and when the revolutionaries demand she marry a commoner; she chooses Sabien.

THE EAGLE AND THE HAWK
Director: Stuart Walker; *Associate Director:* Mitchell Leisen; *Producer:* Bayard Veiller; *Written by:* Bogart Rogers, Seton Miller; *Based on:* "Death In the Morning" by John Monk Saunders; *Cinematographer:* Harry Fishbeck.
Shooting dates: February 27 - April 5, 1933
Release date: May 6, 1933
Running time: 68 mins., reedited in 1939 to 64 mins.
Cast: JEREMIAH YOUNG: Fredric March; HENRY CROCKER: Cary Grant;

Leisen's sketch for Mary Pickford as Marguerite in *Faust* which was abandoned.

MIKE RICHARDS: Jack Oakie; THE BEAUTIFUL LADY: Carole Lombard; MAJOR DUNHAM: Sir Guy Standing; HOGAN: Forrester Harvey; JOHN STEVENS: Kenneth Howell; KINGSFORD: Leyland Hodgson; LADY ERSKINE: Virginia Hammond; GENERAL: Craufurd Kent; TOMMY: Douglas Scott; MAJOR KRUPPMAN: Robert Manning; FANNY: Adrienne D'Ambricourt; FRENCH GENERAL'S AIDE: Jacques Jou - Jerville; FLIGHT SERGEANT: Russell Scott; FRENCH GENERAL: Paul Cremonesi.

Synopsis: Jeremiah Young is a widely admired aviation hero of World War I although he suffers great anguish over the many men he has killed. Given a leave, he goes to Paris but can find no peace of mind. One night at a party, he meets the Beautiful Lady who listens sympathetically to his plight and spends the night with him, but disappears before he awakens the next morning. Returning to the front, he finally commits suicide ingloriously by shooting himself, but his pal, Harry Crocker puts his body in his plane and sends it up so that when it crashes, it appears that Young has died heroically. Years pass and we see a memorial to Young and Crocker, who has become an alcoholic because of guilt over his deception.

CRADLE SONG
Director: Mitchell Leisen; *Associate Director:* Nina Moise;
Producer: E. Lloyd Sheldon; *Written by:* Marc Connelly, Frank Partos, Robert
Sparks; *Based on:* the play by C. M. Martinez Sierra; *Editor:* Anne Bauchens;
Cinematographer: Charles Lang; *Art Direction:* Wiard Ihnen;
Costume Design: Edith Head.
Shooting dates: September 5 - 29, 1933
Release date: November 19, 1933   *Running time:* 76 mins.
Cast: JOANNA: Dorothea Wieck; TERESA: Evelyn Venable; THE DOCTOR: Sir
Guy Standing; THE PRIORESS: Louise Dresser; ANTONIO: Kent Taylor;
MARCELLA: Gertrude Michael; THE VICARESS: Georgia Caine; ALBERTO:
Dickie Moore; SAGRARIO: Nydia Westman; INES: Marion Ballou; MISTRESS
OF NOVICES: Eleanor Wesselhoeft; MARIA LUCIA: Gail Patrick; THE MAYOR:
Howard Lang; CHRISTINA: Diane Sinclair; TORNERO # 1: Gertrude Norman.
Synopsis: Joanna enters a convent but cannot find peace because of longing for her
younger brothers and sisters. A foundling is left at the convent. The nuns adopt
her and name her Teresa. As Teresa approaches womanhood, Joanna hopes that
she too will become a nun, but the Doctor has introduced her to the kindly
Antonio, and they decide to marry leaving Joanna alone with the comfort of her
faith.

DEATH TAKES A HOLIDAY
Director: Mitchell Leisen; *Producer:* E. Lloyd Sheldon; *Written by:* Maxwell Ander-
son, Gladys Lehman, Walter Ferris; *Based on:* the play by Maxwell Anderson
adapted from a play by Alberto Casella; *Cinematographer:* Charles Lang; *Art
Direction:* Ernst Fegte.
Shooting dates: November 4 - December 4, 1933
Release date: February 23, 1934   *Running time:* 78 mins.
Cast: PRINCE SIRKI: Fredric March; GRAZIA: Evelyn Venable; DUKE
LAMBERT: Sir Guy Standing; ALDA: Katherine Alexander; RHODA: Gail
Patrick; STEPHANIE: Helen Westley; PRINCESS MARIA: Kathleen Howard;
CORRADO: Kent Taylor; BARON CESAREA: Henry Travers; ERIC: G.P.
Huntley, Jr.;
FEDELE: Otto Hoffmann; DOCTOR VALLE: Edward Van Sloan; PIETRO:
Hector Sarno; VENDOR: Frank Yaconelli; MAID: Anna De Linsky.
Synopsis: Death comes to Earth to find why men fear him. He assumes the form of
the recently deceased Prince Sirki and during the next three days, no man, plant
or animal dies as Sirki tries to find any element of life as profound as death. At
the end of the third day, he finds true love in Grazia, and as he returns, he realizes
that love is as great as death.

BOLERO
Director: Wesley Ruggles; *Authors:* Carey Wilson, Kubec Glasman, Ruth Ridenour;
Cinematographer: Leo Tover.
Release date: March, 1934
Cast: George Raft, Carole Lombard
(Leisen reshot the dance number at the end of the picture)

MURDER AT THE VANITIES

Director: Mitchell Leisen; *Producer:* E. Lloyd Sheldon; *Written by:* Carey Wilson, Joseph Gollomb, Sam Hellman; *Based on:* the play by Earl Carroll and Rufus King; *Cinematographer:* Leo Tover; *Music:* Leo Robin and Ralph Rainger.

Shooting dates: February 5 - March 12, 1934

Release date: May 18, 1934

Running time: 89 mins.

Cast: ERIC LANDER: Carl Brisson; BILL MURDOCK: Victor McLaglen; JACK ELLERY: Jack Oakie; ANN WARE: Kitty Carlisle; NORMA WATSON: Dorothy Stickney; RITA ROSS: Gertrude Michael; MRS. HELENE SMITH: Jessie Ralph; HOMER BOOTHBY: Charles B. Middleton; SADIE EVANS: Gail Patrick; DR. SAUNDERS: Donald Meek; WALSH: Otto Hoffmann; BEN: Charles McAvoy; BERYL: Beryl Wallace; VIVIEN: Barbara Fritchie; NANCY: Toby Wing; GWEN: Gwenllian Gill; EARL CARROLL GIRLS: Leda Necova, Ernestine Anderson, Anya Taranda, Laurie Shevlin, Wanda Perry, Ruth Hilliard, Evelyn Kelly, Constance Jordan, Dorothy Dawes, Marion Callahan.

Synopsis: Two murders occur on the opening night of Earl Carroll's Vanities, but stage manager Jack Ellery manages to keep the show going and the culprit is apprehended after the final curtain.

BEHOLD MY WIFE

Director: Mitchell Leisen; *Producer:* B. P. Shulberg; *Written by:* Grover Jones, Vincent Lawrence; *Based on:* "Translation of a Savage" by Sir. Gilbert Parker; *Cinematographer:* Leon Shamroy.

Shooting dates: September 26 - October 26, 1934

Release date: February 16, 1935

Running time: 79 mins.

Cast: TONITA STORMCLOUD: Sylvia Sidney; MICHAEL CARTER: Gene Raymond; DIANA CARTER - CURSON: Juliette Compton; MRS. CARTER: Laura Hope Crews; MR. CARTER: H. B. Warner; BOB PRENTICE: Monroe Owsley; JIM CURSON: Kenneth Thomson; MARY WHITE: Ann Sheridan; MRS. SYKES: Charlotte Granville; PETE: Dean Jagger; JUAN STORMCLOUD: Charles B. Middleton; BENSON: Eric Blore; JENKINS: Ralph Remley; GIBSON: Cecil Weston; BRYAN: Dewey Robinson; POLICE CAPTAIN: Charles Wilson; CONNOLLY: Edward Gargan; MATTINGLY: Olin Howland; MEDICINE MAN: Greg Whitespear; INDIAN CHIEF: Jim Thorpe.

Synopsis: Mary White commits suicide when she learns that the family of her fiance, Michael Carter is opposed to their marriage. Michael marries Tonita Stormcloud on the rebound and encounters much opposition from his family but they are eventually reconciled.

FOUR HOURS TO KILL

Director: Mitchell Leisen; *Producer:* Arthur Hornblow Jr.; *Written by:* Norman Krasna; *Based on:* his play, "Small Miracle"; *Editor:* John D. Harrison; *Cinematographer:* Theodore Sparkhul.

Shooting dates: January 28 - February 21, 1935

Release date: April 11, 1935

Running time: 74 mins.
Cast: TONY: Richard Barthelmess; EDDIE: Joe Morrison; HELEN: Helen Mack; SYLVIA: Gertrude Michael; MAE DANISH: Dorothy Tree; JOHNSON: Roscoe Karns; CARL: Ray Milland; TAFT: Charles C. Wilson; MAC. MASON: Henry Travers; CAPT. SEAVERS: Paul Harvey; ANDERSON: Noel Madison; PA (HERMAN): Lee Kohlmar; MA: Bodil Rosing; LITTLE GIRL: Lois Kent; HEALY: Bruce Mitchell.
Synopsis: The lives of the theater staff and members of the audience become intertwined one night during the performance of a musical revue.

HANDS ACROSS THE TABLE
Director: Mitchell Leisen
Producer: E. Lloyd Sheldon
Written by: Norman Krasna, Vincent Lawrence, Herbert Fields
Based on: "Bracelets" by Vina Delmar
Cinematographer: Ted Tetzlaff
Costume Design: Travis Banton
Music: Sam Coslow, Frederick Hollander.
Shooting dates: August 1 - September 5, 1935
Release date: October 25, 1935
Running time: 88 mins.
Cast: REGI ALLEN: Carole Lombard; THEODORE DREW III: Fred MacMurray; ALLEN MACKLYN: Ralph Bellamy; VIVIAN SNOWDEN: Astrid Allwyn; LAURA: Ruth Donnelly; NONA: Marie Prevost; PETER: Joseph Tozer; NATTY: William Demarest; PINKY KELLY: Edward Gargan; MILES, THE BUTLER: Ferdinand Munier; COUTURIER (VALENTINE): Harold Minjir; MAID (FRENCH): Marcelle Corday; SALESLADY: Nell Craig; HEAD WAITER: Jerry Mandy; WAITER IN SUPPER CLUB: Phil Kramer.
Synopsis: Regi Allen, a manicurist determined to marry a wealthy man, tries to get interested in Allen Macklyn, a crippled resident of the hotel where she works. Theodore Drew III similarly intends to marry heiress Vivian Snowden but he and Regi cannot resist each other and in the end, they are married.

THIRTEEN HOURS BY AIR
Director: Mitchell Leisen; *Producer:* E. Lloyd Sheldon; *Written by:* Bogart Rogers, Kenyon Nicholson; *Based on:* "Wild Wings" a story by Bogart Rogers and Frank M. Dazey; *Cinematographer:* Theodore Sparkhul.
Shooting dates: December 23, 1935 - February 8, 1936
Release date: April 30, 1936
Running time: 80 mins.
Cast: JACK GORDON: Fred MacMurray; FELICE ROLLINS: Joan Bennett; MISS HARKINS: Zasu Pitts; PALMER: Alan Baxter; GREGORIE STEPHANI: Fred Keating; DR. EVARTS: Brian Donlevy; FREDDIE SCOTT: John Howard; ANN MCKENNA: Adrienne Marden; VI JOHNSON: Ruth Donnelly; WALDEMAR PITT III: Bennie Bartlett; TRIXIE: Grace Bradley; HAP WALLER: Dean Jagger;

Leisen in a gag bit with Ruth Donnelly that was cut from *Thirteen Hours By Air.*

LANDER: Jack Mulhall; POP ANDREWS: Granville Bates; PETE STEVENS: Arthur Singley; FAT RICKHAUSER: Clyde Dilson.

Synopsis: Heiress Felice Rollins boards a transcontinental flight hoping to reach San Francisco in time to prevent her sister from marrying a fortune hunter. Palmer, an escaped convict, hijacks the plane but pilot Jack Gordon finally manages to complete the flight.

THE BIG BROADCAST OF 1937

Director: Mitchell Leisen; *Producer:* Lewis Gensler; *Written by:* Edwin Gelsey, Arthur Kober, Barry Travers, Walter deLeon, Francis Martin;
Cinematographer: Theodore Sparkhul; *Editor:* Stuart Heisler; *Art Direction:* Hans Dreier, Robert Usher; *Music:* Boris Morros.
Shooting dates: June 22 - August 10, 1936
Release date: October 6, 1936
Running time: 100 mins.
Cast: JACK CARSON: Jack Benny; MR. AND MRS. PLATT: George Burns and Gracie Allen; BOB BLACK: Bob Burns; PATSY: Martha Raye; GWEN HOLMES: Shirley Ross; BOB MILLER: Raymond Milland; FRANK ROSSMAN: Frank Forest; BENNY FIELDS: Benny Fields; SCHLEPPERMAN: Sam Hearn; KAVVY: Stan Kavanaugh; Benny Goodman and His Orchestra.

Synopsis: Various adventures of radio station manager Jack Carson with his sponsors, Mr. and Mrs. Platt, and his many guest artists.

SWING HIGH, SWING LOW

Director: Mitchell Leisen; *Producer:* Arthur Hornblow Jr.;
Written by: Virginia Van Upp, Oscar Hammerstein II; *Based on:* the play BURLESQUE by George Manker Watters and Arthur Hopkins; *Editor:* Eda Warren; *Cinematographer:* Ted Tetzlaff; *Art Direction:* Hans Dreier, Ernst Fegte;*Set Decoration:* Sam Comer; *Costume Design:* Travis Banton;
Music: Boris Morros; songs by Ralph Rainger, Leo Robin, Burton Lane, Ralph Freed, Charley Kisco.
Shooting dates: November 13, 1936
Release date : March 15, 1937
Running time: 92 mins.
Cast: MAGGIE KING: Carole Lombard; SKID JOHNSON: Fred MacMurray; HARRY: Charles Butterworth; ELLA: Jean Dixon; ANITA ALVAREZ: Dorothy Lamour; HARVEY HORNUL: Harvey Stephens; MURPHY: Cecil Cunningham; GEORGIE: Charlie Arnt; HENRI: Franklin Pangborn; THE DON: Anthony Quinn; THE PURSER: Bud Flanagan; TONY: Charles Judels; CHIEF OF

MacMurray, Lamour and Lombard in *Swing High, Swing Low.*

POLICE: Harry Semels; INTERPRETER: Ricardo Mandia; JUDGE: Enrique DeRosas.

Synopsis: Maggie King meets and marries trumpeter Skid Johnson in Panama. He leaves her behind for Anita Alvarez and returns to New York where he goes on a binge and almost dies. Maggie comes to Skid's rescue and helps him get through a radio broadcast.

EASY LIVING

Director: Mitchell Leisen; *Producer:* Arthur Hornblow Jr.; *Written by:* Preston Sturges; *Based on:* an unpublished story by Vera Caspary.

Editor: Doane Harrison; *Cinematographer:* Ted Tetzlaff; *Art Direction:* Hans Dreier Ernst Fegte; *Costume Design:* Travis Banton; *Music:* Boris Morros.

Shooting dates: April 12 - May 24, 1937

Release date: July 7, 1937

Running time: 88 mins.

Cast: MARY SMITH: Jean Arthur; J. B. BALL: Edward Arnold; JOHN BALL, JR.: Ray Milland; MR. LOUIS LOUIS: Luis Alberni; MRS. BALL: Mary Nash; VAN BUREN: Franklin Pangborn; MR. GURNEY: Barlowe Borland; WALLACE WHISTLING: William Demarest; E. F. HULGAR: Andrew Tombes; LILLIAN: Esther Dale; OFFICE MANAGER: Harlan Briggs; MR. HYDE: William B. Davidson; MISS SWERF: Nora Cecil.

Jean Arthur imitating Eleanor Broder's telephone confusion in *Easy Living*.

Synopsis: During an argument with his wife, millionaire J. B. Ball throws her fur coat over the balcony of their Fifth Ave. penthouse. It lands on poor working girl Mary Smith who is soon suspected of being Ball's mistress and is given a luxurious hotel suite. She makes an offhand remark which causes a stock market crisis, but all is resolved in the end and Mary is reunited with John Ball Jr. who she has come to love.

THE BIG BROADCAST OF 1938

Director: Mitchell Leisen; *Producer:* Harlan Thompson; *Written by:* Walter deLeon, Francis Martin, Ken Englund; *Based on:* an adaptation by Howard Lindsay and Russel Crouse of an unpublished story by Frederick Hazlitt Brennan; *Editor:* Eda Warren, Chandler House; *Cinematographer:* Harry Fishbeck; *Art Direction:* Hans Dreier, Ernst Fegte; *Costume Design:* Edith Head; *Music:* Boris Morros, *Songs by* Ralph Rainger and Leo Robin; *Cartoon sequence:* Leon Schlesinger.
Shooting dates: September 13 - November 15, 1937
Release date: February 11, 1938
Running time: 97 mins.
Cast: T. FROTHINGILL BELLOWS S. B. BELLOWS : W. C. Fields; MARTHA BELLOWS: Martha Raye; DOROTHY WYNDHAM: Dorothy Lamour; CLEO FIELDING: Shirley Ross; SCOOP McPHAIL: Lynne Overman; BUZZ FIELDING: Bob Hope; MIKE: Ben Blue; BOB HAYES: Leif Erikson; GRACE FIELDING: Grace Bradley; TURNKEY: Rufe Davis; LORD DROOPY: Lionel Pape; JOAN FIELDING: Dorothy Howe; CAPTAIN STAFFORD: Russell Hicks; IVAN: Leonid Kinskey; HONEY CHILE: Patricia Wilder; Shep Fields and his Rippling Rhythm Orchestra, Kirsten Flagstad of the Metropolitan Opera Company, Wilfred Pelletier, Conductor; STEWARDS: Archie Twitchell, James Craig; OFFICERS: Richard Denning; Michael Brooke; Jack Hubbard.
Synopsis: Two ships are in a race across the Atlantic. The talent director on one of them, Buzz Fielding, is wooing Dorothy Wyndham, but his three ex-wives, Cleo, Grace and Joan are on hand to protect their source of alimony, and Buzz and Cleo eventually decide to give matrimony another chance.

ARTIST AND MODELS ABROAD

Director: Mitchell Leisen; *Producer:* Arthur Hornblow Jr.; *Written by:* Howard Lindsay, Russel Crouse and Ken Englund; *Based on:* an idea by J. P. McEvoy; *Editor:* Doane Harrison; *Cinematographer:* Ted Tetzlaff; *Special effects:* Farciot Edouart; *Art Direction:* Hans Dreier, Ernst Fegte; *Costume Design:* Edith Head; *Music:* Boris Morros; Songs by Ralph Rainger and Leo Robin Musical numbers staged by LeRoy Prinz.
Shooting dates: May 16 - July 16, 1938
Release date: December, 1938
Running time: 90 mins.
Cast: BUCK BOSWELL: Jack Benny; PATRICIA HARPER: Joan Bennett; MRS. ISABEL CHANNING: Mary Boland; JAMES HARPER: Charley Grapewin; CHICKIE: Joyce Compton; SWIFTY: The Yacht Club Boys; DOPEY; JIMMY; KELLY; DUBOIS: Fritz Feld; ELIOT WINTHROP: G. P. Huntley; GANTVOORT:

Monty Woolley; MADAME BRISSARD: Adrienne d'Ambricourt; BRISSARD: Andre Cheron; CHAUMONT: Jules Raucourt.
Synopsis: The adventures of Buck Boswell's crummy theatrical troupe while stranded in Paris.

MIDNIGHT

Director: Mitchell Leisen; *Producer:* Arthur Hornblow Jr.; *Written by:* Charles Brackett, Billy Wilder; *Based on:* an original screen story by Edwin Justus Mayer and Franz Schulz; *Editor:* Doane Harrison; *Cinematographer:* Charles Lang Jr.; *Special effects:* Farciot Edouart; *Art Direction:* Hans Dreier and Robert Usher; *Miss Colbert's gowns by:* Irene;
Music: Frederick Hollander.
Shooting dates: November 14, 1938 - January 16, 1939
Release date: March 15, 1939
Running time: 92 mins.
Cast: EVE PEABODY: Claudette Colbert; TIBOR CZERNY: Don Ameche; GEORGES FLAMMARION: John Barrymore; JACQUES PICOT: Francis Lederer; HELENE FLAMMARION: Mary Astor; SIMONE: Elaine Barrie; STEPHANIE: Hedda Hopper; MARCEL: Rex O'Malley; JUDGE: Monty Wolley; LEBON: Armand Kaliz; EDOUART: Lionel Pape.

John Barrymore and Claudette Colbert in *Midnight.*

Synopsis: Stranded in Paris, chorus girl Eve Peabody is pursued by the taxi-driving Tibor Czerny, but prefers to pose as a Countess for George Flammarion, who wants her to lure Jacques Picot away from Georges' wife Helene. When Czerny poses as Eve's long lost husband, Eve has to undergo a fake divorce, but in the end she decides to marry Czerny after all.

REMEMBER THE NIGHT

Director: Mitchell Leisen; *Producer:* Mitchell Leisen; *Written by:* Preston Sturges; *Editor:* Doane Harrison; *Cinematographer:* Ted Tetzlaff; *Art Direction:* Hans Dreier and Roland Anderson; *Costume design:* Edith Head;
Music: Frederick Hollander.
Shooting dates: July 27 - September 8, 1939
Release date: January 9, 1940
Running time: 94 mins.
Cast: LEE LEANDER: Barbara Stanwyck; JOHN SARGENT: Fred MacMurray; MRS. SARGENT: Beulah Bondi; AUNT EMMA: Elizabeth Patterson; FRANCIS X. O'LEARY: Willard Robertson; WILLIE: Sterling Holloway; JUDGE (NEW YORK): Charles Waldron; DISTRICT ATTORNEY: Paul Guilfoyle; TOM: Charlie Arnt; HANK: John Wray; MR. EMORY: Thomas W. Ross; RUFUS: Snowflake; "FAT" MIKE: Tom Kennedy.
Synopsis: District attorney John Sargent is prosecuting Lee Leander for jewel theft. The trial is adjourned until after Christmas and when Sargent learns that Lee came from Indiana, he offers to drop her off at her mothers on his way home. The mother proves hostile, so Lee spends Christmas with Sargent's family. He falls in love with her and tries to throw the trial, but she pleads guilty. As she begins serving her sentence, he promises to wait for her until she is released.

ARISE MY LOVE

Director: Mitchell Leisen; *Producer:* Arthur Hornblow Jr.; *Written by:* Charles Brackett; *Based on:* an unpublished story by Benjamin Glazer and John S. Toldy; *Adaptation by:* Jacques Thery; *Edited by:* Doane Harrison;
Cinematographer: Charles Lang Jr.; *Art Direction:* Hans Dreier and Robert Usher; *Miss Colbert's gown by:* Irene, *Other costumes* by Edith Head and Mitchell Leisen; *Music:* Victor Young.
Shooting dates: June 24 - August 15, 1940
Release date: October 17, 1940
Running time: 100 mins.
Cast: AUGUSTA NASH: Claudette Colbert; TOM MARTIN: Ray Milland; SHEP: Dennis O'Keefe; PHILLIPS: Walter Abel; PINK: Dick Purcell; PRISON GOVERNOR: George Zucco; FATHER JACINTO: Frank Puglia; SUSIE: Esther Dale; BRESSON: Paul Leyssac; MME. BRESSON: Anne Codee; COL. TUBBS-BROWN: Stanley Logan; LORD KETTLEBROOK: Lionel Pape; ACHILLE: Aubrey Mather; BOTZELBERG: Cliff Nazarro; BOTZELBERG'S ASSISTANT: Michael Mark.
Synopsis: Reporter Augusta Nash rescues Tom Martin from a Spanish prison by pretending to be his wife. Various romantic and melodramatic adventures ensue as they fall in love and decide to leave Europe which in on the brink of war. Their ship, the Athenia, however, is torpedoed and they decide to remain in Europe and fight the German oppression.

George Zucco, Milland, and Colbert in *Arise My Love*.

I WANTED WINGS

Director: Mitchell Leisen; *Producer:* Arthur Hornblow Jr.;
Written by: Richard Maibaum, Lieutenant Beirne Lay Jr. and Sid Herzig;
Based on: a story by Eleanore Griffin and Commander Frank Wead from the book by Beirne Lay Jr.; *Editor:* Hugh Bennett; *Cinematographer:* Leo Tovar; *Aerial Photography:* Elmer Dyer; *Process Photography:* Farciot Edouart; *Special effects:* Gordon Jennings; *Art Direction:* Hans Dreier and Robert Usher; *Music:* Victor Young; song "Born to Love" by Victor Young and Ned Washington, song "Spirit of the Air Corps" by William J. Clinch.
Shooting dates: August 26 - December 19, 1940 (Leisen took over September 7)
Release date: March 27, 1941
Running time: 130 mins.
Cast: JEFF YOUNG: Ray Milland; AL LUDLOW: William Holden; TOM CASSIDY: Wayne Morris; CAPT. MERCER: Brian Donlevy; CAROLYN BARTLETT: Constance Moore; SALLY VAUGHN: Veronica Lake; "SANDBAGS" RILEY: Harry Davenport; JIMMY MASTERS: Phil Brown; PRESIDENT OF THE COURT: Edward Fielding; JUDGE ADVOCATE: Willard Robertson; FLIGHT COMMANDER: Richard Lane; FLIGHT SURGEON: Addison Richards; MICKEY: Hobart Cavanaugh.
Synopsis: The adventures of three men training to be pilots just before World War II.

Boyer and de Havilland in *Hold Back the Dawn.*

HOLD BACK THE DAWN
(working titles: MEMO TO A MOVIE DIRECTOR, THE GOLDEN DOOR)
Director: Mitchell Leisen; *Producer:* Arthur Hornblow Jr.; *Written by:* Charles
Brackett and Billy Wilder; *Based on:* the novel by Ketti Frings;
Editor: Doane Harrison; *Cinematographer:* Leo Tover; *Art Direction:* Robert Usher;
Costume Design: Edith Head; *Music:* Victor Young.
Shooting dates: February 18 - May 5, 1941
Release date: July 31, 1941
Running time: 115 mins.
Cast: GEORGES ISCOVESCU: Charles Boyer; EMMY BROWN: Olivia de Havil-
land; ANITA DIXON: Paulette Goddard; VAN DEN LUECKEN: Victor Francen;
INSPECTOR HAMMOCK: Walter Abel; BONBOIS: Curt Bois; BERTA KURZ:
Rosemary DeCamp; JOSEF KURZ: Eric Feldary; FLORES: Nestor Paiva; LUPITA:
Eva Puig; CHRISTINE: Micheline Cheirel; ANNI: Madeleine LeBeau; TONY:
Billy Lee; MECHANIC: Mikhail Rasumny; MR. SAXON: Mitchell Leisen; AC-
TOR: Brian Donlevy; ACTOR: Richard Webb; ACTRESS: Veronica Lake.
Synopsis: Georges Iscovescu is denied entry into the U. S. because his nationality's
quota is filled. Stuck in a Mexican border town, he encounters his old mistress,
Anita, who tells him that marrying an American citizen will get him across the
border. He woos and marries a naive schoolteacher, Emmy Brown, who leaves
him when Anita reveals his past. Learning that Emmy has been seriously injured,

Georges crosses the border illegally and is apprehended, but is finally reunited with her.

THE LADY IS WILLING (Columbia)
(working title: MISS MADDEN IS WILLING)
Director: Mitchell Leisen; *Producer:* Mitchell Leisen; A Charles K. Feldman Group Production; *Written by:* James Edward Grant and Albert McCleery; *Based on:* an unpublished story by James Edward Grant; *Editor:* Eda Warren; *Cinematographer:* Ted Tetzlaff; *Art Direction:* Lionel Banks;
Miss Dietrich's gowns by Irene *(other costumes by* Mitchell Leisen*)Music:* W. Frankie Harling, M. W. Stoloff; song "I Find Love" by Jack King and Gordon Clifford.
Shooting dates: September, October 1941
Release date: February 17, 1942
Running time: 92 mins.
Cast: ELIZABETH MADDEN: Marlene Dietrich; DR. COREY MCBAIN: Fred MacMurray; BUDDY: Aline MacMahon; KENNETH HANLINE: Stanley Ridges; FRANCES: Arline Judge; VICTOR : Roger Clark; MARY LOU: Marietta Canty; BABY COREY: David James; MYRTLE: Ruth Ford; ARTHUR MIGGLE: Sterling Holloway; DR. GOLDING: Harvey Stephens; DETECTIVE SERGEANT BARNES: Harry Shannon; MRS. CUMMINGS: Elisabeth Risdon; K. K. MILLER: Charles Lane.

"I wish you could have known Marlene then, David. She was the most fascinating woman who ever lived." To the left, screenwriter Albert McCleery.

Synopsis: Broadway star Elizabeth Madden finds an abandoned baby, and needing a husband to adopt the infant, arranges a marriage of convenience with Dr. Cory McBain. Jealousy breaks them up, but they are reunited when the baby becomes ill and Dr. McBain pulls him through.

TAKE A LETTER, DARLING
Director: Mitchell Leisen; *Producer:* Fred Kohlmar; *Written by:* Claude Binyon; *Based on:* an unpublished story by George Beck; *Edited by:* Doane Harrison; *Cinematographer:* John Mescall; *Art Direction:* Hans Dreier, Roland Anderson; *Costume Design:* Mitchell Leisen; *Rosalind Russell's gowns by* Irene; *Constance Moore's gowns by* Mitchell Leisen; *Music:* Victor Young.
Shooting dates: November 27, 1941 - January 16, 1942
Release date: May 6, 1942
Running time: 93 mins.
Cast: A. M. MACGREGOR: Rosalind Russell; TOM VERNEY: Fred MacMurray; JONATHAN CALDWELL: Macdonald Carey; ETHEL CALDWELL: Constance Moore; G. B. ATWATER: Robert Benchley; FUD NEWTON: Charles Arnt; UNCLE GEORGE: Cecil Kellaway; AUNT MINNIE: Kathleen Howard; AUNT JUDY: Margaret Seddon; MOSES: Dooley Wilson; SAM: George H. Reed; SALLY: Margaret Hayes; MICKEY DOWLING: Sonny Boy Williams.
Synopsis: Advertising executive A. M. MacGregor hires Tom Verney to act as her personal secretary and keep the wolves away from her door. She gets provoked when Tom gets interested in client Ethel Caldwell and although Ethel's brother Jonathan pursues her, A. M. finally realizes she loves Tom.

NO TIME FOR LOVE
Director: Mitchell Leisen; *Producer:* Mitchell Leisen; *Associate Producer:* Fred Kohlmar; *Written by:* Claude Binyon; *Adaption by:* Warren Duff; *Based on:* a story by Robert Lees and Fred Rinaldo; *Editor:* alma Macrorie; *Cinematographer:* Charles Lang Jr.; *Art Direction:* Hans Dreier, Robert Usher; *Set decoration:* Sam Comer; *Costume Design:* Edith Head; *Claudette Colbert's gowns by* Irene; *Music:* Victor Young.
Shooting dates: June 8 - July 29, 1942
Release date: November 10, 1943
Running time: 83 mins.
Cast: KATHERINE GRANT: Claudette Colbert; JIM RYAN: Fred MacMurray; HOPPY GRANT: Ilka Chase; ROGER: Richard Hayden; HENRY FULTON: Paul McGrath; DARLENE: June Havoc; SOPHIE: Marjorie Gateson; CHRISTLEY: Bill Goodwin; KENT: Robert Herrick; DUNBAR: Morton Lowry; CLANCY: Rhys Williams; MORAN: Murray Alper; MORRISEY: John Kelly; LEON BRICE: Jerome De Nuccio; PETE HANAGAN: Grant Withers; TAYLOR: Rod Cameron; PRESIDENT OF CONSTRUCTION COMPANY: Willard Robertson; VICE-PRESIDENT: Arthur Loft; SAND HOGS: Fred Kohler, Jr.,Tom Neal, Max Laur, Oscar G. Hendrian, Tex Harris, Art Foster, Sammy Stein, Jack Roper, Woodrow W. Strode.
Synopsis: Sandhog Jim Ryan is working on a crew digging a tunnel under the Hudson River and photographer Katherine Grant comes to take pictures. She

falls for Ryan and gives him a job when he gets fired, but he leaves her in disgust and returns to save the tunnel from disaster and finally comes back to Katherine in the end.

LADY IN THE DARK

Director: Mitchell Leisen; *Producer:* Richard Blumenthal; *Executive Producer:* B. G. De Sylva; *Written by:* Frances Goodrich, Albert Hackett (Mitchell Leisen); *Based on:* the play by Moss Hart; *Editor:* Alma Macrorie;
Cinematographer: Ray Rennahan; *Technical Effects:* Paul Lerpae;
Color by Technicolor; *Special Effects:* Gordon Jennings; *Process Photography:* Farciot Edouart; *Art Direction:* Hans Dreier; *Dream Sequence Settings and Costumes:* Raul Pene DuBois; *Costumes executed by:* Madame Karinska; *Modern Costumes:* Edith Head (Mitchell Leisen) Babs Wilomez; *Set Decoration:* Ray Moyer; *Songs:* Ira Gershwin and Kurt Weill; "Suddenly It's Spring" by Johnny Burke and James Van Husen; *Vocal arrangements:* Joseph J. Lilley; *Orchestrations:* Robert Russell Bennett; Miss Rogers' dance, "Suddenly It's Spring: by and with Don Loper; "The Circus" staged by Billy Daniels; *Music Associate:* Arthur Franklin.
Shooting dates: 1942 - March 20, 1943
Release date: February 10, 1944
Running time: 100 mins.
Cast: LIZA ELLIOTT: Ginger Rogers; CHARLEY JOHNSON: Ray Milland; KENDALL NESBITT: Warner Baxter; RANDY CURTIS: Jon Hall; DR. BROOKS: Barry Sullivan; RUSSELL PAXTON: Mischa Auer; ALLISON DUBOIS: Phyllis Brooks; MAGGIE GRANT: Mary Phillips; DR. CARLTON: Edward Fielding; GIRL WITH RANDY CURTIS: Frances Robinson; ADAMS: Don Loper; MISS PARKER: Mary Parker; MISS FOSTER: Catherine Craig; MARTHA: Marietta Canty; MISS EDWARDS: Virginia Farmer; MISS BOWERS: Fay Helm; BARBARA: Gail Russell; MISS STEVENS: Marian Hall; LIZA'S MOTHER: Kay Linaker; LIZA'S FATHER: Harvey Stephens; OFFICE BOY: Billy Daniels; MISS SULLIVAN: Georgia Backus; BEN: Rand Brooks.
Synopsis: Fashion magazine editor Liza Elliott faces a crisis in her life and cannot decide what to do. She consults a psychiatrist, and after experiencing three hallucinatory dreams, comes to a true understanding of herself, realizing even that she really loves Charley Johnson, her old nemesis at the office.

FRENCHMAN'S CREEK

Director: Mitchell Leisen; *Producer:* B. G. DeSylva; *Associate Producer;* David Lewis; *Written by:* Talbot Jennings; *Based on:* the novel by Daphne DuMaurier; *Editor:* Alma Macrorie; *Cinematographer:* George Barnes (and Charles Lang); *Color by* Technicolor; *Art Direction:* Hans Dreier, Ernst Fegte; *Set Decoration:* Sam Comer; *Costume Design:* Raoul Pene Du Bois (and Mitchell Leisen); *Music:* Victor Young.
Shooting dates: June 18 - October 20, 1943
Release date: September 20, 1944
Running time: 110 mins.
Cast: DONA ST. COLUMB: Joan Fontaine; THE FRENCHMAN–JEAN BENOIT AUBREY: Arturo De Cordova; LORD ROCKINGHAM: Basil Rathbone; LORD

Kellaway and Fontaine in *Frenchman's Creek.*

GODOLPHIN: Nigel Bruce; WILLIAM: Cecil Kellaway; HARRY ST. COLUMB: Ralph Forbes; EDMOND: Harald Ramond; PIERRE BLANC: Billy Daniels; LADY GODOLPHIN: Moyna MacGill; HENRIETTA: Patricia Barker; JAMES: David James.

Synopsis: Donna St. Columb leaves London to escape her dull husband and his lecherous best friend Lord Rockingham. Domiciled at her Cornwall estate, she meets a French pirate and has many amusing adventures with him, but, in the end, refuses to become his mistress and returns to her husband and children.

PRACTICALLY YOURS

Director: Mitchell Leisen; *Producer:* Mitchell Leisen; *Associate Producer:* Harry Tugend; *Written by:* Norman Krasna; *Cinematographer:* Charles Lang Jr.; *Art Direction:* Hans Dreier, Robert Usher; *Set decoration:* Stephen Seymour; *Claudette Colbert's gowns by:* Howard Greer; *Music:* Victor Young.

Shooting dates: February 4 - April 15, 1944

Release date: December 20, 1944

Running time: 90 mins.

Cast: PEGGY MARTIN: Claudette Colbert; LT. (S. G.) DANIEL BELLAMY: Fred MacMurray; ALBERT BEAGELL: Gil Lamb; MARVIN P. MEGLIN: Cecil Kellaway; JUDGE OSCAR STIMSON: Robert Benchley; COMMANDER HARPE: Tom Powers; MUSICAL COMEDY STAR: Jane Frazee; ELLEN MACY: Rosemary De Camp; MRS. MEGLIN: Isabel Randolph; LA CROSSE: Mikhail Rasumny; UNCLE BEN BELLAMY: Arthur Loft; HARVEY (BUTLER): Edgar

Norton; SAM: Donald MacBride; MEGLIN'S CHAUFFEUR: Donald Kerr; MEGLIN'S MAID: Clara Reid; DON BARCLAY: Himself; PIGGY (A DOG): Rommie (A DOG).

Synopsis: Lt. Daniel Bellamy is shot down after completing a heroic mission in the Pacific. In his last words he talks of Piggy his dog, which is misinterpreted to be Peggy, a girl he hardly knows in his office. The mistake soon becomes apparent when Bellamy is rescued, but he and Peggy eventually fall in love anyway.

KITTY

Director: Mitchell Leisen; *Producer:* Karl Tunberg; *Written by:* Darrel Ware, Karl Tunberg; *Based on:* the novel by Rosamund Marshall; *Editor:* Alma Macrorie; *Cinematographer:* Daniel L. Fapp; *Process Photography:* Farciot Edouart; *Special Effects:* Gordon Jennings; *Art Direction:* Hans Dreier, Walter Tyler; *Settings and Costumes:* Raoul Pene Du Bois; costumes executed by Madame Karinska; *Music:* Victor Young.

Shooting dates: June 22 - September 9, 1944
Release date: October 16, 1945
Running time: 103 mins.

Cast: KITTY: Paulette Goddard; SIR HUGH MARCY: Ray Milland; BRETT HARDWOOD, EARL OF CARSTAIRS: Patric Knowles; DUKE OF MALMUNS-TER: Reginald Owen; THOMAS GAINSBOROUGH: Cecil Kellaway; LADY SUSAN DOWITT: Constance Collier; JONATHAN SELBY: Dennis Hoey; OLD MEG: Sara Allgood; DOBSON: Eric Blore; SIR JOSHUA REYNOLDS: Gordon Richards; H. R. H. THE PRINCE OF WALES: Michael Dyne; EARL OF CAMPTON: Edgar Norton; ELAINE CARLISLE: Patricia Cameron; DOCTOR HOLT: Percival Vivian; NANNY: Mary Gordon; NULLENS: Anita Bolster; LIL: Heather Wilde; MAJOR DOMO: Charles Coleman; MOLLY: Mae Clarke.

Synopsis: Thomas Gainsborough discovers Kitty, a beautiful beggar in the streets of London. He cleans her up, paints her portrait and introduces her to Sir Hugh Marcy, who teaches her manners and arranges two very advantageous marriages for her. After her second husband dies, Marcy marries Kitty himself.

MASQUERADE IN MEXICO

Director: Mitchell Leisen; *Producer:* Karl Tunberg; *Written by:* Karl Tunberg; *Based on:* MIDNIGHT, story by Edwin Justus Mayer and Franz Schulz; *Editor:* Alma Macrorie; *Cinematographer:* Lionel Lindon; *Art Direction:* Hans Dreier, Roland Anderson; *Costume Design:* Edith Head (and Mitchell Leisen); *Music:* Victor Young.

Shooting dates: January 8 - March 15, 1945
Release date: December 3, 1945
Running time: 98 mins.

Cast: ANGEL O'REILLY: Dorothy Lamour; MANOLO SEGOVIA: Arturo De Cordova; THOMAS GRANT: Patric Knowles; HELEN GRANT: Ann Dvorak; BORIS CASSALL: George Rigaud; IRENE DENNY: Natalie Schafer; PABLO: Mikhail Rasumny; RICO FENWAY: Billy Daniels; THE GUADALAJARA TRIO: Lamberto Leyva, Mario Santos, Jesus Castillon; JOSE: Martin Garralaga.

Dorothy Lamour's wardrobe is the subject of this big huddle on the set of *Masquerade in Mexico*. (l. to r.) Asst. Director Tex Harris, dancer Billy Daniels, Art Director Roland Anderson, Costume Designer Edith Head and Leisen.

Leisen discusses scene with de Havilland and John Lund for *To Each His Own*.

TO EACH HIS OWN

Director: Mitchell Leisen; *Producer:* Charles Brackett; *Written by:* Charles Brackett, Jacques Thery; *Edited by:* Alma Macrorie; *Cinematographer:* Daniel L. Fapp; *Art Direction:* Hans Dreier, Roland Anderson; *Set decorators:* Sam Comer and James M. Walters; *Costume Design:* Edith Head; *Music:* Victor Young;
Shooting dates: June 25 - September 6, 1945
Release date: March 12, 1946
Running time: 100 mins.
Cast: MISS NORRIS: Olivia de Havilland; CAPTAIN COSGROVE (GREGORY): John Lund; CORINNE PIERSEN: Mary Anderson; LORD DESHAM: Roland Culver; ALEX PIERSEN: Phillip Terry; MAC TILTON: Bill Goodwin; LIZ LORIMER: Virginia Welles; DAISY GINGRAS: Victoria Horne; MR. NORRIS: Griff Barnett; BELLE INGHAM: Alma Macrorie; GRIGGSY (5 1/2 YEARS): Bill Ward; BABE: Frank Faylen; DR. HUNT: Willard Robertson; MR. CLINTON: Arthur Loft; MRS. CLINTON: Virginia Farmer.
Synopsis: Josephine Norris is a middle aged businesswoman living in London During World War II. She learns that a soldier named Gregory Piersen is due to arrive, and she goes to the station to meet him. While waiting, she recalls how during World War I she had fallen in love with an aviator, had become pregnant and then learned he had been killed. Her child was adopted by another family while she watched on; she finally left the U.S. when she could bear it no longer. Returning to the present, she meets the son and invites him to stay with her. He

accepts, not knowing who she is, for she refuses to tell him, despite the urging of her beau, Lord Desham, who eventually reveals the truth after the boy is married.

SUDDENLY IT'S SPRING

Director: Mitchell Leisen; *Producer:* Claude Binyon; *Written by:* Claude Binyon and P. J. Wolfson; *Based on:* "Sentimental Journey" by P. J. Wolfson; *Cinematographer:* Daniel L. Fapp; *Editor:* Alma Macrorie; *Art Direction:* Hans Dreier, John Meehan; *Set Decorations:* Sam Comer, Grace Gregory; *Costume Design:* Mary Kay Dodson; *Music:* Victor Young.
Shooting dates: February 25 - April 19. 1946
Release date: February 13, 1947
Running time: 87 mins.
Cast: MARY MORELY: Paulette Goddard; PETER MORELY: Fred MacMurray; JACK LINDSAY: Macdonald Carey; GLORIA FAY: Arleen Whelan; MARY'S MOTHER: Lilian Fontaine; HAROLD MICHAELS: Frank Faylen; CAPTAIN ROGERS: Frances Robinson; LIEUT. BILLINGS: Victoria Horne; MAJOR CHEEVER: Georgia Backus; WAC CORP. MICHAELS: Jean Ruth; WAC SER-GEANT: Roberta Jonay; PORTER ON TRAIN: Willie Best.
Synopsis: Marriage counselor Mary Morely has been separated form her husband Peter by the war and when the war ends, she learns that Peter wants to divorce her and marry Gloria Fay. Jack Lindsay also pursues Mary, but eventually she gets Peter back.

GOLDEN EARRINGS

Director: Mitchell Leisen; *Producer:* Harry Tugend; *Written by:* Abraham Polonsky, frank Butler and Helen Deutsch; *Based on:* the novel by Yolanda Foldes; *Cinematographer:* Daniel L. Fapp; *Editor:* Alma Macrorie; *Art Direction:* Hans Dreier and John Meehan; *Set decoration:* Sam Comer and Grace Gregory; *Costume Design:* Mary Kay Dodson;
Special effects: Gordon Jennings; *Process photography:* Farciot Edouart;
Music: Victor Young; *Song:* "Golden Earrings" by Victor Young, Jay Livingston and Ray Evans.
Shooting dates: August 6 - October 17, 1946
Release date: August 27, 1947
Running time: 100 mins.
Cast: COL. RALPH DENISTOUN: Ray Milland; LYDIA: Marlene Dietrich; ZOLTAN: Murvyn Vye; BYRD: Bruce Lester; HOFF: Dennis Hoey; QUENTIN REYNOLDS: Himself; PROFESSOR KROSIGK: Reinhold Schunzel MAJOR REIMANN: Ivan Triesault; GRETA KROSIGK: Hermine Sterler; ZWEIG: Eric Feldary; 1ST AGENT: Fred Nurney; 2ND AGENT: Otto Reichow; DOWAGER: Gisela Werbiseck; PAGE BOY: Larry Simms.
Synopsis: Col. Ralph Denistoun receives a pair of gold earrings at his club in London and departs immediately. On the plane he relates to Quentin Reynolds how he had been imprisoned in Germany for espionage and had managed to escape. He met Lydia, a gypsy woman, who dressed him as a gypsy and led him to safety. Now that the war is over, he returns to Germany and Lydia.

VARIETY GIRL

Director: George Marshall
Producer: Daniel Dare
Release date: August 29, 1947
Cast: Mary Hatcher, Olga San Juan, many Paramount contract players. Mitchell Leisen appeared as himself in a scene with several other Paramount directors.

DREAM GIRL

Director: Mitchell Leisen; *Producer:* P. J. Wolfson; *Based on:* the play by Elmer Rice; *Edited by:* alma Macrorie; *Cinematographer:* Daniel L. Fapp;
Art Direction: Hans Dreier, John Meehan; *Set decoration:* Sam Comer, Grace Gregory; *Costume Design:* Edith Head; *Music:* Victor Young.
Shooting dates: April 28 - June 26, 1947
Release date: July 27, 1948
Running time: 85 mins.
Cast: GEORGINA ALLERTON: Betty Hutton; CLARK REDFIELD: Macdonald Carey; JIM LUCAS: Patric Knowles; MIRIAM ALLERTON LUCAS: Virginia Field; GEORGE ALLERTON: Walter Abel; LUCY ALLERTON: Peggy Wood; CLAIRE BLEAKLEY: Carolyn Butler; PROFESSOR MEELY: John Abbott; GEORGE HAND: Lowell Gilmore; MME. KIMMELOFF (MUSIC TEACHER): Zamah Cunningham; ANTONIO: Frank Puglia; JUDGE 'JED' ALLERTON: Selmar Jackson; EDNA: Georgia Backus; CHARLES: Charles Meredith; MOLLIE HAND: Dorothy Christy; LOVELITA: Antonia Morales; RADIO ANNOUNCER: John Dehner.
Synopsis: Rich girl Georgina Allerton runs a book shop for fun and imagines what life would be like with her brother-in-law, Jim Lucas. In her fantasies, she is alternately Madame Butterfly and Sadie Thompson until reporter Clark Redfield makes her face reality and she falls in love with him.

MISS TATLOCK'S MILLIONS

Director: Richard Haydn
Producer: Charles Brackett
Release date: November 19, 1948
Cast: John Lund, Wanda Hendrix. Leisen again appeared as himself in this comedy which took place in Hollywood.

SONG OF SURRENDER

(*working titles:* THE SIN OF ABBY HUNT; NOW AND FOREVER; ABIGAIL, DEAR HEART.)
Director: Mitchell Leisen; *Producer:* Richard Maibaum; *Written by:* Richard Maibaum; *Based on:* an unpublished story by Ruth McKenney and Richard Bransten; *Cinematographer:* Daniel L. Fapp; *Special Effects:* Gordon Jennings; *Process Photography:* Farciot Edouart; *Art Direction:* Hans Dreier, Henry Bumstead; *Costume Design:* Mary Kay Dodson; *Music:* Victor Young; song, "Song of Surrender," music by Victor Young, lyrics by Jay Livingston, Ray Evans, sung by Buddy Clark. "Shubert's Serenade" sung by Richard Tucker; Enrico Caruso recordings on RCA.
Shooting dates: January 12 - February 27, 1948

Release date: October 28, 1949
Running time: 93 mins.
Cast: ABIGAIL HUNT: Wanda Hendrix; ELISHA HUNT: Claude Rains; BRUCE ELDRIDGE: Macdonald Carey; PHYLLIS CANTWELL: Andrea King; DEACON PARRY: Henry Hull; MRS. BEECHAM: Elizabeth Patterson; MR. WILLIS: Art Smith; DUBOIS: John Beal; COUNTESS MARINA: Eva Gabor; CLYDE ATHERTON: Dan Tobin; GENERAL SECKLE: Nicholas Joy; SIMON BEECHAM: Peter Miles;
AUCTIONEER: Ray Walker; FAITH BEECHAM: Gigi Perreau; MR. BEECHAM: Ray Bennett; MR. TORRANCE: Clancy Cooper.
Synopsis: Elisha Hunt, a stern middle-aged museum curator is married to Abigail, who is many years his junior. To relieve the monotony of her life, Abigail turns to Bruce Eldridge, a visitor from New York who introduces her to the pleasures of fashionable society. Elisha is enraged upon learning of this and dies of a stroke, leaving Abigail free to marry Eldridge.

BRIDE OF VENGEANCE
(*working title:* A MASK FOR LUCRETIA)
Director: Mitchell Leisen; *Producer:* Richard Maibaum; *Written by:* Cyril Hume, Michael Hogan; *Added dialogue:* Clemence Dane (and John Lund);
Based on: "Chalice" by Michael Hogan; *Editor:* Alma Macrorie;
Cinematographer: Daniel L. Fapp; *Special effects:* Gordon Jennings; *Process Photography:* Farciot Edouart; Art *Direction:* Hans Dreier, Roland Anderson, Albert Nozaki; *Set decoration:* Sam Comer, Ray Moyer; Costume *Design:* Mitchell Leisen, Mary Grant; *Music:* Hugo Friedhofer.
Shooting dates: September 1 - October 22, 1948
Release date: April 7, 1949
Running time: 91 mins.
Cast: LUCRETIA BORGIA: Paulette Goddard; ALFONSO D'ESTE: John Lund; CESARE BORGIA: Macdonald Carey; VANETTI: Albert Dekker; BISCEGLIE: John Sutton; MICHELOTTO: Raymond Burr; BASTINO: Charles Dayton; TIZIANO: Donald Randolph; ELEANORA: Rose Hobart; CHAMBERLAIN: Nicholas Joy; FILIPPO: Fritz Leiber; BEPPO: Billy Gilbert; PERUZZI: William Farnum; GEMMA: Kate Drain Lawson; CAPTAIN OF THE GUARD: Anthony Caruso.
Synopsis: Cesare Borgia tells his sister Lucretia that Alfonso D'este, the Duke of Ferrara, murdered her husband. Lucretia marries the Duke and plots to poison him, but learns the truth and joins her husband in a victorious battle against Cesare.

CAPTAIN CAREY, U. S. A.
(*working title:* AFTER MIDNIGHT)
Director: Mitchell Leisen; *Producer:* Richard Maibaum; *Written by:* Robert Thoeren; *Based on:* DISHONORED by Martha Albrand; *Editor:* Alma Macrorie;
Cinematographer: John F. Seitz; *Art Direction:* Hans Dreier, Roland Anderson; *Set decoration:* Sam Comer, Ray Moyer; *Costume Design:* Mary Kay Dodson; *Music:* Hugo Friedhofer; *Song:* "Mona Lisa" by Ray Evans, Jay Livingston.

Shooting dates: February 14 - March 26, 1949; retakes March 30, April 5, May 3, 4. 7
Release date: February 21, 1950
Running time: 83 mins.
Cast: WEBSTER CAREY: Alan Ladd; GUILIA de GREFFI: Wanda Hendrix; BARON ROCCO de GREFFI: Francis Lederer; DR. LUNATI: Joseph Calleia; COUNTESS FRANCESCA de CRESCI: Celia Lovsky; SERA FINA: Angela Clarke; NANCY: Jane Nigh; LUIGI: Frank Puglia; SANDRO: Luis Alberni; MANFREDO ACUTO: Roland Winters; COUNT CARLO de CRESCI: Richard Avonde; FRANK: Paul Lees; PIETRO: Rusty Tamblyn; ANGELINA: Virginia Farmer; BLIND MUSICIAN: David Leonard.
Synopsis: Webster Carey, enamored of Giullia de Greffi in Post-war Italy, is involved in an obscure intrigue.

NO MAN OF HER OWN
(*working titles:* I MARRIED A DEAD MAN, THE LIE)
Director: Mitchell Leisen; *Producer:* Richard Maibaum; *Written by:* Sally Bensen, Catherine Turney (and Mitchell Leisen); *Based on:* I MARRIED A DEAD MAN by Cornell Woolrich; *Edited by:* Alma Macrorie; *Cinematographer:* Daniel L. Fapp; *Art Direction:* Hans Dreier, Henry Bumstead; *Costume Design:* Edith Head; *Music:* Hugo Friedhofer.
Shooting dates: May 31 - July 25, 1949
Release date: February 21, 1949
Running time: 98 mins.

Barbara Stanwyck in *No Man of Her Own.*

Cast: HELEN FERGUSON: Barbara Stanwyck; BILL HARKNESS: John Lund; MRS. HARKNESS: Jane Cowl; PATRICE HARKNESS: Phyllis Thaxter; STEPHEN MORLEY: Lyle Bettger; MR. HARKNESS: Henry O'Neill; HUGH HARKNESS: Richard Denning; BLONDE: Carole Mathews; JOSIE: Esther Dale; PLAIN CLOTHES MAN: Milburn Stone; DR. PARKER: Griff Barnett; TY WINTHROP: Harry Antrim; ROSALIE BAKER: Catherine Craig; NURSE: Georgia Backus; DINING CAR WAITER: Dooley Wilson; PORTER: Ivan Browning; COP: William Haade.

Synopsis: Helen Ferguson, pregnant and unmarried, is shunned by her lover, Stephen Morley, but he gives her a transcontinental train ticket. En route to San Francisco, she meets Hugh Harkness and his wife Patrice, who is also pregnant. The train crashes and when Helen awakens, she has given birth and been falsely identified as Patrice. She moves in with the Harkness family. Morley turns up, tries to blackmail Patrice and is murdered, but Patrice and her fiance Bill Harkness are cleared of guilt.

THE MATING SEASON

(*working title:* RELATIVE STRANGERS)

Director: Mitchell Leisen; *Producer:* Charles Brackett; *Written by:* Charles Brackett, Walter Reisch, Richard Breen; *Based on:* MAGGIE, an unproduced play by Caesar Dunn; *Cinematographer:* Charles B. Lang, Jr.; *Art Direction:* Hal Pereira, Roland Anderson; *Miss Tierney's clothes designed by:* Oleg Cassini; *Music:* Joseph J. Lilley.

Shooting dates: May 18 - July 1, 1950

Release date: January 12, 1951

Running time: 101 mins.

Cast: MAGGIE CARLETON: Gene Tierney; VAL McNULTY: John Lund; FRAN CARLETON: Mirian Hopkins; ELLEN McNULTY: Thelma Ritter; BETSY: Jan Sterling; MR. KALINGER, SR.: Larry Keating; GEO. C. KALINGER, JR.: James Lorimer; MRS. CONGER: Gladys Hurlbut; MRS. WILLIAMSON: Cora Witherspoon; MR. WILLIAMSON: Malcolm Keen; ANNIE: Ellen Corby; MUGSY: Billie Bird; COLONEL CONGER: Samuel Colt; MRS. FAHNSTOCK: Grayce Hampton; DR. CHORLEY: Stapelton Kent.

Synopsis: Poor and ambitious Val McNulty marries wealthy Maggie Carleton and when his hardworking mother Ellen comes to call, Maggie mistakes her for the new maid. She is thus installed with her real identity unknown to Maggie, whose bitchy mother, Fran, moves in as well. Complications ensue and Val almost loses his job, but his mother manages to straighten everything out.

DARLING, HOW COULD YOU!

(*working title:* RENDEZVOUS)

Director: Mitchell Leisen; *Producer:* Harry Tugend; *Written by:* Dodie Smith, Lesser Samuels; *Based on:* ALICE-SIT-BY-THE-FIRE, a play by James Barrie; *Cinematographer:* Daniel L. Fapp; *Art Direction:* Hal Pereira and Roland Anderson; *Costume Design:* Edith Head; *Music:* Fredrick Hollander.

Shooting dates: November 10 - December 19, 1950

Release date: August 8, 1951

Running time: 96 mins.

Miriam Hopkins and Gene Tierney in a scene from *The Mating Season.*

Cast: ALICE GREY: Joan Fontaine; DR. ROBERT GREY: John Lund; AMY: Mona Freeman; DR. STEVE CLARK: Peter Hanson; COSMO: David Stollery; FANNY: Virginia Farmer; NURSE: Angela Clarke; LORD AUBREY QUAYNE: Lowell Gilmore; MR. ROSSITER: Robert Barrat; MRS. ROSSITER: Gertrude Michael; SYLVIA: Mary Murphy; SIMMS: Frank Elliott; ROSIE: Billie Bird; THEATRE MANAGER: Willard Waterman; MAN: Gordon Arnold.

Synopsis: Dr. Robert Grey and his wife Alice return from a long trip abroad to realize that they are strangers to their children, Amy and Cosmo. After seeing a lurid melodrama, Amy thinks, her mother is having an affair with Dr. Steve Clark, and goes to Clark's apartment to seduce him, but has to hide when both her parents arrive. When all is straightened out, Amy and her mother have become much closer friends.

YOUNG MAN WITH IDEAS (MGM)

(working title: YOUNG MAN IN A HURRY)

Director: Mitchell Leisen; *Producer:* Gottfried Reinhardt, William H. Wright; *Written by:* Arthur Sheekman; *Editor:* Fredrick Y. Smith;

Cinematographer: Joseph Ruttenburg; *Art Direction:* Cedric Gibbons, Arthur Lonergan; *Set decorations:* Edwin B. Willis, Hugh Hunt; *Costume Design:; Music:* David Rose.

Shooting dates: August - September, 1951

Release date: May 2, 1952

Running time: 84 mins.

Cast: MAX WEBSTER: Glenn Ford; JULIE WEBSTER: Ruth Roman; JOYCE LARAMYE: Nina Foch; DORIANNE GRAY: Denise Darcel; CAROLINE WEBSTER: Donna Corcoran; SUSAN WEBSTER: Nadine Ashdown; MRS. GILPIN: Mary Wicks; WILLIS GILPIN: Bobby Diamond; BRICK DAVIS: Sheldon Leonard; EDDIE: Dick Wessel; TUX CULLERY: Carl Milletaire; GUESTS AT PARTY: Will Wright, Bess Flowers, Jean Acker, Margaret Farrell, Emmett Vogan, Isabel Randolf, Rodney Bell, Jack Gogan, Cameron Grant.

Synopsis: Max Webster, a young lawyer with a family, leaves the Midwest and comes to California looking for a better life. He gets into all sorts of trouble, including a mix-up with some gangsters, but in the end, he makes a good case for himself at a trial and gets a good job with a law firm.

TONIGHT WE SING (20th Century Fox)

Director: Mitchell Leisen; *Producer:* George Jessel; *Written by:* Harry Kurnitz and George Oppenheimer; *Based on:* an autobiographical work by Sol Hurok and Ruth Goode; *Edited by:* Dorothy Spencer; *Cinematographer:* Leon Shamroy; *Color by:* Technicolor; *Art Direction:* Lyle Wheeler, George W. Davis; *Set Decorations:* Thomas Little, Walter M. Scott; *Costume Design:* Renie; *Music:* Alfred Newman; *Choral Direction:* Ken Darby;
Ballet Choreography: David Lichine.
Release date: January 26, 1953
Running time: 124 mins.

Cast: SOL HUROK: David Wayne; FEODOR CHALIAPIN: Ezio Pinza; ELSA VALDINE: Roberta Peters; ANNA PAVLOVA: Tamara Toumanova; EMMA HUROK: Anne Bancroft; EUGENE YSAYE: Issac Stern; GREGORY LAWRENCE: Byron Palmer; BENJAMIN GOLDER: Oscar Karlweis; NICOLAI: Mikhail Rasumny; PRAGER: Steven Geray; GRITTI: Walter Woolf King; ALLBRECHT: Serge Perault; SOL HUROK (AGE 10): John Meek; MRS. GOLDER: Eda Reis Merin; EDDIE GOLDER: Russell Cantor; EUGENE YSAYE'S ACCOMPANIST: Alex Zakin; CONDUCTOR: Alex Steinart; DR. MARKOFF: Oscar Beregi; PETUKOFF: Leo Mostovoy; CHARLES DILLINGHAM: Ray Largay; JULES MASSENET: Wolfgang Fraenkel; MRS. GRANEK: Lela Bliss; MR. GRANEK: Harry Hayden.

Synopsis: A biography of Sol Hurok, covering his early life in Russia, the beginnings of his career in America and his relationships with artists like Anna Pavlova, Feodor Chaliapin, Eugene Ysaye and Jules Massenet.

RED GARTERS

Directors: George Marshall & Mitchell Leisen; *Producer:* Pat Duggan;
Written by: Michael Fessier; *Editor:* Arthur Schmidt; *Cinematographer:* Arthur E. Arling; *Art Direction:* Hal Pereira, Roland Anderson; *Women's Costumes:* Edith Head; *Men's Costumes:* Yvonne Wood; *Music:* Joseph J. Lilley.
Shooting dates: started May 11, 1953
Cast: Rosemary Clooney, Joanne Gilbert, Don Taylor (replaced by Gene Barry) Guy Mitchell. (Leisen started shooting RED GARTERS May 11, 1953, and was fired May 19. None of his footage remained in the final cut.)

Anne Baxter and Steve Forrest in *Bedevilled.*

BEDEVILLED (MGM)
(working titles: THE LOVED AND THE LOST; THE PARIS STORY)
Director: Mitchell Leisen; *Producer:* Henry Berman; *Written by:* Jo Eisinger; *Editor:* Frank Clark; *Cinematographer:* F. A. Young; *In Cinemascope and Eastman Color; Art Direction:* Alfred Judge; *Costume Design:* Jean Dessus; Miss Baxter's costumes by Helen Rose; *Music:* William Allwyn.
Release date: April 28, 1955
Running time: 89 mins.
Cast: MONICA JOHNSON: Anne Baxter; GREGORY FITZGERALD: Steve Forrest; FRANCESCA: Simone Renant; TREVELLE: Maurice Teynac; TONY: Robert Christopher; MAMA LUGACETTA: Ina de la Haye; FATHER DU ROCHER: Victor Francen; FATHER CUNNINGHAM: Joseph Tometly; HOTEL MANAGER: Olivier Hussenot; TAXI DRIVER: Jacques Hilling; CONCIERGE: Raymond Bussieres.
Synopsis: Gregory Fitzgerald, studying to be a priest, in Paris, gets involved with chanteuse Monica Johnson without realizing that she has killed a man. He helps her to hide, but in the end, she turns herself in.

THE GIRL MOST LIKELY (RKO—Universal)
Director: Mitchell Leisen; *Producer:* Stanley Rubin; *Written by:* Devery Freeman;
Based on: TOM, DICK AND HARRY, a screenplay by Paul Jarrico;
Editors: Henry Marker, Dean Harrison; *Cinematographer:* Robert Planck;

Color by Technicolor; *Art Direction:* Albert D'Agostino, George W. Davis; *Set Decoration:* Eli Benneche; *Costume Design:* Renie; *Music:* Nelson Riddle; *Choreography:* Gower Champion.*Release date:* December 17, 1957
Cast: DODIE: Jane Powell; PETE: Cliff Robertson; NEIL: Keith Andes; BUZZ: Tommy Noonan; MARGE: Kaye Ballard; MOTHER: Una Merkel; PAULINE: Judy Nugent; SAM: Kelly Brown; POP: Frank Cady; PHOTOGRAPHER: Nacho Galindo; STEWARD: Chris Essay; YOUNG DADDY: Valentin de Vargas; MR. SCHLOM: Joseph Kearns; BASKET VENDOR: Julia Montoya; MAN IN PENNY ARCADE: Paul Garay; SPECIALTY DANCERS: Gloria DeWerd,Gail Ganley,Harvey Hohnecker, Bob Banas,Joyce Blunt,Tex Brodus, Buddy Bryant,Maurice Kelly, Tommy Ladd,Todd Miller,Dean Myles,Howard Parker,Donna Pouget,Paul Rees, Bruce Stowell, Lida Thomas.
Synopsis: Dodie finds herself engaged to Pete, Neil and Buzz at the same time and dreamily imagines what being married to each of them would be like.

SPREE (a Trans America release)
Directors: Mitchell Leisen, Walon Green
Written by: Sydney Field
Release date: November 1967
Color
Running time: 84 mins.
Cast: Vic Damone, Juliet Prowse, Jayne Mansfield, Constance Moore.
Synopsis: A documentary including some footage Leisen shot in 1964 for an abandoned documentary entitled HERE'S LAS VEGAS.
TELEVISION

G.E. THEATRE (Revue, 1955, 1958 - 1961)
Director: Mitchell Leisen
Producer: various, including William Morwood, Harry Tugend
Program Supervisor for General Electric: Ronald Reagan
Episodes:
THE BACHELOR'S BRIDE (Fred MacMurray, Pat Crowley, Virginia Field, Lawrence Keating, Sarah Selby)
THE GIRL WITH THE FLAXEN HAIR (Ray Bolger, Gena Rowland, Irving Bacon, Hal Dawson, Mabel Forrest)
NIGHT CLUB (Glenda Farrell, Barbara Hale, Jeanie Cooper, Bea Benaderet, Joi Lansing, Amanda Blake, June Lockhart, Kathleen Freeman, Rosemary DeCamp, Sue Randall, Lori Nelson)
MIRACLE OF THE OPERA (Ed Wynn, Barbara Morrison, Sig Ruman, Fortunio Bonanova, Maggie Pierce, Cyril Delevanti)
THE MINUS SIGN (Ronald Reagan, Bess Flowers)
ABSALOM, MY SON (Burl Ives, Edgar Barrier, Ted de Corsia, Jack Lambert, Patricia Medina)
THE HOUSE OF TRUTH (Ronald Reagan, Phyllis Thaxter, Philip Ahn, Alice Backes, Allen Jung)
THE UGLY DUCKLING (Oscar Homolka, Linda Watkins, Joanna Barnes, Richard Haydn, Bill Allyn, Joyce Jansen)

THE OTHER WISE MAN (Henry Towns, Abraham Sofaer, Charlotte Fletcher, Rebecca Welles, Michael Ferris, Dennis McCarthy, Francis X. Bushman)
MOTHER CLIMBS TREES (Jan Clayton, Suzanne Cupito, Melinda Plowman, Frank McHugh, Dennis Holmes, Donald Woods, Dan Tobin) This was intended as a pilot for a series.

SHIRLEY TEMPLE'S STORYBOOK
(Jaffee Enterprises - Screen Gems, 1958)
Director: Mitchell Leisen
Producer: Alvin Cooperman
Episodes:
SLEEPING BEAUTY (Alexander Scourby, Nancy Marchand, Anne Helm, Olive Deering, Pernell Roberts)
HIAWATHA (John Ericson, Katherine Warren, J. Carrol Naish, Pernell Roberts, Felix Locher)
MOTHER GOOSE (Shirley Temple, Rod McKuen, Elsa Lanchester, Gene Nash, Billy Gilbert, Carleton Carpenter, Lori Black, Susan Black, Charles Black, Fidor Owen)
Leisen also directed Shirley Temple's introductions to the rest of the episodes in the series.

TWILIGHT ZONE (Revue, 1959)
Director: Mitchell Leisen
Producer: Rod Serling
Episodes:
ESCAPE CLAUSE (David Wayne, Virginia Christine, Thomas Gomez, Raymond Bailey)
PEOPLE ARE THE SAME ALL OVER (Roddy McDowall, Susan Oliver, Paul Coni, Byron Morrow, Vic Perrin, Vernon Gray)
16 MM SHRINE (Ida Lupino, Martin Balsam, Alice Frost, Jerome Cowan, Bob McCord)

MARKAM (Revue, 1960)
Director: Mitchell Leisen
Producers: Ray Milland, Joseph Sistrom, Warren Duff
Episodes:
THE LAST OASIS (Ray Milland, Arthur Franz, Roy Bancroft)
FATEFUL REUNION (Milland, Vaughn Taylor, Charles Watts)
THE ANXIOUS ANGEL (Milland, Bert Freed, Dennis Patrick, Carol Ohmart)
THE PRIZE (Milland, Constance Moore, Tudor Owen)
THE SITTING DUCK (Milland, Nester Paiva, Larry Perron)
CRASH IN THE DESERT (Milland, Jeff Morrow, Julie Adams; Leisen collaborated on the teleplay with Maureen Kelly)
FATEFUL REUNION (Milland, Frank Overton, Vaughn Taylor, Charles Watts)
THE RINGER (Milland, Edmond Ryan, Jocylin Brandon)
A CRY FROM THE PENTHOUSE (Milland, Jack Weston, Willard Waterman)
FALSE COLORS (Milland, Erika Peters, Ann Codee, Dick Wilson)

THE SPECIALISTS (Milland, Suzanne Lloyd, Paul Picerni, John Petruzzi)
13 AVENIDA MUERTE (Milland, Ted DiCorsia, Donna Martell)
THE SNOWMAN (Milland, Jim Davis, Marion Ross, Jackie Russell)
THE BAD SPELL (Milland, Ellen Willard, Gale Robbins, Bobby Troup)

THRILLER (Revue, 1960)
Director: Mitchell Leisen
Producer: Hubbell Robinson
Episodes:
GIRL WITH A SECRET (Fay Bainter, Cloris Leachman, Paul Hartman, Anne Seymour, Ellen Corby, Esther Dale, Victor Buono, Myrna Fahey, Rhodes Reason)
WORSE THAN MURDER (Constance Ford, Christine White, Dan Tobin, Shirley O'Hara, Pat O'Malley, Ross Bender, John Baragrey)

THE WOMAN IN THE CASE (CBS 1960)
Director: Mitchell Leisen
Episode: OPEN WINDOWS (Maureen O'Hara and Tony Randall)
A pilot for an anthology hosted by and occasionally starring Maureen O'Hara. It did not sell.

WAGON TRAIN (Revue - 1960)
Director: Mitchell Leisen
Producer: Howard Christie
Episodes:
QUAKER MEDICINE WOMAN (Robert Horton, Rhonda Fleming, Michael Ansara, Terry Burnham, Jason Robards Sr., Morgan Woodward)
THE PRAIRIE STORY (Robert Horton, Jan Clayton, Beulah Bondi, Frank McGrath, Terry Wilson, Virginia Christine, Jack Beutel)

FOLLOW THE SUN (20th Century Fox, 1961)
Director: Mitchell Leisen
Episodes:
CHICAGO STYLE (Gary Lockwood, Gigi Perreau, Keenan Wynn, Lee Patrick, Howard Caine, Eduardo Ciannelli)
BUSHMAN'S HOLIDAY (Barry Coe, Gary Lockwood, Gigi Perreau, Jack Klugman, Richard Fong, Don Beddoe, Peter Coe)
MELE KALIKIMAKA TO YOU (Barry Coe, Gary Lockwood, Gigi Perreau, Edward Andrews, Ellen Corby, Walter Hong, Jr.)

AD' ENTURES IN PARADISE
(20t . Century Fox, 1961)
Director: Mitchell Leisen
Episodes:
SHOW ME A HERO (Gardner McKay, Guy Stockwell, David Jansen, Robert Faulk, Jim Holden)
THE VELVET TRAP (Gardner McKay, James Holden, Linda Watkins, Tuesday Weld, Addison Myers, Ed Peck, Gregg Martell)

PETE AND GLADYS (El Camino Productions)
Director: Mitchell Leisen
Episode: THE LIVE IN COUPLE (Cara Williams, Henry Morgan, Lee Patrick, Byron Foulger, Sandra Gould, Allen Jenkins.)

ALEXANDER THE GREAT (1963)
Producer: Albert McCleery
Costumes: Mitchell Leisen
An hour-long television pilot which was never aired.

EVE ARDEN SHOW (Universal Television 1965)
Director: Mitchell Leisen
Producer: Lester Colodny
Episode: BE CAREFUL, IT'S MY ART (Eve Arden AND Steve Franken)
A pilot for a projected series that did not sell.

THE GIRL FROM U.N.C.L.E. (MGM, 1966)
Director: Mitchell Leisen
Producer: Douglas Benton
Episodes:
THE DANISH BLUE AFFAIR (Stephanie Powers, Noel Harrison, Leo G. Carroll, Randy Kirby, Dom de Luise, Lloyd Bochner)
THE PETIT PRIX AFFAIR (Stephanie Powers, Noel Harrison, Leo G. Carroll, Randy Kirby)
THE DRUBLEGRATZ AFFAIR (Stephanie Powers, Noel Harrison, Leo G. Carroll)

Leisen not only posed Paulette Goddard in special advertising stills for *Kitty*, he also made her up. Goddard's hairdresser, Hedvig, looked on.